access to history

1 week loan

£14.99

WITHDRAWN

Reaction and Revolution: Russia

1894–1924

MICHAEL LYNCH

FOURTH EDITION

HODDER
EDUCATION
AN HACHETTE UK COMPANY

The Publishers would like to thank Robin Bunce and Sarah Ward for their contribution to the Study Guide.

The Publishers would like to thank the following for permission to reproduce copyright material:

Photo credits: p6 David King; **p17** Library of Congress, LC-USZ62-128298; **p37** TopFoto; **p38***l, r* British Film Institute; **p47** Library of Congress, LC-DIG-ggbain-07327; **pp53, 72** Punch Limited; **p83** Library of Congress, LC-H261-4489; **p100** Hulton Archive/Getty Images; **p104** Library of Congress, LC-USZ62-101877; **p109** The Granger Collection/TopFoto; **p110** ITAR-TASS/TopFoto; **p117** TopFoto; **p144** Hulton-Deutsch Collection/Corbis; **p147** Library of Congress, LC-B2- 5858-2; **p157** Roger-Viollet/TopFoto; **p163** David King.

Acknowledgements: Blackwell, *Russia and the Last Tsar: Opposition and Subversion 1894–1917* by A. Geifman (editor), 1999. Jonathan Cape, *Soviet Government: A Selection of Official Documents on Internal Policies* by M. Matthews (editor), 1974. Collins Harvill, *The Russian Revolution* by R. Pipes, 1990. Granada, *Russia in Revolution 1890–1918* by L. Kochan, 1966. Izdatel'stro Z-oe, *O Samagone* by D.N. Voronov, 1929. Lawrence & Wishart, *Reminiscences of Lenin* by K.K. Krupskaya, 1959. Macmillan, *Imperial and Soviet Russia* by D. Christian (editor), 1997; *Lenin* by R. Service, 2000; *The Russian Revolution & the Soviet State 1917–21: Documents* by M. McCauley, 1984; *The Russian Revolution and the Soviet State* by M. McCauley (editor), 1975. Oxford University Press, *Endurance and Endeavour: Russian History 1812–1980* by J.N. Westwood, 1985. Paladin, *Russia in Revolution*, by L. Kochan, 1974. Penguin, *An Economic History of the USSR* by A. Nove, 1973; *Lenin* by D. Shub, 1976; *Lenin and the Russian Revolution* by C. Hill, 1971; *Nicholas II: The Last of the Tsars* by M. Ferro, 1990; *The Bolshevik Revolution* by E.H. Carr, 1973. Pimlico, *Nicholas II* by D. Lieven, 1993; *Three Whys of the Russian Revolution* by R. Pipes, 1998. Pluto Press, *The History of the Russian Revolution* by L. Trotsky, 1985. Prentice-Hall, *Russia 1917: The February Revolution*, by G. Katkov, 1967. Progress Publishers, *Selected Works* by V.I. Lenin, 1971. Random House, *The Structure of Russian History* by M. Cherniavsky (editor), 1970. University of Chicago Press, *Readings in Russian Civilization* by T. Riha (editor), 1964. University of Exeter Press, *The Soviet Union: A Documentary History* by E. Acton (editor), 2005. Yale University Press, *A Source Book for Russian History from Early Times to 1917* by G. Vernadsky (editor), 1973.

Every effort has been made to trace all copyright holders, but if any have been inadvertently overlooked the Publishers will be pleased to make the necessary arrangements at the first opportunity.

Although every effort has been made to ensure that website addresses are correct at time of going to press, Hodder Education cannot be held responsible for the content of any website mentioned in this book. It is sometimes possible to find a relocated web page by typing in the address of the home page for a website in the URL window of your browser.

Hachette UK's policy is to use papers that are natural, renewable and recyclable products and made from wood grown in sustainable forests. The logging and manufacturing processes are expected to conform to the environmental regulations of the country of origin.

Orders: please contact Bookpoint Ltd, 130 Milton Park, Abingdon, Oxon OX14 4SB. Telephone: +44 (0)1235 827720. Fax: +44 (0)1235 400454. Lines are open 9.00a.m.–5.00p.m., Monday to Saturday, with a 24-hour message answering service. Visit our website at www.hoddereducation.co.uk

© Michael Lynch 2015

First published in 2015 by
Hodder Education
An Hachette UK Company
338 Euston Road
London NW1 3BH

Impression number	10	9	8	7	6	5	4	3	2	1
Year			2019	2018	2017	2016	2015			

Cover photo by © RIA Novosti/TopFoto
Produced, illustrated and typeset in Palatino LT Std by Gray Publishing, Tunbridge Wells
Printed and bound by CPI Group (UK) Ltd, Croydon CR0 4YY

A catalogue record for this title is available from the British Library

ISBN 978 1471838569

Contents

Dedication

Keith Randell (1943–2002)

The *Access to History* series was conceived and developed by Keith, who created a series to 'cater for students as they are, not as we might wish them to be'. He leaves a living legacy of a series that for over 20 years has provided a trusted, stimulating and well-loved accompaniment to post-16 study. Our aim with these new editions is to continue to offer students the best possible support for their studies.

CHAPTER 1

Introduction: Russia in 1894

Tsar Nicholas II came to the throne of the Russian Empire in 1894. The nation he ruled was beset by many long-standing difficulties that threatened to prevent its becoming a modern political and economic state. This chapter describes the basic geographical, social, political and economic features of the Russian Empire at the beginning of Nicholas II's reign, and suggests reasons why the tsar's government was reluctant to undertake the reforms that many deemed necessary for effective modernisation to be achieved. The analysis falls under two main headings:

★ The land, the people and tsardom

★ The problem of reform

Key dates

1854–6	The Crimean War		**1881**	Statute of State Security
1855–81	Reign of Alexander II		**1887**	The University Statute
1861	Emancipation of the serfs		**1890**	The Zemstva Act
1881	Assassination of Alexander II		**1894**	Start of Nicholas II's reign
1881–94	Reign of Alexander III			

1 The land, the people and tsardom

▶ *How had Russia's geography helped to shape its history?*

▶ *What was the relationship between the tsar and the people?*

Russia's geography and peoples

In 1894, Imperial Russia covered over 22 million square kilometres (8 million square miles), an area equivalent to two and a half times the size of the USA today (see Figure 1.1 on page 3). At its widest, from west to east, it stretched for 8000 km (5000 miles); at its longest, north to south, it measured 3200 km (2000 miles). It covered a large part of two continents. European Russia extended eastward from the borders of Poland to the Urals mountain range. Asiatic Russia extended eastward from the Urals to the Pacific Ocean. The greater part of the population, which between 1815 and 1914 quadrupled from 40 million to 165 million, was concentrated in European Russia. It was in that part of the empire that the major historical developments had occurred and it was there that Russia's principal cities, Moscow and St Petersburg, the capital, were situated.

The sheer size of the Russian Empire tended to give an impression of great unity and strength. This was misleading. The population contained a wide variety of peoples of different race, language, religion and culture (see Table 1.1). Controlling such a variety of peoples over such a vast territory had long been a major problem for Russian governments.

Table 1.1 The major nationalities of the Russian Empire according to the census of 1897 (in millions, defined according to mother tongue)

Great Russia	55.6	German	1.8	Mordvinian	1.0
Ukrainian	22.4	Azerbaijani	1.7	Georgian	0.8
Turkic/Tatar	13.4	Latvian	1.4	Tadzhik	0.3
Polish	7.9	Bashkir	1.3	Turkmenian	0.3
White Russian	5.8	Lithuanian	1.2	Greek	0.2
Yiddish (Jewish)	5.0	Armenian	1.2	Bulgarian	0.2
Kirgiz/Kaisats	4.0	Romanian/Moldavian	1.1		
Finnic	3.1	Estonian	1.0		

The tsar

The peoples of the Russian Empire were governed by one person, the tsar (emperor). Since 1613, the Russian tsars had been members of the **Romanov dynasty**. By law and tradition, the tsar was an **autocrat**. There were no restrictions on his power. The people owed him total obedience. This had been clearly expressed in the **Fundamental Laws of the Empire** issued by Nicholas I in 1832. The tsar's absolute rule was exercised through three official bodies:

- The Imperial Council: a group of honorary advisers directly responsible to the tsar.
- The Cabinet of Ministers, which ran the various government departments.
- The Senate, which supervised the operation of the law.

These bodies were much less powerful than their titles suggested. They were appointed, not elected, and they did not govern; their role was merely to give advice. They had no authority over the tsar, whose word was final in all governmental and legal matters.

Russia's political backwardness

What the tsar's power showed was how little Russia had advanced politically compared with other European nations. By the beginning of the twentieth century all the major western European countries had some form of

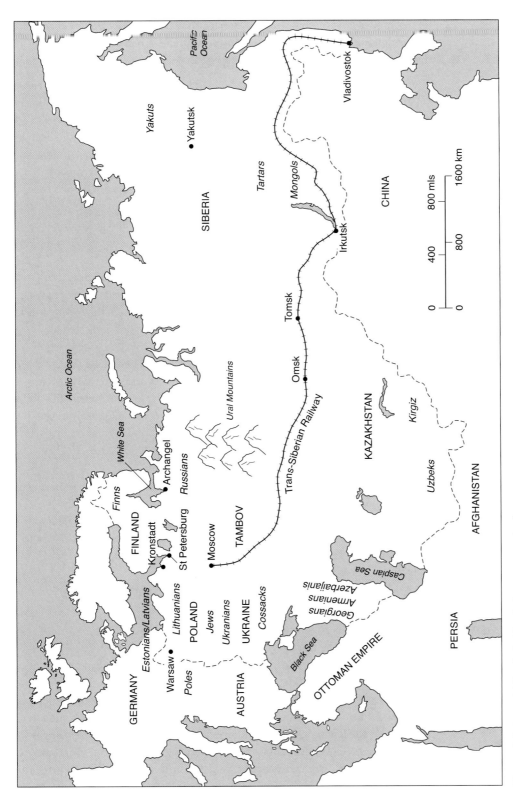

Figure 1.1 Imperial Russia (with ethnic groups marked).

representative government. Not so Russia; although it had been frequently involved in European diplomatic and military affairs, it had remained outside the mainstream of European political thought.

There had been reforming tsars, such as Peter I (1683–1725), Catherine II (1762–96) and Alexander II (1855–81), who had tried to modernise the country by such measures as rebuilding Moscow and St Petersburg, improving the transport system, and making the army more efficient. But their achievements had been in practical areas; they had not included the extension of political rights. In Russia in 1881 it was still a criminal offence to oppose the tsar or his government. There was no parliament, and although political parties had been formed they had no legal right to exist. There had never been a free press in Imperial Russia. Government censorship was imposed on published books and journals.

Repression

Government restrictions had not prevented **liberal** ideas from seeping into Russia, but it did mean that they could not be openly expressed. The result was that supporters of reform or change had to go underground. In the nineteenth century, there had grown up a wide variety of secret societies dedicated to political reform or revolution. The noun 'liberals' came to refer to those who wanted political or social change in Russia, but who believed that it could be achieved by reforming rather than destroying the tsarist system. Yet such relatively moderate views were still unacceptable to the Russian authorities and the liberal groups were frequently infiltrated by agents of the **Okhrana**. As a result, arrests, imprisonment and general harassment were regular occurrences.

Extremism

The denial of free speech tended to drive **political activists** towards extremism. The outstanding example of this occurred in 1881 when Tsar Alexander II was blown to bits by a bomb detonated by a terrorist group known as 'The People's Will' (see page 23). In a society in which state oppression was met with revolutionary terrorism, there was no moderate middle ground on which a tradition of ordered political debate could develop.

The Russian Orthodox Church

The tsars were fully supported in their claims to absolute authority by one of the great pillars of the tsarist system, the Orthodox Church. This was a branch of Christianity that, since the fifteenth century, had been entirely independent of any outside authority such as the **papacy**. Its detachment from foreign influence had given it an essentially Russian character. The great beauty of its liturgy and music had long been an outstanding expression of Russian culture. However, by the late nineteenth century it had become a deeply conservative body, opposed to political change and determined to preserve the tsarist system in its **reactionary** form. The detachment of the Orthodox Church from Russia's growing industrial population was illustrated by the statistic that, in 1900, a Moscow suburb with 40,000 people had only one church and one priest.

The Church did contain some priests who strongly sympathised with the political revolutionaries, but, as an institution, it used its spiritual authority to teach the Russian people that it was their duty to be totally obedient to the tsar as **God's anointed**. The **catechism** of the Church included the statement that 'God commands us to love and obey from the inmost recesses of our heart every authority, and particularly the tsar.'

The social structure of tsarist Russia

The striking features of the social structure were the comparatively small commercial, professional and working classes and the great preponderance of peasants in the population. This is depicted in Figure 1.2, which shows the class distribution of the population as measured by Russia's 1897 census.

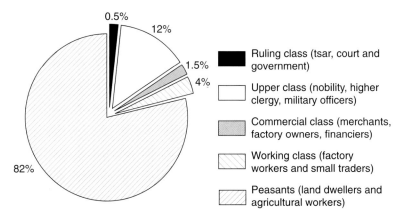

Figure 1.2 The class distribution of the Russian population, 1897.

The Russian economy

The remarkable difference in size between the urban professional and working classes and the rural peasants illustrated a critical feature of Imperial Russia – its slow economic development. The low numbers of urban workers was a sign that Russia had not achieved the major industrial growth that had taken place in the nineteenth century in such countries as Germany, Britain and the USA.

This is not to say that Russia was entirely without industry. The Urals region produced considerable amounts of iron, and the chief western cities, Moscow and St Petersburg, had extensive textile factories. Most villages had a smelting works, which enabled them to produce iron goods, and most peasant homes engaged in some form of cottage industry, producing wooden, flaxen or woollen goods to supplement their income from farming. However, these activities were all relatively small scale. The sheer size of Russia and its undeveloped transport system had limited the chances for industrial expansion.

KEY TERMS

God's anointed The anointing of the tsar with holy oil at his coronation symbolised that he governed by divine right.

Catechism A primer of religious instruction, explaining essential dogmas.

SOURCE A

? Study Source A. How effectively does it portray the relationship between the various social classes in tsarist Russia?

A mocking socialist cartoon of 1900 showing the social pyramid in Imperial Russia. The Russian caption for each layer reads (in ascending order): 'We work for them while they ...' '... shoot at us.' '... eat on our behalf.' '... pray on our behalf.' '... dispose of our money.'

🔑 KEY TERMS

Capital The essential supply of money that provides investment for economic expansion.

Entrepreneurialism The dynamic attitude associated with individual commercial and industrial enterprise.

Agrarian economy Food and goods produced by arable and dairy farming, and then traded.

A further restriction had been the absence of an effective banking system. Russia found it hard to raise **capital** on a large scale. It had not yet mastered the art of successful borrowing and investment, techniques that help to explain why expansion had been so rapid in western countries. Russia's financial sluggishness had discouraged the rise of **entrepreneurialism**.

Agriculture in tsarist Russia

Russia's unenterprising industrial system was matched by its inefficient pattern of agriculture. Even though four-fifths of the population were peasants, a thriving **agrarian economy** had failed to develop. Indeed, the land in Russia was a source of national weakness rather than strength. Not all the empire's vast acres were good farming country. Much of Russia lay too far north to enjoy a climate or a soil suitable for crop growing or cattle rearing. Arable farming was restricted mainly to the Black Earth region, the area of European Russia stretching from Ukraine to Kazakhstan.

The great number of peasants in the population added to the problem. There was simply not enough fertile land available. Under the terms of the **Emancipation Decree of 1861**, the ex-serfs were entitled to buy land, but they invariably found the price too high. This was caused both by a shortage of suitable farming territory and by the government's taxation of land sales, imposed in order to raise the revenue needed to compensate the landowners for their losses caused by emancipation. The only way the peasants could raise the money to buy land was by borrowing from a special fund provided by the government. Consequently, those peasants who did manage to purchase property found themselves burdened with large mortgage repayments that would take them and their families generations to repay.

The peasant problem

Among Russia's governing class, which was drawn from less than one per cent of the population, there was a deeply ingrained prejudice against granting rights to the mass of the people. Over 80 per cent of the population were peasants. They were predominantly illiterate and uneducated. Their sheer size as a social class and their coarse ways led to their being regarded with a mixture of terror and contempt by the governing élite, who believed that these dangerous '**dark masses**' could be controlled only by severe repression. This was what Nicholas II's wife, the Empress Alexandra, meant by saying that Russia needed always to be 'under the whip'.

The existence in the second half of the nineteenth century of an uneducated peasantry, suspicious of change, and living with large debts and in great poverty, pointed to the social, political and economic backwardness of Imperial Russia. Various attempts to educate the peasants had been made in the past, but such efforts had been undermined by the fear among the ruling class that any improvement in the conditions of the 'dark masses' might threaten its own privileges. It was commonplace for officials in Russia to speak of the 'safe ignorance' of the population, implying that any attempt to raise the educational standards of the masses would prove highly dangerous, socially and politically.

The Russian army

One common method of keeping the 'dark masses' in check was to recruit them into the Russian armed services. The lower ranks of the army and navy were largely filled by **conscription**, which was also regularly used as a form of punishment for law-breakers. Ordinary Russians dreaded this sentence; they knew that life in the armed forces was a brutal experience for the common soldier or sailor. The Russian army was notorious in Europe for the severity of its discipline and the grimness of the conditions in which its soldiers lived. Special

KEY TERMS

Emancipation Decree of 1861 Granting of freedom to the serfs (peasant land workers), who had formerly been bound to the landowners.

Dark masses The dismissive term used in the royal court and government circles to describe the peasants.

Conscription Compulsory enlistment of people (in Russia's case, largely peasants) into the armed services.

military camps had been set up in the remoter regions of the empire, which operated as penal colonies rather than as training establishments. The rigours of service life had accounted for the deaths of over a million soldiers in peacetime during the reign of Nicholas I (1825–55).

It was a widespread belief that Russia, as a large empire, needed a large army. Throughout the nineteenth century, the imperial forces were kept at a strength of around 1.5 million men. The cost of maintaining the army and the navy accounted on average for 45 per cent of the government's annual expenditure. This was by far the largest single item of state spending, and, when compared with the four per cent devoted to education, shows how unbalanced government priorities were.

Weaknesses within the army

The higher ranks of the army were the preserve of the aristocracy. **Commissions** were bought and sold, and there was little room for promotion on merit. This weakened it as a fighting force, but the truth of this tended to remain hidden because, with the exception of the Crimean War (1854–6), Russia was not engaged in a major conflict with a western European power for a whole century after 1815. The army's active service was essentially a matter of putting down national risings or serious disturbances within the empire or on its frontiers. There were frequent border clashes with Turkey throughout the nineteenth century, and, at various times, Russian forces saw action in Poland, Armenia and Persia.

The bureaucracy (civil service)

Ironically, it was in the area where there had been the largest attempted reform that the greatest corruption had developed. At the beginning of the eighteenth century, Peter I (1683–1725) had tried to modernise Russia by establishing a full-scale civil service with the aim of maintaining central government control throughout the empire. However, by the middle of the nineteenth century, many Russian critics had begun to condemn this civil service as a corrupt bureaucracy whose **nepotism** and incompetence were the principal reasons for Russia's backwardness. Writing in 1868, **Alexander Herzen** claimed that the bureaucracy had become 'a civilian priesthood, sucking the blood of the people with thousands of greedy, unclean mouths'.

By the middle of the nineteenth century, Herzen asserted, tsarist Russia was run by a bureaucratic class that, for all its incompetence, still possessed the power to control the lives of the Russian masses. At local and national levels, the law, the government, the police and the **militia** were in the hands of a set of men whose first thought was their own convenience and advantage. Against this injustice the ordinary citizen had no redress, since any challenge to the system was lost in bureaucratic procedures. Herzen's savage attack provided powerful ammunition for those in Russia who wished to ridicule and undermine the tsarist system

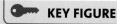
KEY TERMS

Commissions Official appointments of individuals to the various officer ranks.

Nepotism The corrupt practice in which officials distributed positions and offices to their family or friends.

Militia Local citizens called together and given arms to control social disorder.

KEY FIGURE

Alexander Herzen (1812–70)

A leading revolutionary thinker and writer.

itself. However, it is important to remember that Herzen was a revolutionary propagandist intent on painting the blackest picture he could of tsardom. Efforts were made in the nineteenth century to reform the administration and limit its abuses.

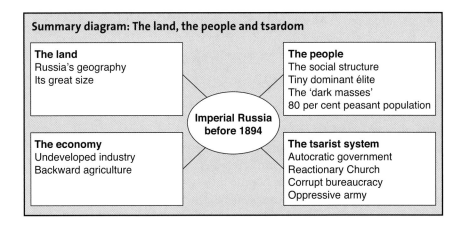

Summary diagram: The land, the people and tsardom

The land
Russia's geography
Its great size

The people
The social structure
Tiny dominant élite
The 'dark masses'
80 per cent peasant population

Imperial Russia before 1894

The economy
Undeveloped industry
Backward agriculture

The tsarist system
Autocratic government
Reactionary Church
Corrupt bureaucracy
Oppressive army

2 The problem of reform

▶ *Why was it difficult to introduce reform in Imperial Russia?*

'Westerners' versus 'Slavophiles'

Many members of the ruling class accepted that major reforms were needed if Russia was to overcome its social and economic backwardness. However, a major barrier to reform was a basic disagreement within the governing élite over Russia's true character as a nation. Since the days of Peter the Great there had been serious differences between 'Westerners' and 'Slavophiles':

- 'Westerners' were those who believed that if Russia wished to remain a great nation it would have to adopt the best features of the political and economic systems of the countries of western Europe.
- 'Slavophiles' were those who regarded western values as corrupting and urged the nation to preserve itself as 'holy Russia', by glorying in its Slav culture and its separate historical tradition.

The dispute between these groups made it difficult to achieve reform in an ordered and acceptable way.

Another bar to planned reform was the autocratic structure of Russia itself. Change could come only from the top. There were no representative institutions, such as a parliament, with the power to alter things. The only possible source of change was the tsar. From time to time, there were progressive tsars (see page 4). Yet it was hardly to be expected that any tsar, no matter how enlightened, would go so far as to introduce measures that might weaken his authority. The result was that reform in Russia had been piecemeal, depending on the inclinations of the individual tsar, rather than a systematic programme of change. It is notable that the significant periods of reform in Russia were invariably a response to some form of national crisis or humiliation. This was certainly true of the reforms introduced in Alexander II's reign (1855–81). His accession coincided with the defeat of Russia at the hands of France and Britain in the Crimean War. The shock of this prompted the new tsar into adopting a reform programme.

Local government reform

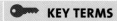

KEY TERMS

Zemstvos Local elected councils, dominated by the landowners since the voting regulations largely excluded peasants.

Mir The traditional village community.

Intelligentsia Educated and more enlightened members of Russian society who had been influenced by Western ideas and wanted to see Russia adopt progressive changes.

Alexander II's reforms began with the Emancipation of the Serfs in 1861, followed three years later by the setting up of a network of elected rural councils, known as the *zemstvos*. Although these were not truly democratic, they did provide Russia with a form of representative government, no matter how limited, which offered some hope to those who longed for an extension of political rights. The authorities complemented their introduction of the *zemstvos* by re-emphasising the valuable role played in the countryside by the *mir*, which government officials saw as a local organisation that would provide an effective means of keeping order, as well as a cheap method of collecting taxes and mortgage repayments.

Legal reforms

In addition, a number of legal reforms were introduced with the aim of simplifying the notoriously cumbersome court procedures whose delays had led to corruption and injustice. Of even greater importance was Alexander II's relaxation of the controls over the press and the universities. Greater freedom of expression encouraged the development of an **intelligentsia**.

The limited nature of the reforms

Alexander II was not a supporter of reform for its own sake. Rather, he saw it as a way of lessening opposition to the tsarist system. He said that his intention was to introduce reform from above in order to prevent revolution from below. His hope was that his reforms would attract the support of the intelligentsia. In this, he was largely successful. Emancipation, greater press and university freedoms, and the administrative and legal changes were greeted with enthusiasm by progressives.

However, no matter how progressive Alexander II himself may have appeared, he was still an autocrat. It was unthinkable that he would continue with a process that might compromise his power as tsar. Fearful that he had gone too far, he abandoned his reformist policies and returned to the tsarist tradition of oppression. His assassination by a group of Social Revolutionaries, known as the

People's Will (see page 23), led to even more severe measures being imposed by his successor, Alexander III (1881–94). These were so oppressive that they earned the title 'the Reaction' (see box).

> ## Key measures of 'the Reaction'
>
> ### *The Statute of State Security, 1881*
>
> - Special government-controlled courts were set up that operated outside the existing legal system.
> - Judges, magistrates and officials who were sympathetic towards liberal ideas were removed from office.
> - The powers of the *Okhrana*, the tsarist secret police, were extended, and censorship of the press was tightened.
>
>   At its introduction in 1881, this statute was described as temporary but it remained in place until 1917.
>
>   The University Statute in 1887 brought the universities under strict government control. The *Zemstva* Act in 1890 decreased the independence of the local councils and empowered government officials to interfere in their decision-making.

Summary diagram: The problem of reform

Tension between 'Westerners' and 'Slavophiles'
↓
Conflict over character of Imperial Russia
↓
Alexander II's reforms: *zemstvos* and intelligentsia, but still autocratic
↓
The People's Will and assassination of Alexander II:
Alexander III's even harsher rule in 'the Reaction'

Chapter summary

Russia in 1894 was a vast empire ruled by the tsar, Nicholas II, head of the Romanov dynasty. Detached from the mainstream of European political and economic developments, Russian leaders had tended to regard reform as unnecessary. As Slavophiles, they regarded Russia as unique among nations and not requiring modernisation, despite its economy lagging behind those of the advanced nations of Europe. Over 80 per cent of the population, of which half were non-Russians, were illiterate peasants. Their great numbers meant they were constantly feared by the governing élite, who believed that these dangerous 'dark masses' had to be held in check by whatever means necessary.

The result was that the nation's great problems of deprivation and social inequality remained largely unaddressed. The tsarist government relied on a privileged bureaucracy, a peasant army officered by an élite group of aristocrats, and the Orthodox Church, which preached the duty of obedience. Supported in this way, it met protest and criticism with suppression. This was strikingly illustrated by Nicholas II's predecessor, Alexander III, who began as a reformer, then changed course and resorted to a series of repressive measures known as 'the Reaction'.

Refresher questions

Use these questions to remind yourself of the key material covered in this chapter.

1 Why was the Russian peasantry often referred to as the 'dark masses'?

2 What function did the *Okhrana* perform?

3 How unbalanced was the distribution of the classes in Russian society?

4 How did the Emancipation Decree of 1861 affect 'the peasant problem'?

5 Why was the Russian economy backward compared to those of other European countries?

6 What function did the army serve in tsarist Russia?

7 What was the fundamental weakness of the tsarist bureaucracy?

8 What were the key measures of 'the Reaction'?

9 Why had there been so little political progress in Russia by 1894?

10 Why was it so difficult for Russia to reform itself?

CHAPTER 2

Nicholas II's early rule 1894–1905

The period 1905–14 was a testing time for Imperial Russia. At issue was the question of whether it could become a modern state. In 1905, the tsarist system was shaken by the most open challenge it had yet faced. It survived, but only by making concessions to its opponents. A parliament was granted and political parties were legalised. Whether such concessions weakened or strengthened tsardom is the underlying theme of this chapter, which sees Imperial Russia wrestling with its internal and external enemies. The key areas examined are:

★ Nicholas II: character and policies

★ Economic reform 1893–1903

★ The opponents of tsardom

★ The Russo-Japanese War 1904–5

★ The 1905 Revolution

Key dates

1890s	The great spurt	1904–5	Russo-Japanese War
1894	Start of Nicholas II's reign	1904	Union of Liberation formed
1894–1906	Sergei Witte's economic reforms	1905	Revolution
1897	Jewish Bund formed		Bloody Sunday
1898	Social Democrats (SD) party formed		All-Russian Union of Peasants formed
1901	Social Revolutionaries (SR) party formed		October Manifesto
1903	SD party split into Bolsheviks and Mensheviks		Formation of the Kadets and the Octobrists

Nicholas II: character and policies

 How did Nicholas II approach the problem of governing Russia?

Nicholas II came to the throne in 1894. It was an irony of history that, at the very time when Russia most needed a tsar of strength and imagination, it was a man of weakness and limited outlook who ruled the nation. Whatever his private virtues (he was, for example, a devoted husband and father), he never showed the statesmanship the times required. There are two main aspects to Nicholas II's reign:

- the problems he faced as tsar at a particularly critical stage in Russian history
- the growth of opposition in Russia to the tsarist system.

The issue of modernity

The most pressing question facing Russia at the start of Nicholas's reign was whether Imperial Russia could modernise itself sufficiently to be able to compete with the other European nations. Would the new tsar be a reformer or a reactionary? There was little doubt what the answer would be. The assassination of a progressive tsar, Alexander II, followed by a fierce period of repression under his successor Alexander III, had made it highly unlikely that the new tsar would reverse his predecessor's policy. Furthermore, Nicholas's upbringing and education made him suspicious of change. It was no surprise that he continued the repressive policies he had inherited. This further angered the intelligentsia and the critics of the tsarist regime; they began to prepare to challenge tsardom.

Nicholas II's upbringing: the role of Pobedonostsev

As a young man, Nicholas had been tutored at court by **Konstantin Pobedonostsev**, a man of great influence in late Imperial Russia. Known as the 'Grand Inquisitor' because of his repressive attitudes, Pobedonostsev was an arch-conservative who had a deep distaste for all forms of democracy. He condemned the growth of parliamentary democracy in western Europe as a betrayal of their duty by the political leaders there. He dismissed the idea of **representative government** as 'the great lie of our time'. To his mind, autocracy was the only possible government for Imperial Russia. Pobedonostsev personified the obstructions in the way of Russia's necessary political and social reform. As personal tutor to Alexander III and Nicholas II, he played a major part in shaping the reactionary attitudes of the last two tsars. Nicholas took to heart the lessons he learned from Pobedonostsev.

One of the quirks of the Russian history of this period was that 'the Reaction', associated with Alexander III and Pobedonostsev, coincided with a time of remarkable economic expansion. It is this that gives added weight to the

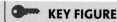 **KEY FIGURE**

Konstantin Pobedonostsev (1827–1907)

Chief minister in the Russian government from 1881 to 1905 and also the Procurator (lay head) of the Synod, the governing body of the Russian Orthodox Church.

 KEY TERM

Representative government A system in which the people of a nation elect a government into office, and subsequently vote it out if they so choose.

argument that in the late nineteenth and early twentieth centuries, the tsarist government through its reactionary policies threw away its last chance of survival. At a critical phase, when economic developments seemed to offer Russia the opportunity to modernise, tsardom showed a fatal resistance to change. By restricting itself to a narrow form of **nationalism** and **orthodoxy**, the tsarist government blindly denied itself the chance to adapt successfully to a changing world.

Russification

A policy of particular note that had begun under Alexander III and which Nicholas II carried on was **Russification**. This was a severely enforced policy of restricting the influence of the non-Russian national minorities by emphasising the superiority of all things Russian. The aim was to impose Russian ways on all the peoples within the empire.

Officials everywhere in the empire now had a vested interest in maintaining the dominance of Russian values at the expense of the other national cultures. Discrimination against non-Russians, which had previously been a hidden feature of Russian public life, became more open and vindictive in the 1890s. The nationalities that suffered most from this were the Baltic Germans, the Poles, the Finns, the Armenians and the Ukrainians. State interference in their education, religion and culture became widespread and systematic.

Anti-Semitism

Among the chief victims of Russification were the Jews. Over 600 new measures were introduced, imposing heavy social, political and economic restrictions on the Jewish population. Since the majority of Jews lived in **ghettos**, they were easily identifiable scapegoats who could be blamed for Russia's difficulties. Anti-Semitism was deeply ingrained in tsarist Russia. **Pogroms** had long disfigured Russian history. A group of ultra-conservative Russian nationalists, known as the 'Black Hundreds', were notorious for their attacks on Jews. During the reign of Nicholas II the number of pogroms increased sharply. This was proof of the tsarist regime's active encouragement of the terrorising of the Jews. But what was equally noticeable was the eagerness with which local communities followed the lead from above in organising the bloodletting.

The response to Nicholas II's policies

The tight controls that Nicholas II tried to impose did not lessen opposition to tsardom. The reverse happened; despite greater police interference, opposition became more organised. A number of political parties, ranging from moderate reformers to violent revolutionaries, came into being. The government's policies of reaction and Russification produced a situation in which many political and national groups grew increasingly frustrated by the mixture of coercion and incompetence that characterised the tsarist system.

 **KEY TERMS**

Nationalism The conviction that the nation state is the highest form of social organisation; in Russian tradition, the belief that Russia was a 'holy' nation that did not need to embrace modernity.

Orthodoxy Conformity to an unchanging set of political ideas or religious beliefs.

Russification Russian was declared to be the official first language; all legal proceedings and all administration had to be conducted in Russian. Public office was closed to those not fluent in the language.

Ghettos Discrete districts where Jews were concentrated and to which they were restricted.

Pogroms Fierce state-organised persecutions that often involved the wounding or killing of Jews and the destruction of their property.

The failings of Russification

As a policy, Russification proved remarkably ill-judged. At a critical stage in Russia's development, when cohesion and unity were needed, its leaders chose to treat its national minorities, who made up half the population, as inferiors or potential enemies. The persecution of the Jews was especially ill-judged. It alienated the great mass of the 5 million Jews in the Russian population, large numbers of whom fled in desperation to western Europe and North America, carrying with them an abiding hatred of tsardom. Those who could not escape stayed to form a large and disaffected community within the empire. It was no coincidence that the 1890s witnessed a large influx of Jews into the various anti-tsarist movements in Russia. In 1897, Jews formed their own revolutionary 'Bund' or union.

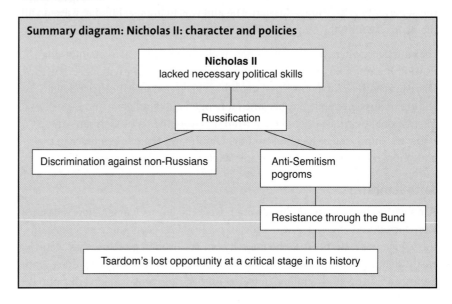

Summary diagram: Nicholas II: character and policies

Nicholas II
lacked necessary political skills

Russification

Discrimination against non-Russians

Anti-Semitism
pogroms

Resistance through the Bund

Tsardom's lost opportunity at a critical stage in its history

② Economic reform 1893–1903

▶ *What methods did Witte use to develop the Russian economy?*

For all the difficulties that Russia faced, the period was one of rapid economic expansion. For a time it seemed that Russia might become a modern industrial nation. This was largely due to the work of two outstanding ministers: Count Sergei Witte, who served during the early part of Nicholas II's reign, and Peter Stolypin (see pages 46–50). In the face of resistance from the very regime they were trying to serve, Witte and Stolypin sought to modernise Russia.

In the 1890s, Russian industry grew so rapidly that the term the **'great spurt'** was used to describe the period. A major reason for the exceptional growth

Sergei Witte

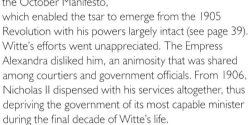

1849	Born in Tbilisi
1870s–80s	Administrator in private businesses
1892–1903	Reforming minister of finance
1903–6	Chairman of the Committee of Ministers
1905	Negotiated end of Russo-Japanese War
1906	Dismissed by Nicholas II
1915	Died

Academically gifted and experienced in management, Witte was brought into government in 1892 as minister of finance. He set about modernising Russia's backward economy. Despite constant criticism from his less talented colleagues, who resented his ability, he achieved a series of major financial and economic reforms that led to the great spurt of the 1890s, which suggested that Russia had the potential to become a modern industrial power. However, after a decade in office, he was dismissed by the tsar, who believed fabricated stories that Witte was implicated in a Jewish conspiracy to undermine the Russian state. Despite this, the tsar recalled him in 1905 to extricate Russia from its war with Japan, a task which Witte accomplished

by skilfully negotiating a peace that left Russia militarily defeated but not diplomatically humiliated. Witte showed similar brilliance in drafting the October Manifesto, which enabled the tsar to emerge from the 1905 Revolution with his powers largely intact (see page 39). Witte's efforts went unappreciated. The Empress Alexandra disliked him, an animosity that was shared among courtiers and government officials. From 1906, Nicholas II dispensed with his services altogether, thus depriving the government of its most capable minister during the final decade of Witte's life.

Witte's prickly personality and reluctance to suffer fools gladly meant that he easily made enemies. Yet, he remained Russia's last best hope. His enlightened economic reforms showed what Russia might have accomplished had he remained in office long enough. In hindsight, there is a strong case for saying that the tsar's dismissal of Witte, at a critical juncture in Russia's fortunes, inadvertently threw away the best chance of his dynasty's survival. Witte's tragedy, and ultimately tsardom's, was that he was never trusted by those in charge of the nation he was trying to save.

---

was the increase in the output of coal in Ukraine and of oil in the Caucasus. Economic historians are agreed that, although this sudden acceleration was the result of **private enterprise**, it was sustained by deliberate government policy.

However, the motives of the tsarist government were military rather than economic. It is true that Russia's **capitalists** did well out of the great spurt, but it was not the government's primary intention to help them. Economic expansion attracted the tsar and his ministers because it was a means of improving the strength of the Russian armed forces. A growing industry would produce more and better guns, equipment and ships.

The outstanding individual involved in Russia's development at this time was Sergei Witte. As Minister of Finance from 1892 to 1903, he set himself the huge task of modernising the Russian economy to a level where it could compete with the advanced nations of the West. To help bring this about, he invited foreign experts and workers to Russia to advise on industrial planning. Engineers and managers from France, Belgium, Britain, Germany and Sweden played a vital role in the great spurt.

 KEY TERMS

Private enterprise
Economic activity organised by individuals or companies, not the government.

Capitalists Financiers and factory owners.

State capitalism

While not opposed to private enterprise, Witte considered that modernisation could be achieved only through **state capitalism**. He was impressed by the results of the industrial revolutions in western Europe and the USA, and argued that Russia could successfully modernise by planning along the same lines. He admitted that, given the backwardness of Russia, this presented particular difficulties.

SOURCE A

From Witte's memorandum to the tsar in 1899, quoted in T. Riha, editor, *Readings in Russian Civilization*, volume 2, University of Chicago Press, 1964, p. 431.

The economic relations of Russia to Western Europe are fully comparable to the relations of colonial countries with their metropolises [mother countries]. The latter consider their colonies as advantageous markets in which they can freely sell the products of their labor and of their industry, and from which they can draw with a powerful hand the raw materials necessary for them. Russia was, and to a certain extent still is, such a hospitable colony for all industrially developed states, generously providing them with the cheap products of her soil and buying dearly the products of their labor. But there is a radical difference between Russia and a colony: Russia is an independent and strong power. She has the right and the strength not to want to be the handmaiden of states which are more developed economically.

? According to Witte in Source A, what is the relationship between Russia and the advanced industrial nations?

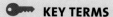

KEY TERMS

State capitalism The direction and control of the economy by the government, using its central authority.

Tariffs Duties imposed on foreign goods to keep their prices high and thereby discourage importers from bringing them into the country.

Gold standard The system in which the rouble had a fixed gold content, thus giving it strength when exchanged with other currencies.

Rouble Russia's basic unit of currency.

Witte judged that, for Russia to avoid remaining 'the handmaiden' of the advanced industrial states, its greatest need was to acquire capital for investment in industry. To raise this, he negotiated large loans and investments from abroad, while imposing heavy taxes and high interest rates at home. At the same time as he encouraged the inflow of foreign capital, Witte limited the import of foreign goods. Protective **tariffs** were set up as a means of safeguarding Russia's young domestic industries, such as steel production. In 1897, the Russian currency was put on the **gold standard**. The hope was that this would create financial stability and so encourage international investment in Russia. The aim was largely successful but it penalised the consumers at home since they had to pay the higher prices that traders introduced to keep pace with the increased value of the **rouble**. Furthermore, prices tended to rise as a result of tariffs making goods scarcer.

The importance of the railways

Much of the foreign capital that Witte was successful in raising was directly invested in railways. He believed that the modernisation of the Russian economy ultimately depended on developing an effective railway system. His enthusiasm was an important factor in the extraordinary increase in lines and rolling stock that took place between 1881 and 1913. It would not be an exaggeration to describe this as a transport revolution (see Figure 2.1).

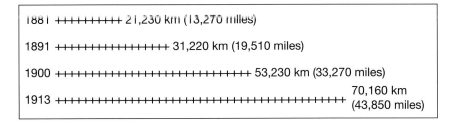

Figure 2.1 The growth of Russian railways.

Witte's special project was the trans-Siberian railway, which was constructed between 1891 and 1902. The line stretched for 6000 km (3750 miles) from Moscow to Vladivostok (see the map on page 3) and was intended to connect the remoter regions of the central and eastern empire with the industrial west, and so encourage the migration of workers to the areas where they were most needed. However, it promised more than it delivered. Sections of it were still incomplete in 1914 and in the event it did not greatly improve east–west migration. The trans-Siberian railway proved more impressive as a symbol of Russian enterprise than as a project of real economic worth.

One of Witte's main hopes was that the major improvements in transport would boost exports and foreign trade. The trade figures suggest that his hopes were largely fulfilled (see Table 2.1 and Figure 2.2 on page 20).

These figures of increased production are not so impressive when it is remembered that Russia was experiencing a massive growth in population. Production **per capita** was lower than the overall figures suggested (see Table 2.2). Although total production rose during this period, the average amount produced by each person dropped.

 **KEY TERM**

Per capita 'Per head', calculated by dividing the amount produced by the number of people in the population.

Table 2.1 The Russian economy: annual production (in millions of tonnes)

Year	Coal	Pig iron	Oil	Grain*
1890	5.9	0.89	3.9	36
1900	16.1	2.66	10.2	56
1910	26.8	2.99	9.4	74
1913	35.4	4.10	9.1	90
1916	33.8	3.72	9.7	64

* European Russia only.

Table 2.2 Population of Imperial Russia 1885–1913

Region	1885	1897	1913
European Russia	81,725,200	93,442,900	121,780,000
Caucasus	7,284,500	9,289,400	12,717,200
Siberia	4,313,700	5,758,800	9,894,500
Steppes and Urals	1,588,500	2,465,700	3,929,500
Central Asia	3,738,600	5,281,000	7,106,000
Total	98,650,500	116,237,800	155,427,200

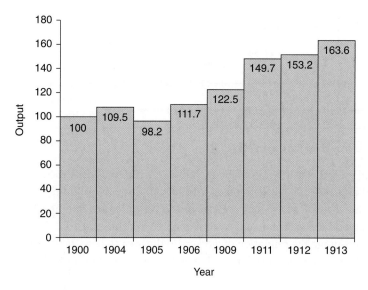

Figure 2.2 Industrial output in the Russian Empire (calculated to base unit of 100 in 1900).

Nevertheless, Russia was enjoying real economic growth. Figure 2.3 shows how favourably its industrial output compared with other European countries. Again, one has to be cautious in interpreting the data. Given its backwardness, Russia was starting from a much lower level of production. For example, although its 96.8 per cent growth looks to be over twice that of Britain's, it was playing catch-up and had a long way to go.

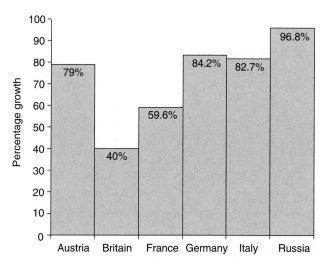

Figure 2.3 Growth in national production 1898–1913.

Witte's problems

There is no doubt that Witte's policies had a major impact on the expansion of the Russian economy. However, what can be questioned is whether the results were wholly beneficial for Russia. Critics have pointed to three drawbacks in his economic reforms:

- Witte made Russia too dependent on foreign loans and investments.
- In giving priority to heavy industry, Witte neglected vital light engineering areas, such as machine tool production, which would have helped to modernise manufacturing.
- Witte paid no attention to Russia's agricultural needs.

Yet, any criticism of Witte should be balanced by reference to the problems he faced. The demands of the military commanders that their transport and equipment needs should have priority in economic planning too often interfered with his schemes for railway construction and the building of new industrial plant. Moreover, Witte's freedom of action was restricted by the resistance to change that he met from the court and the government. The main purpose of his economic policies was to make the nation strong and thus protect tsardom against the disruptive forces in Russian society, but he was disliked by the royal court and the government, which seldom gave him the support he needed. In 1903, the tsar forced him to resign as finance minister.

Witte was an abrasive individual who made enemies easily, but in ability he towered above all the other ministers and officials in the government. His tragedy was that despite his great talents, which, if properly recognised, might have led Russia towards peaceful modernisation, he was never fully trusted by the people of the tsarist court and system he was trying to save.

The end of the great spurt by 1900

The improvement of the Russian economy in the 1890s was not simply the result of the work of Witte. It was part of a worldwide industrial boom. However, by the turn of the century, the boom had ended and a serious international **trade recession** had set in. The consequences for Russia were especially serious. The industrial expansion at the end the century had led to a ballooning of the population of the towns and cities (see Table 2.3 on page 22). This increase had not been organised or supervised; the facilities for accommodating the influx of workers were wholly inadequate. The result was severe overcrowding. Furthermore, when boom turned to recession there was widespread unemployment which increased unrest in the cities and urban areas.

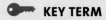 **KEY TERM**

Trade recession A fall in the demand for goods, which leads to production being cut back and workers laid off.

Table 2.3 Growth of population in Russia's two main cities

Year	St Petersburg	Moscow	Year	St Petersburg	Moscow
1881	928,000	753,500	1900	1,439,600	1,345,000
1890	1,033,600	1,038,600	1910	1,905,600	1,617,700
1897	1,264,700	1,174,000	1914	2,217,500	1,762,700

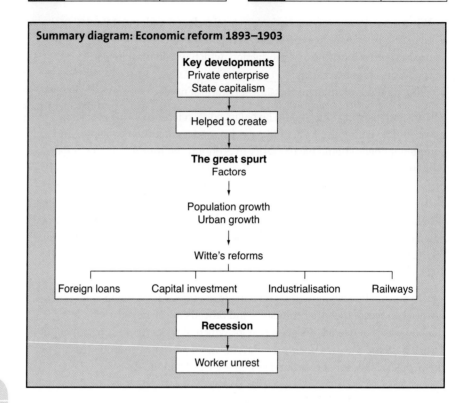

Summary diagram: Economic reform 1893–1903

Key developments
Private enterprise
State capitalism

↓

Helped to create

↓

The great spurt
Factors

↓

Population growth
Urban growth

↓

Witte's reforms

Foreign loans — Capital investment — Industrialisation — Railways

↓

Recession

↓

Worker unrest

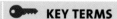

KEY TERMS

Revolutionaries Those who believed that Russia could not progress unless the tsarist system was destroyed.

Reformers Strong critics of the tsarist system but who believed it could be changed for the better by pressure from without and reform from within.

Populists *Narodniks*, from the Russian word for 'the people'.

Social Democrats The All-Russian Social Democratic Workers' Party.

③ The opponents of tsardom

▶ *What forms did opposition to tsardom take?*

Two main groups opposed to tsardom can be identified in Nicholas II's reign: **revolutionaries** and **reformers** (liberals).

Revolutionaries

The revolutionaries comprised three major groups:

- **Populists**
- Social Revolutionaries (SRs)
- **Social Democrats** (SDs).

The Populists (*Narodniks*)

The **Populists** regarded the future of Russia as being in the hands of the peasants who made up the overwhelming mass of the population. The peasants must take the lead in transforming Russia, beginning with the overthrow of the tsarist system itself.

Populism dated from the 1870s. As with all the significant political movements of this period, the Populist leaders were drawn, not from the peasants, but from the middle and upper classes. These leaders regarded it as their duty to educate the uninformed peasantry into an awareness of its revolutionary role. This involved 'going to the people', a policy under which the educated Populists went from the universities into the countryside to live for a period with the peasants in an attempt to turn them into revolutionaries. The policy was seldom a success. The peasants tended to regard the students as airy-fairy thinkers and prattlers who had no knowledge of real life.

In desperation, some Populists turned to terrorism as the only way of achieving their aims. In 1879, a group calling itself 'The People's Will' was founded with the declared intention of murdering members of the ruling class. This movement, which was no more than 400 strong, gained notoriety two years later when it successfully planned the assassination of Alexander II, who was blown to pieces by a bomb. However, this act weakened rather than strengthened the Populist movement. The murder of a tsar who had initiated many reforms seemed to discredit the idea of reform itself and so justified the repression imposed in the wake of the assassination.

The importance of Populism lay in its methods rather than in its ideas. Its concept of a peasant-based revolution was unrealistic; the Russian peasantry were simply not interested in political revolution. What was lasting about Populism was the part it played in establishing a violent anti-tsarist tradition. All the revolutionaries in Russia after 1870 were influenced, if not inspired, by the example of the Populist challenge to tsardom.

The Social Revolutionaries (SRs)

The Social Revolutionary Party grew directly out of the Populist movement. The economic spurt of the 1890s had produced a quickening of interest in political and social issues. Seeing this as an opportunity to gain recruits from the rapidly growing urban workforce, the SRs began to agitate among the workers. The intention was to widen the concept of the '**people**', so that it encompassed not simply the peasants but all those in society who had reasons for wishing to see the end of tsardom.

An important figure in the reshaping of Populist strategy was Victor Chernov, who played a key part in the formation of the Social Revolutionary Party in 1901 and became its leader. He was a member of the intelligentsia, and sought to provide a firmer base for Populism than its previous passionate but vague ideas

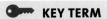

KEY TERM

People That part of the population that the Social Revolutionaries believed truly represented the character and will of the Russian nation.

had produced. However, as with all the revolutionary groups in tsarist Russia, the SRs were weakened by disagreements among themselves. Leon Trotsky, who was later to play a major role as a revolutionary, pointed to this division when he described the SRs as being made up of two competing groups: 'Left Social Revolutionaries' and 'Right Social Revolutionaries'.

In distinguishing between the left and the right elements, Trotsky was referring to the division of the SRs into anarchists and revolutionaries. The Left SRs were the faction who wanted to continue the policy of terrorism inherited from 'The People's Will'. The Right SRs were the more moderate element, who, while believing in revolution as their ultimate goal, were prepared to co-operate with other parties in working for an immediate improvement in the conditions of the workers and peasants. Between 1901 and 1905, it was the terrorist faction that dominated. During those years the SRs were responsible for over 2000 political assassinations, including Plehve, the interior minister, and the tsar's uncle, the Grand Duke Sergei. These were spectacular successes but they did little to bring about the desired link with the urban workers.

The 1905 Revolution, which saw the first serious open challenge to tsardom in Nicholas II's reign (see page 35), brought more gains to the liberals than to the revolutionaries. One effect of this was that the more moderate Right SRs gained greater influence over party policy. This began to show dividends. From 1906, the SRs experienced a growing support from the professional classes, from the trade unions and from the All-Russian Union of Peasants, which had been set up in 1905. At its first congress in 1906, the SR Party committed itself to **revolutionary socialism** and gave a special pledge to the peasants that it would end 'the bourgeois principle of private ownership by returning the land to those who worked it'.

It was their land policy that largely explains why the SRs remained the most popular party with the peasants. However, at the time, the congress decisions brought disruption rather than unity. The left wing protested that the party's programme ignored the industrial workers, while the right asserted that congress policy was unworkable in current Russian conditions. Chernov tried to hold the factions together, but from 1906 onwards the SRs were a collection of radical groups rather than a united party. Nevertheless, until they were outlawed by the Bolsheviks after the 1917 Revolution (see page 171), the SRs remained the party with the largest popular following in Russia.

The Social Democrats (SDs)

The Social Democrats came into being in 1898; their aim was to achieve revolution in Russia by following the ideas of Karl Marx (1818–83), the German revolutionary, who had advanced the idea that human society operated according to scientific principles. He had asserted that, just as the physical universe was governed by the laws of chemistry and physics, so too, the behaviour of human beings was determined by social laws. These could be

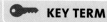 **KEY TERM**

Revolutionary socialism
The belief that change could be achieved only through the violent overthrow of the tsarist system.

scientifically studied and applied. Marx claimed that the critical determinant of human behaviour was **class struggle**, a process that operated throughout history. He referred to this process as the **dialectic**.

For revolutionaries in the nineteenth century, the most exciting aspect of Marx's analysis was his conviction that the contemporary industrial era marked the final stage of the dialectical class struggle. Human history was about to reach its culmination in the revolutionary victory of the **proletariat** over the **bourgeoisie**, which would usher in 'the dictatorship of the proletariat'. This dictatorship would be the last but one stage of history in which the workers, having overthrown the bourgeoisie in revolution and taken power, would hunt down and destroy all the surviving reactionaries. It would be a violent and bloody affair but, once these final class enemies had been obliterated, all conflict would end and the perfect, harmonious society would emerge.

The attraction of Marx for Russian revolutionaries is easy to understand. His ideas had been known in Russia for some time, but what gave them particular relevance was the great spurt of the 1890s. This promised to create the industrial conditions in Russia that would make a successful revolution possible. The previously unfocused hopes for revolution could now be directed on the industrial working class.

The first Marxist revolutionary of note in Russia was **George Plekhanov**. He had translated Marx's writings into Russian and had worked to promote the idea of proletarian revolution. Despite his pioneering work, and his founding of the SD Party, a number of the members soon became impatient with Plekhanov's leadership. They found him too theoretical in his approach; they wanted a much more active revolutionary programme. The outstanding spokesman for this viewpoint was Vladimir Ulyanov, better known as Lenin.

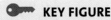 **KEY TERMS**

Class struggle A continuing conflict at every stage of history between those who possessed economic and political power and those who did not – in simple terms, 'the haves' vs 'the have-nots'.

Dialectic The violent struggle between opposites which takes place in nature and in human society.

Proletariat The exploited industrial workers who would supposedly triumph in the last great class struggle.

Bourgeoisie The owners of capital, the boss class, who exploited the workers but who supposedly would be overthrown by them in revolution.

KEY FIGURE

George Plekhanov (1856–1918)

Often referred to as 'the father of Russian Marxism'; it was under his leadership that the SD Party was formed in 1898.

Lenin and Marxism

By the age of 20, Lenin's study of Marx's writings had turned him into a committed Marxist for whom revolution was a way of life. By the age of 30, his dedication to the cause of revolution in Russia had led to arrest, imprisonment and internal exile. Indeed, he was in exile in Siberia when the SD Party was formed in 1898.

Lenin's greatest single achievement as a revolutionary was to reshape Marxist theory to make it fit Russian conditions. The instrument that he chose for this was the Bolshevik Party. Because the party was the vehicle of historical change, its role was not to win large-scale backing, but to direct the revolution from above, regardless of the scale of popular support. 'No revolution', Lenin wrote, 'ever waits for formal majorities.' (See page 104 for a full profile of Lenin.)

Lenin's impact on the SDs

When Lenin returned from exile to western Russia in 1900, he set about turning the SDs into his idea of what a truly revolutionary party must be. With a colleague, Julius Martov, he founded a party newspaper, *Iskra* (*The Spark*), which he used as the chief means of putting his case to the party members. Lenin criticised Plekhanov for being more interested in reform than revolution. He said that under Plekhanov the SDs, instead of transforming the workers into a revolutionary force for the overthrow of capitalism, were following a policy of '**economism**'. Lenin wanted living and working conditions to get worse, not better. In that way the bitterness of the workers would increase, and so drive the Russian proletariat to revolution.

In 1902, Lenin wrote his strongest attack yet on Plekhanov in a pamphlet called, *What Is To Be Done?* In it he berated him for continuing to seek allies among as broad a group of anti-tsarist elements as possible. Lenin insisted that this would lead nowhere. Revolution in Russia was possible only if it was organised and led by a party of dedicated, professional revolutionaries.

For Lenin, revolution was not a haphazard affair; it was a matter of applied science. He regarded the teachings of Karl Marx as having already provided the key to understanding how revolutions operated. It was the task of those select members of the SD Party who understood scientific Marxism to lead the way in Russia. The workers could not be left to themselves; they did not know enough. They had to be directed. It was the historical role of the informed members of the SD Party to provide that direction. Only they could rescue the Russian working class and convert it to true socialism.

The Bolshevik–Menshevik split

The dispute between Lenin and Plekhanov came to a head during the second congress of the SD Party in 1903. Plekhanov tried to avoid confrontation, but Lenin deliberately made an issue of who had the right to belong to the party. His aim was to force members to choose between Plekhanov's idea of a broad-based party, open to all revolutionaries, and his own concept of a small, tightly knit and exclusive party. The congress that met in a number of different places, including Brussels and London, was a heated affair, which frequently descended into a series of slanging matches over points of procedure. The London police, who had been asked by the Russian authorities to keep an eye on proceedings, tended to find the SDs a comical bunch. Their reports spoke of 'funny foreign gentlemen' all speaking at the same time and trying to out-shout each other.

No matter how much the SDs may have amused the London bobbies, they took themselves very seriously. A deep divide developed between Lenin and one of his *Iskra* co-editors, Julius Martov, who shared Plekhanov's viewpoint about membership. Their quarrel was as much to do with personality as with politics. Martov believed that behind Lenin's tactics was a fierce determination to become dictator of the party. Martov's view was supported by Alexander

Potresov, another co-editor of *Iskra*, who wrote the description of Lenin in Source B.

SOURCE B

From the papers of Alexander Potresov, writing in 1903, quoted in David Shub, *Lenin*, Penguin, 1976, p. 76.

Lenin [showed] great cunning and a readiness to do anything to make his opinion prevail. Frequently my colleagues and I felt out of place in our own newspaper office. Lenin divided the world sharply between those who were with him and those who were against him. For him there existed no personal or social relationship outside of the two classes. When the political principle was enunciated that in the fight against the common enemy – the Tsarist government – it was desirable to present a common front by combining with other groups and parties, Lenin accepted it reluctantly and only in theory. In practice, it remained an idle phrase. He could not have acted on that principle even if he had wanted to, because he was incapable of co-operating with other people. It went against his grain.

According to Source B, why was Lenin unwilling to join a common front against the tsarist government?

In a series of votes, the SD congress showed itself to be evenly divided between Lenin and Martov. However, after a particular set of divisions had gone in his favour, Lenin claimed that he and his supporters were the majority. This led to their being called **Bolsheviks** while Martov's group became known as **Mensheviks**. Initially, the main point dividing Bolsheviks and Mensheviks was simply one of procedure. However, following the split in 1903 the differences between them hardened into a set of opposed attitudes. These are shown in Figure 2.4.

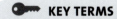

KEY TERMS

Bolsheviks From *bolshinstvo*, Russian for majority.

Mensheviks From *menshinstvo*, Russian for minority.

By 1912, Bolsheviks and Mensheviks had become two distinct, conflicting Marxist parties. Lenin deliberately emphasised the difference between himself and Martov by resigning from the editorial board of *Iskra* and starting his own journal, *Vyperod* (*Forward*), as an instrument for Bolshevik attacks on the Mensheviks. A Bolshevik daily paper, *Pravda* (*The Truth*), was first published in 1912.

Lenin and the Bolsheviks before 1917

An important point to note is that the later success of Bolshevism in the October Revolution has tempted writers to overstate the importance of Lenin in the period before 1917. For example, Trotsky, who joined Lenin in 1917 after having been a Menshevik, argued in his later writings that the Bolsheviks had been systematically preparing the ground for revolution since 1903. But the fact was that during the years 1904–17 Lenin was largely absent from Russia. He lived variously in Finland, France, Switzerland and Austria, and his visits to Russia were rare and fleeting. Although he continued from exile to issue a constant stream of instructions to his followers, he and they played only a minor role in events in Russia before 1917.

Menshevik view	Issue	Bolshevik view
Russia not yet ready for proletarian revolution – the bourgeois stage had to occur first.	Revolution	Bourgeois and proletarian stages could be telescoped into one revolution.
A mass organisation with membership open to all revolutionaries.	The party	A tight-knit, exclusive, organisation of professional revolutionaries.
Open, democratic discussion within the party – decisions arrived at by votes of members.	Decision-making	Authority to be exercised by the central committee of the party – this was described as **'democratic centralism'**.
• Alliance with all other revolutionary and bourgeois liberal parties. • Support of trade unions in pursuing better wages and conditions for workers ('economism').	Strategy	• No co-operation with other parties. • 'Economism' dismissed as playing into hands of bourgeoisie. • Aimed to turn workers into revolutionaries.

Figure 2.4 Main differences between the Mensheviks and Bolsheviks.

KEY TERM

'Democratic centralism'
Lenin's notion that democracy in the Bolshevik Party lay in obedience to the authority and instructions of the leaders. In practice, Bolsheviks did what Lenin told them to do.

Bolshevik tactics

Lenin and his fellow exiles set up training schools for revolutionaries who were then smuggled back into Russia to infiltrate worker organisations such as the trade unions. The Bolsheviks who remained in Russia spent their time trying to raise money for their party. This frequently involved direct terrorism and violence; post offices were favourite targets for Bolshevik attack. In one notorious episode in Tiflis (present-day Tbilisi) in Georgia, a Bolshevik gang bomb-blasted their way into a post office and killed some twenty people before making off with a quarter of a million roubles. The money stolen in such raids was used to finance the printing of masses of handbills, leaflets and newspapers attacking the tsarist regime and calling for revolution.

Yet, the truth was that, despite such activities, Lenin's revolutionaries were regarded by the authorities during this period as merely a fringe group of extremists. Interestingly, the Bolsheviks were not listed by the police as a major challenge to the tsarist system. In the pre-1914 period the numerical strength of the Bolsheviks varied between 5000 and 10,000; even in February 1917 it was no more than 25,000. Before 1917, the Mensheviks invariably outnumbered them. Numbers, of course, are not everything. Determination is arguably more important. Whatever the apparent lack of influence of Lenin's Bolsheviks before 1917, the fact is that when a revolutionary situation developed in 1917 it was they who proved the best prepared to seize the opportunity to take over government (see page 118). The Bolsheviks' readiness was one of Lenin's major political achievements.

Reformers and Liberals

There were a number of reforming groups seeking change. These are usually referred to as liberals but they never came together to form a common front. Until the issuing of the October Manifesto in 1905 (see page 40), political parties had been illegal in Russia. This had not actually prevented their formation, but it had made it very difficult for them to develop as genuinely democratic bodies. There was no tradition of open debate. Since they were denied legal recognition, they often resorted to extreme methods in order to spread their ideas. As a result, during the brief period of their permitted existence from 1905 to 1921, before they were again outlawed, the Russian political parties proved to be suspicious and intolerant of each other. This made co-operation and collective action difficult to organise. Yet, although they were to have a short and inglorious life, the Russian liberal parties should not be ignored. In historical study, losers deserve as much attention as winners.

The economic boom of the 1890s saw the rapid development of a small but ambitious class of industrialists, lawyers and financiers. It was among such social groups that liberal ideas for the modernising of Russia began to take hold. There was also often a strong national element in Russian liberalism. The national minorities viewed the liberal movement as a means of advancing their claim to be independent of Russian imperial control. Three principal liberal parties came to prominence in the pre-1914 period: the Union of Liberation, the Octobrists and the Kadets.

Union of Liberation

The first significant reforming movement to emerge was the Union (also sometimes called League) of Liberation. Its principal leaders were academics **Paul Milyukov** and **Peter Struve**. Formed in 1904, the Union drew up a programme which expressed its basic aim.

SOURCE C

Extract from the programme of the Union of Liberation, 1904, quoted in David Christian, *Imperial and Soviet Russia*, Macmillan, 1997, p. 135.

The first and foremost aim of the Union of Liberation is the liberation of Russia. Considering political liberty in even its most minimal form completely incompatible with the absolute character of the Russian monarchy, the union will seek before all else the abolition of autocracy and the establishment in Russia of a constitutional regime. In determining the concrete forms in which a constitutional regime can be reduced to Russia, the Union of Liberation will make all efforts to have the political problems resolved in the spirit of extensive democracy. Above all, it recognises as fundamentally essential that the principle of universal equal, secret, and direct elections be made the basis of the political reform.

 KEY FIGURES

Paul Milyukov (1859–1943)
An outstanding liberal critic of tsardom, he grew increasingly disillusioned with the tsar and doubted that the system he represented could be saved.

Peter Struve (1870–1944)
A radical thinker and writer who had first been attracted to Marxism and for a short time was an SD member.

According to Source C, what is the basic aim of the Union of Liberation?

The union tried to bring the various liberal groups together by pointing out where there was common ground between them. Its influence helped to prepare the way for the 1905 Revolution and it continued to operate as a party until 1917. However, the union was unable to create a single coherent reforming movement with a single purpose. The union's deeper significance was in indicating the range of anti-tsarist feeling that existed and in advancing the arguments and ideas that the more progressive members of the government, such as Witte, took to heart. The union's programme was expressed in the type of language with which all liberal and reforming parties subsequently asserted their claims.

The Octobrists

This group dated from the issuing of the tsar's manifesto of October 1905, which created the *duma*. The Octobrists were moderates who were basically loyal to the tsar and his government. They believed in the maintenance of the Russian empire and regarded the manifesto and the establishment of the *duma* as major constitutional advances.

The Octobrists were mainly drawn from the larger commercial, industrial and landowning interests. Their leading members were **Alexander Guchkov** and **Mikhail Rodzianko**, both of whom were later to take a major part in the Provisional Government of 1917 (see page 99). How relatively restricted the Octobrists were in their aims can be gauged from their programme, issued in November 1905, which called for unity among all those who wanted the 'rule of law'. It appealed for the continuation of a 'strong and authoritative regime' to work with 'the representatives of the people' in bringing peace to the country.

The limited aims of the Octobrists led to their being dismissed by revolutionaries as bourgeois reactionaries who were unwilling to challenge the existing system. This was not wholly accurate. In the *dumas*, the Octobrists frequently voiced serious criticisms of the short-sightedness or incompetence of the tsarist government. They may not have wanted the overthrow of tsardom, but they were very willing to point out its failings.

The Constitutional Democrats (Kadets)

The Constitutional Democrats also came into being as a party at the time of the 1905 Revolution. The Kadets, the largest of the liberal parties, wanted Russia to develop as a **constitutional monarchy** in which the powers of the tsar would be restricted by a democratically elected constituent (national) assembly. They believed that such a body, representative of the whole of Russia, would be able to settle the nation's outstanding social, political and economic problems. Lenin dismissed this as bourgeois political naïvety, but there is no doubt that the dream of a constituent assembly remained a source of inspiration to Russian reformers in the period before the 1917 Revolution.

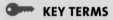

KEY TERMS

Duma The Russian parliament, which existed from 1906 to 1917.

Constitutional monarchy A system of government in which the king or emperor rules but only through elected representatives whose decisions he cannot countermand.

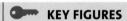

KEY FIGURES

Alexander Guchkov (1862–1936)

A major industrialist and factory owner.

Mikhail Rodzianko (1859–1924)

A large landowner.

The Kadet Party contained progressive landlords, the smaller industrial entrepreneurs and members of the professions. Academics were prominent in it, as typified by its leader, Paul Milyukov, who was a professor of history and had been a founder member of the Union of Liberation. In the *duma*, the Kadets proved to be the most outspoken critics of the tsarist system. They were to play a significant role in the events surrounding the February Revolution in 1917 (see page 86).

The Kadet Programme

- An All-Russian Constituent Assembly.
- Full equality and civil rights for all citizens.
- The ending of censorship.
- The abolition of the mortgage repayments on land.
- The recognition of trade unions and the right to strike.
- The introduction of universal, free education.

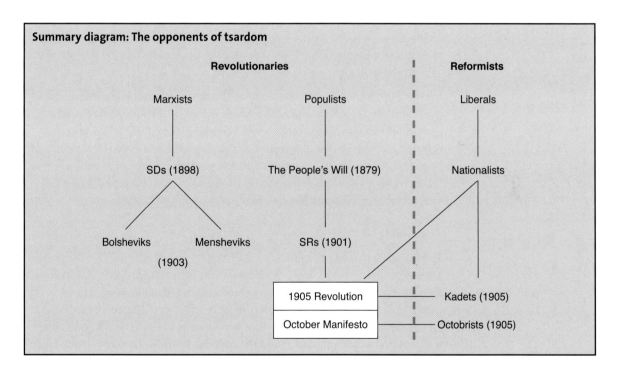

Summary diagram: The opponents of tsardom

The Russo-Japanese War 1904–5

▶ *Why did Russia go to war with Japan in 1904?*

The foreign policy that Nicholas II inherited and continued was largely determined by the size of the Russian empire. The protection of its many frontiers was a constant preoccupation. In 1904, Nicholas II faced his first major test in foreign affairs when his country went to war with its far-eastern neighbour, Japan. It was a war largely of Russia's own making. The Russian government had three main motives:

- to pursue an expansionist policy in the Far East, to make up for what it saw as its relative decline in Europe
- to obtain an ice-free port, something for which Russia had yearned for centuries, all its major ports being unusable in the winter months when they froze
- to distract attention from Russia's domestic troubles by rallying the nation in a patriotic struggle.

In regard to the last motive, it used to be thought that Vyacheslav Plehve, the interior minister, was the main force pushing for war. His words 'We need a small, victorious war to avert a revolution' were often quoted. However, research has shown that Plehve was deliberately misrepresented by his political opponent, Witte. We now know that Plehve was reluctant to go to war, whereas Witte, wishing to see Russia expand economically into the Far East, knew full well that this made conflict with Japan a very strong possibility.

The path to war

The Russians looked on Japan as an inferior nation and no match for themselves. They expected an easy victory. Pretexts for war were not hard to find. Territorial disputes between Russia and Japan over Korea and Manchuria were long-standing. In 1904, the Russian government curtly rejected Japanese proposals for the settlement of the two countries' rival claims to Korea. The Russian hope was that this would provoke a military response from the Japanese. It did: Japan opened hostilities by attacking the Russian fleet in Port Arthur.

The course of the conflict

The war itself soon revealed that Russia had greatly underestimated the strength of Japan. It was not the backward state the Russians had imagined. Under the Emperor Meiji (1869–1914), Japan had embarked upon a series of major reforms aimed at rapid modernisation along Western lines. The Japanese army and navy were far better prepared and equipped than the Russian forces and won a series

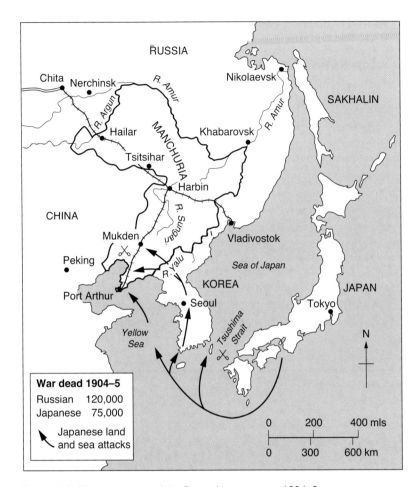

Figure 2.5 The main areas of the Russo-Japanese war, 1904–5.

of striking victories over them. For Russia, the conflict was a tale of confusion and disaster. After a long siege, Port Arthur fell to Japan in January 1905. The following month, the Japanese exploited their advantage by seizing the key Manchurian town of Mukden.

The final humiliation for Russia came at sea. The Russian Baltic fleet, dispatched to the Far East in 1904, took eight months to reach its destination, only to be blown out of the water immediately on its arrival by the Japanese fleet at Tsushima in May 1905. Such defeats obliged the tsarist government to make peace. In the Treaty of Portsmouth, Russia agreed to withdraw its remaining forces from Manchuria and accepted Japanese control of Korea and Port Arthur.

Russia's defeat

Russia lost the war not because its troops fought badly, but because its military leaders had not prepared effectively:

- The commanders understood neither the enemy they were fighting nor the territory in which the struggle took place.
- Their unimaginative strategy allowed the Japanese to outmanoeuvre the Russian forces.
- The distance over which men and materials had to be transported from western Russia made it impossible to provide adequate reinforcements and supplies.
- The trans-Siberian railway, still incomplete in a number of sections, proved of little value. Russia's defeat at the hands of a small, supposedly inferior, Asian country was a national humiliation.

Within Russia, the incompetence of the government, which the war glaringly exposed, excited the social unrest that it had been specifically designed to dampen. Russia's dismal performance was a potent factor in the increasing tension which eventually led to an open challenge to tsardom – the 1905 Revolution.

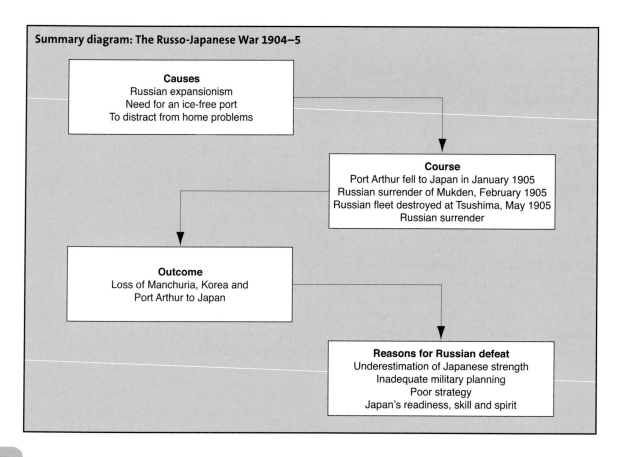

Summary diagram: The Russo-Japanese War 1904–5

Causes
Russian expansionism
Need for an ice-free port
To distract from home problems

Course
Port Arthur fell to Japan in January 1905
Russian surrender of Mukden, February 1905
Russian fleet destroyed at Tsushima, May 1905
Russian surrender

Outcome
Loss of Manchuria, Korea and
Port Arthur to Japan

Reasons for Russian defeat
Underestimation of Japanese strength
Inadequate military planning
Poor strategy
Japan's readiness, skill and spirit

5 The 1905 Revolution

▶ *How far was the tsarist government responsible for the 1905 Revolution?*

The reasons for the revolution

The situation created by the government's policy of political repression was graphically described by Leo Tolstoy (1828–1910), the world-renowned Russian novelist and philosopher. In 1902, in an 'Open address to Nicholas II', he detailed the persecution under which Russia groaned. Prisons were overflowing with convicts innocent of any real crime, the city streets were full of soldiers ready to shoot the people on a whim, and the censors' power stretched everywhere, denying freedom of religious and political expression. Things were no better in the countryside, where famine was a constant source of peasant misery. Presiding over this grim scene, Tolstoy asserted, was a government that squeezed money from the people through heavy taxation but was incapable of providing leadership. The result was 'the general dissatisfaction of all classes with the government and their open hostility against it'. Tolstoy's dispiriting conclusion was that it was 'impossible to maintain this form of government except by violence'.

The bleak picture which Tolstoy painted did not necessarily mean that confrontation, still less revolution, was unavoidable. After all, if oppression is applied firmly enough it prevents effective challenges to government. What weakened the tsarist regime in the period before 1917 was not its tyranny but its incompetence. It is certainly true that the crisis that occurred in Russia in 1905 was in large measure due to the mishandling of the situation by the tsar and his government. This was shown by the speed with which the government reasserted its authority once it had recovered its nerve.

The year 1905 marked the first time the tsarist government had been faced by a combination of the three main opposition classes in Russia: the industrial workers, the peasantry and the reformist middle class. This was the broad-based revolt that most revolutionaries had been awaiting. Yet, when it came, it was accidental rather than planned. Despite the efforts of the various revolutionary parties to politicise events, the strikes and demonstrations in the pre-1905 period had been the result of economic rather than political factors. They had been a reaction to industrial recession and bad harvests. It was the tsarist regime's ill-judged policies that turned the disturbances of 1905 into a direct challenge to its own authority.

The course of events

Bloody Sunday

The 1905 Revolution began with what has become known as Bloody Sunday. On 22 January, Father Georgi Gapon, an Orthodox priest, attempted to lead a peaceful march of workers and their families to the Winter Palace in St Petersburg. The marchers' intention was to present a loyal petition to the tsar, begging him to use his royal authority to relieve their desperate conditions. However, the march induced panic in the police forces in the capital. The marchers were fired on and charged by cavalry. There are no precise casualty figures, but estimates suggest that up to 200 marchers may have been killed, with hundreds more being injured. The deaths were depicted by opponents of the tsarist regime as a deliberate massacre of unarmed petitioners. Although Nicholas II was in fact absent from St Petersburg when these events took place, they gravely damaged the traditional image of the tsar as the '**Little Father**'. In the midst of the death and confusion, Gapon had repeatedly cried out: 'There is no God any longer. There is no Tsar.'

Disorder spreads

The immediate reaction to Bloody Sunday in Russia at large was a widespread outbreak of disorder, which increased as the year went on. Strikes occurred in all the major cities and towns. Terrorism against government officials and landlords, much of it organised by the Social Revolutionaries, spread to the countryside. The situation was made worse by Russia's humiliation in the war against Japan (see page 32). The government was blamed for Russia's defeat, which led to further outrages, including the assassination of Plehve by SR terrorists. Public buildings in towns and large private estates in the country were attacked. Land and properties were seized by the peasants, who then squatted in the landlords' houses. An important factor motivating the peasants was the fear that the government was about to repossess the homes of those families who had failed to pay off the mortgages taken out in the post-emancipation years (see page 46).

The unrest and the government's difficulties in containing it encouraged the non-Russian minorities to assert themselves. Georgia declared itself an independent state, the Poles demanded **autonomy** and the Jews pressed for equal rights. In May, Paul Milyukov, leader of the Union of Liberation, persuaded the majority of the liberal groups to join in forming a 'Union of Unions', with the aim of organising a broad-based alliance that would include the peasants and the factory workers. A 'Union of Unions' declaration was issued, which referred to the government as 'a terrible menace' and called for a constituent assembly to replace 'the gang of robbers' now in power. It was from this Union of Unions that the Kadet party, also led by Milyukov, would be formed in 1905 (see page 31).

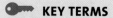

KEY TERMS

Little Father A traditional term denoting the tsar's paternal care of his people.

Autonomy National self-government.

Father Georgi Gapon

1903	Helped found the Assembly of Russian Workers
1904	Involved in organising a mass strike
1905	January, led workers' march to present a petition to the tsar
	February, fled to Geneva after Bloody Sunday massacre
	December, returned to St Petersburg
1906	March, murdered

Gapon remains an intriguing character. There were strong suspicions that he was an *Okhrana* **double-agent**. Sometimes he genuinely sympathised with the workers, as suggested by his efforts in organising the Assembly of Russian Factory and Plant Workers. He said he wanted to 'build a nest among the factory and mill workers where a truly Russian spirit would prevail'. Yet, on other occasions, he was willing to inform on those he led and to betray them to the authorities.

At the time of Bloody Sunday he appeared to be sincere in his wish to lead the workers in protest; indeed, he ignored a direct order from the authorities to call off the march. Having escaped serious injury or arrest during the suppression of the protest, he immediately fled from Russia to join a group of SDs in Geneva. It was there that he met Lenin. Krupskaya, Lenin's wife, recorded that her husband learned a great deal about Russian peasant problems from Gapon. For his part, Lenin tried to convert Gapon to Marxism.

Yet, by the end of 1905, Gapon had returned to St Petersburg, declaring that he no longer believed in revolution and that he wished to help the government to track down its enemies. This may have been a ruse. Perhaps he intended to infiltrate government circles as an SD spy. The only hard fact is that in March 1906 he was murdered, apparently by *Okhrana* agents, although even this is unclear.

Modern historians tend to agree that Gapon was naïve politically and became involved in events he never fully grasped. A contemporary was once asked whether Gapon was a supporter of constitutionalism. He replied, 'Support it? He can't even say it.' Whatever Gapon's real intentions may have been, his lack of understanding of political realities made him a fascinating but ultimately powerless participant in the 1905 Revolution.

The *Potemkin* mutiny

The summer of 1905 brought the still more disturbing news for the tsarist authorities of mutinies in the army and navy. The rank and file soldiers in the army were peasants who were naturally reluctant to attack their own kind – workers on strike or rebellious peasants in the countryside. There were several instances of troops disobeying orders to shoot unarmed strikers or to use force to drive peasants from the properties they had occupied.

In June there were even worse tidings for the government. The crew of the battleship *Prince Potemkin*, of the Black Sea naval squadron, mutinied while at sea. The incident began as a protest by the sailors at having to eat rotting food and drink foul water; particular horrors were **borsch**, and scraps of meat crawling with maggots. The sailors elected a representative, Peter Vakulenchuk, to approach the captain with their complaints. The captain's immediate response was to have the man shot. In retaliation, the crew attacked the officers, killed several of them and then took over the ship. This was a desperate act and could have worked only if the other ships in the squadron had mutinied also.

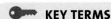

KEY TERMS

Double-agent
A government spy who pretends to be working for the opposition against the authorities but who reports plans and secrets back to the authorities.

Borsch A thin soup made from rotting beetroot.

SOURCE D

How valuable are the photos in Source C when studying the impact of the *Potemkin* mutiny?

There are no photographs of the *Potemkin* mutiny. These two stills are taken from the feature film *Battleship Potemkin*, made in 1925 by Sergei Eisenstein, the pro-Bolshevik director. The images from his silent film are so powerful that they have conditioned the way the actual event itself is now visualised.

But they did not; despite the equally grim conditions in the other ships, the captains managed to maintain control. The crew of the *Potemkin* was on its own.

Hoping to arouse support on land, the crew sailed to the port of Odessa, where a serious anti-government strike was taking place. The strikers welcomed the crew as heroes and formally honoured the body of Vakulenchuk by laying it on an elevated platform and surrounding it with flowers. It was a defiant gesture of solidarity but it enraged the authorities, who could not tolerate strikers and mutineers making common cause. Troops were ordered to disperse the crowds who had gathered in the harbour at the foot of a deep and wide flight of steps. With bayonets fixed, the soldiers marched resolutely down the steps, trampling on those who fell in front of them and driving hundreds into the sea. The civilian death toll ran into thousands.

The massacre forced the *Potemkin* to leave Odessa. Since no other ships had sided with them, the sailors decided to cut their losses. They sailed around the Black Sea looking for a safer area to land. Eventually they abandoned the ship in a Romanian port, hoping to find sanctuary for themselves in this remoter part of the Russian empire.

Although the mutiny was restricted to one ship, there was no doubt that the affair was deeply troubling to the Russian authorities. A government that cannot rely on the loyalty of its armed services, particularly in time of war, is in a very vulnerable position. The end of the Russo-Japanese War in August did little to ease the situation. Indeed, Witte feared that the returning troops would join the revolution. If this happened, he said, 'then everything would collapse'.

Witte's role

Nicholas II had shown his distaste for Sergei Witte years earlier when he had relieved him of his post as finance minister after ten years' loyal service (see page 17). However, it was to Witte that the tsar now turned in June 1905. Witte's first task was to negotiate peace terms with the Japanese. With this successfully completed, he then became chairman of the council of ministers, the effective head of the tsar's government. Yet, Witte remained frustrated by the inability of the tsar and his ministers to understand the crisis Russia was in. He referred to government policy as a 'mixture of cowardice, blindness and stupidity'. Nevertheless, he remained at his post, driven by a sense of duty to do his best to steer the regime through its difficulties.

Failure of the August Manifesto

It was on Witte's advice that the tsar issued the August Manifesto, an attempt to lessen the tensions by making concessions, the principal one being a promise to create a state assembly of elected representatives of the 51 provinces of the empire, which would begin sitting in January 1906. However, the powers the assembly would have were not clearly defined. Moreover, since the tsar added the clause, 'We reserve to ourselves exclusively the care of perfecting the organisation of the Assembly', the clear implication was that he did not intend his royal authority to be restricted in any way. The limited concession the manifesto represented did not work. In September a series of strikes had begun in both St Petersburg and Moscow. Striking workers were joined by striking students, whose activities brought the universities to a standstill and added to the general disorder in the capital.

Soviets

By October 1905, the industrial unrest had grown into a general strike. It was in this atmosphere that a development of particular moment occurred. In a number of cities, most notably in St Petersburg and Moscow, workers formed themselves into an elected **soviet**. The soviets began as organisations to represent the workers' demands for better conditions, but their potential as bases for political agitation was immediately recognised by revolutionaries. The Menshevik, Leon Trotsky, became chairman of the St Petersburg soviet and organiser of several strikes in the capital.

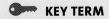 **KEY TERM**

Soviet Russian word for a council made up of elected representatives.

Government recovery

By October, the tsar was faced by the most united opposition in Romanov history. But, recognising the danger, the regime now began to show the sense of purpose that it had so far lacked. Concession was unavoidable, but, by giving ground, the government intended to divide the opposition forces ranged against it:

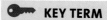

KEY TERM

Legislative *duma*
A parliament with law-making powers.

- The liberals were the first to be appeased. On Witte's advice, the tsar issued the October Manifesto in which, going further than he had in the August Manifesto, he accepted the creation of a **legislative *duma***: 'Our will is that no law can be made without the agreement of the State *Duma*.' Since the manifesto, which Witte had written, also contained a promise to introduce a range of civil rights, including freedom of speech, assembly and worship, and the legalising of trade unions, the liberals could claim a remarkable success. Their appetite for reform was satisfied, at least temporarily.
- The peasants were the next to be pacified by an announcement in November that the mortgage repayments which had so troubled them were to be progressively reduced and then abolished altogether. The response was an immediate drop in the number of land-seizures by the peasants and a decline in the general lawlessness in the countryside.
- Having won over the liberals and peasants, the government was now seriously opposed by only one major group – the industrial workers. Here the policy was one not of concession but of suppression. The government felt strong enough to attempt to crush the soviets. Despite the mutinies earlier in the year, the troops who returned from the Far East at the end of the war proved sufficiently loyal to be used against the strikers. After a five-day siege, the headquarters of the St Petersburg soviet were stormed and the ringleaders, including Trotsky, were arrested. The destruction of an uprising in Moscow proved even more violent.

Moscow uprising suppressed

On 7 December, a group of Bolsheviks, Mensheviks and SRs came together in the recently formed Moscow soviet to organise a general strike. Encouraged by their success in this, they then seized a number of key installations, including post offices and railway stations, in an attempt to take over the whole city. However, tsarist regiments, some of whom had recently suppressed the St Petersburg soviet, were rushed to Moscow. There they used heavy artillery to force the insurgents into an increasingly confined area. To avoid being slaughtered, the soviet resisters surrendered on 18 December. Lenin, who had encouraged the uprising but had played no direct part in it, arrived in Moscow just in time to witness the flames of the gutted soviet buildings, set ablaze by government troops. The twelve-day uprising had led to the deaths of over 1000 people.

The significance of the 1905 Revolution

A notable feature of the 1905 Revolution was how minor a part was played by the revolutionaries. Hardly any of them were in St Petersburg or Moscow when it began. Revolution occurred in spite, rather than because, of them. With the exception of Trotsky, none of the SDs made an impact on the course of events. This throws doubt on the notion of 1905 as a revolution.

There is the further fact that in a number of important respects tsardom emerged from the disturbances stronger rather than weaker. Despite its disastrous failure in the war against Japan, which produced protest throughout Russia and united the classes in opposition, the tsarist regime survived 1905 remarkably unscathed. The mutinies in the armed services did not spread and did not continue after the war. Loyal troops returned to destroy the soviets. The readiness of the liberals and the peasants to accept the government's political and economic bribes indicated that neither of those groups was genuinely ready for revolution.

It is true that the tsar appeared to grant significant concessions in the October Manifesto, but these were expedients rather than real reforms. The *duma* was not intended to be, nor did it become, a limitation on the tsar's autocratic powers. This was evident from the Fundamental Laws, which Nicholas II promulgated in April 1906: 'The Sovereign Emperor possesses the initiative in all legislative matters … The Sovereign Emperor ratifies the laws. No law can come into force without his approval.'

The lesson of the 1905 Revolution

What 1905 showed was that as long as the tsarist government kept its nerve and the army remained loyal, the forces of protest would find it very difficult to mount a serious challenge. The events of 1905 also raised questions about the extent to which the liberals wanted change in Russia. Few of them enjoyed their experience of mixing with the workers during the revolution. They found proletarian coarseness unattractive and were frightened by the primitive forces they had helped to unleash. One middle-class proprietor, who had thrown his house open to the strikers, remarked on the difficulty of sustaining his belief in the goodness of people who abused his hospitality by molesting his daughters, urinating on his carpets and stealing everything they could carry. Peter Struve, who had been a founder member of the Union of Liberation before joining the Kadets in 1905, spoke for all frightened liberals when he said 'Thank God for the tsar, who has saved us from the people.'

Leon Trotsky reflected that 1905 had failed as a revolution because the protestors were disunited and inexperienced. Furthermore, the liberals had backed out of the revolution and betrayed the workers by leaving them to be crushed by government troops. He concluded that the tsarist system, 'although with a few broken ribs, had come out of the experience of 1905 alive and strong'.

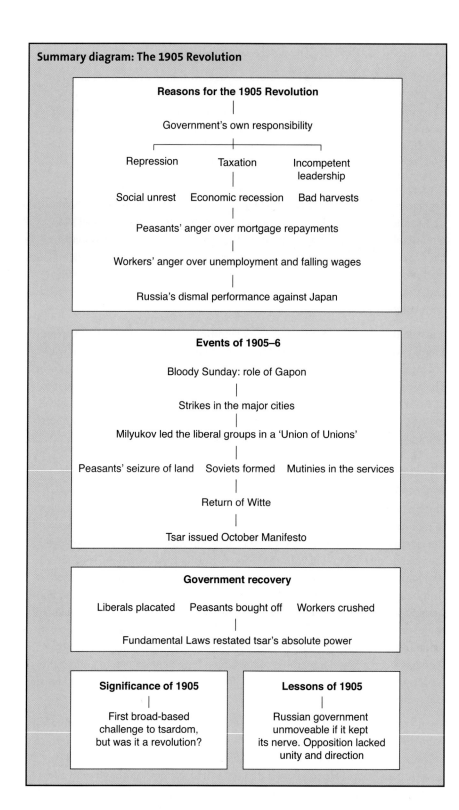

Chapter summary

Led by a tsar and a government that were reluctant to engage in reform, Russia faced the problem of how to achieve modernity. The answer of tsardom's leading statesman, Witte, was to shape the economy in such a way that the nation could compete at parity with its European rivals. He encouraged industrial expansion and urged the state to take the lead in this by encouraging foreign investments. His efforts undoubtedly contributed to Russia's achieving the 'great spurt' of the 1890s.

Notwithstanding its economic growth, Russia's slowness in reforming politically led to the development of opposition from liberals and revolutionaries. While liberals believed that tsardom could be reformed into a constitutional monarchy, revolutionaries were convinced that only by the destruction of tsardom could Russia be modernised. Choosing to go to war with Japan in 1904, the government was shocked by Russia's defeat, which proved a major factor in the outbreak of the 1905 Revolution when a loose alliance of peasants, industrial workers and liberals joined in resistance and protest. The government recovered its nerve and survived for the time being by satisfying the peasants with the cancelling of their mortgage repayments, placating the liberals by political concessions, and physically suppressing the protesting workers.

Refresher questions

Use these questions to remind yourself of the key material covered in this chapter.

1 Why was it so difficult for Russia to reform itself?

2 What was Russification intended to achieve?

3 What methods did Sergei Witte use to develop the Russian economy?

4 How successful were Witte's policies?

5 What were the main ideas of the Social Revolutionaries (SRs)?

6 What was the impact of Marxism on the Social Democrats (SDs)?

7 What led to the divide in the SD Party?

8 How strong were the Bolsheviks before 1917?

9 What had encouraged the growth of a liberal movement in tsarist Russia?

10 How sweeping was the Kadet Programme for the reform of tsarist Russia?

11 How critical were the Octobrists of the tsarist system?

12 Why did Russia perform so badly in the Russo-Japanese war?

13 What pattern did the 1905 Revolution follow?

14 Why was the *Potemkin* mutiny such a serious threat to the tsarist regime?

15 What steps did the government take to deal with the challenge facing it in 1905?

Question practice

ESSAY QUESTIONS

1 'The only policy Nicholas II's government genuinely followed between 1894 and 1904 was one of repression.' How far do you agree with this statement?

2 How far did Witte succeed in his plans to reform Russian industry in the years 1892–1903?

3 How accurate is it to say that by 1905, Russia's revolutionary parties had failed to make any real advance towards their goal of undermining tsardom?

4 To what extent was the 1905 Revolution the result of the mistakes made by the tsarist regime?

SOURCE QUESTIONS

1 Why is Source 1 valuable to the historian for an enquiry into the causes of Bloody Sunday in January 1905? Explain your answer, using the source, the information given about it and your own knowledge of the historical context.

2 How much weight do you give the evidence of Source 1 for an enquiry into the attitude of the Petrograd workers towards the tsar in January 1905? Explain your answer, using the source, the information given about it and your own knowledge of the historical context.

SOURCE I

From a petition intended to be delivered by striking industrial workers to Tsar Nicholas II on Sunday 9 January 1905 ('Bloody Sunday'), quoted in Lionel Kochan, *Russia in Revolution 1890–1918*, Granada, 1966, p. 99.

We working men and inhabitants of St Petersburg, our wives and children, and our parents, helpless and aged men and women, have come to You, our ruler, in quest of justice and protection. We have no strength at all, O Sovereign. Our patience is at an end. We are approaching that terrible moment when death is better than continuance of intolerable sufferings.

Our first request was that our employers should discuss with us but this they refused to do. They regarded as illegal our other demands: reduction of the working day to eight hours, the fixing of wage rates in consultation with us, and investigation of our grievances against the factory managements. We have been in bondage [slavery] with the help and co-operation of Your officials. Anyone who dares to speak up in defence of the interests of the working class and ordinary people is jailed or exiled. Is this, O Sovereign, in accordance with the laws of God, by whose grace you reign?

CHAPTER 3

Romanov rule 1906–14

In the aftermath of the 1905 Revolution, the tsarist government entertained thoughts of limited reform. Stolypin attempted to modernise Russia's agriculture while the newly permitted political parties vied for influence in the *duma*. On the industrial front, tensions increased, taking their most serious form in a general strike in 1914. Whether such experiments and developments weakened or strengthened tsardom is the underlying theme of this chapter. It also looks at foreign policy before 1914, examining Russia's long-term reasons for entering the First World War, before concluding with an assessment of the tsar's standing in 1914. The key areas examined are:

★ Economic policy under Stolypin

★ The *dumas* 1906–14

★ Growing tensions in Russia 1911–14

★ Russia's foreign policy before 1914

★ The tsar's position at the outbreak of war in 1914

The key debate on *page 65* of this chapter asks the question: Was tsardom already doomed in 1914?

Key dates

1906	Fundamental Laws issued	1911–14	Period of growing political and social tension
	First *duma*	1912	Lena goldfields episode
1906–11	Stolypin's years as chief minister	1912–14	Fourth *duma*
1907	Second *duma*	1914	General strike in St Petersburg
1907–12	Third *duma*		Germany declared war on Russia

Economic policy under Stolypin

 ▶ *What was Stolypin aiming to achieve in his dealings with the peasants?*

Stolypin and land reform

Peter Stolypin was appointed president of the council of ministers in July 1906. Like Witte before him, he was dedicated to strengthening tsardom in a time of crisis. He was a political conservative, whose attitude was clearly expressed in the coercive measures he introduced between 1906 and 1911. He declared his guiding principle to be 'suppression first and then, and only then, reform'. However, he also considered that, where possible, reform should be introduced as a way of reducing the social bitterness on which opposition fed. It was in this spirit that he approached the land problem in Russia.

Rural crisis

Stolypin started from the conviction that industrial progress by itself could not solve Russia's most pressing need: how to feed the nation's rapidly growing population. The marked increase in population that occurred in the late nineteenth century had resulted in land shortage and rural overpopulation. This **rural crisis** was deepened by a series of bad harvests; the years 1891 and 1897 witnessed severe famines which left millions starving. The government's land policies following the emancipation of the serfs in 1861 had not helped. The scheme under which state mortgages were advanced to the emancipated serfs to enable them to buy their properties had not created the system of stable land tenure that the government had expected. The high price of land, which led to heavy mortgage repayments being undertaken, had impoverished the peasantry. Their sense of insecurity both inhibited them from being efficient food-producers and made them a dangerous social force.

'De-revolutionising' the peasantry

One of the reasons why the peasants had joined the revolution in 1905 was their fear that the government was about to repossess the land of the mortgage-holders who had defaulted on their payments. When, under Stolypin's prompting, the government came to understand this fear, it bought off the peasants by announcing that the outstanding repayments would be cancelled. Stolypin referred to this tactic as 'de-revolutionising' the peasants.

The 'wager on the strong'

Stolypin planned to build on this successful treatment of the peasantry. In 1906–7, he introduced measures to restore the peasants' sense of security:

- Farmers were urged to abandon the inefficient strip system and replace it with fenced fields, based on the pattern that existed in western Europe.

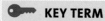 **KEY TERM**

Rural crisis Land shortage and overpopulation in the countryside resulting from the huge number of people living in Russia by the late nineteenth century.

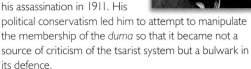

Peter Stolypin

1862	Born into an aristocratic family
1902	Appointed as a regional governor
1906	April, appointed interior minister
	July, appointed prime minister
1906–11	Served as prime minister
1906–7	Introduced 'wager on the strong'
1907	Effective liaison with the second *duma*
1911	Assassinated

Stolypin studied agriculture at university and went on to hold minor government posts before rising to become governor of Kovno and then Saratov. His experience of the peasants led him to believe that to improve their conditions and make them more productive they needed both encouragement and stern political control. He followed both approaches. He wanted to break the peasants' dependence on collective and communal farming by giving them incentives to farm efficiently and profitably. This was not done out of pure altruism; if the peasants were left aggrieved, they would continue to be a dangerous source of social unrest. Stolypin's complementary policy of suppressing the 'dark masses' to prevent their becoming a disruptive force was evident in the harshness of the social policies he enforced until his assassination in 1911. His political conservatism led him to attempt to manipulate the membership of the *duma* so that it became not a source of criticism of the tsarist system but a bulwark in its defence.

Stolypin was faced by the same problem that had confronted Witte; the leading members of the Russian establishment he was trying to save never fully appreciated what he was doing or gave him the support he needed. His attempt to convince them of the paradox that in order to conserve they had to be less conservative proved unavailing. They approved his repressive measures but never grasped that repression alone would not solve Russia's crises and that it had to be coupled with economic modernisation. Stolypin's uncompromising political stance, mixed with a strong sense of economic realism, offered a way out of the institutional crisis that threatened to destroy Imperial Russia. Tsardom's tragedy was that it never understood this.

- The current trend of peasants grouping in **obschina** was discouraged and incentives were given to peasants to return to individual farming.
- A special Land Bank was established to provide funds for the independent peasant to buy his land.
- Schemes for large-scale voluntary resettlement of the peasants were implemented, the aim being to populate the empire's remoter areas, such as Siberia, and turn them into food-growing areas.

 KEY TERM

Obschina Peasant communes set up within the localities.

Stolypin defined his policy as a 'wager on the strong'. His intention was to create a layer of prosperous, productive peasants who would farm independently of the communes and whose new wealth would turn them into natural supporters of the tsarist system.

Difficulties confronting Stolypin

The standard view of most scholars in this field has been that Stolypin had little real chance of reforming agriculture since the Russian peasantry was so backward and he had so little time to change things. Others, however, have argued that, while it is true that the conservatism of most peasants prevented them from embracing progressive change, Stolypin was right, nonetheless,

Figure 3.1 Strip farming as practised in central Russia c.1900. Each scattered black strip represents the land farmed individually by one of the various nineteen households. The thicker the line, the larger the amount of land owned by a family.

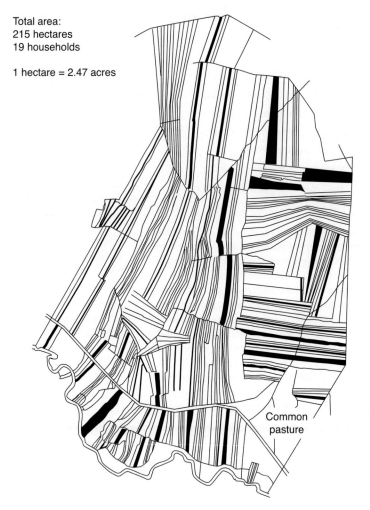

Total area:
215 hectares
19 households

1 hectare = 2.47 acres

Common pasture

in thinking that he could 'wager on the strong' since there was, indeed, a layer of strong peasant farmers. This argument is based on evidence drawn from tsarist tax returns, which show that a significant minority of peasants were paying increasingly higher taxes in the decade before 1914, a sign that their farming was producing high profits.

However, even if one accepts that there was a progressive element among the peasants, there is no certainty that this would have been enough to modernise Russian agriculture. Even in advanced economies land reform takes time to work. Stolypin was well aware that, in a country as relatively backward as Russia, the changes would take even longer to become effective. He spoke of needing twenty years for his 'wager on the strong' to bring results. In the event, his assassination in 1911 allowed him personally only five years, and the coming of the war in 1914 allowed Russia only eight.

The doubt remains whether, even without the interruption of murder and war, Stolypin's peasant policy would have succeeded. The deep conservatism of the mass of the Russian peasants made them slow to respond. In 1914, the strip system was still widespread. As Table 3.1 shows, only some fifteen per cent of the land had been consolidated into farms. Most peasants were reluctant to leave the security of the commune for the uncertainty of individual farming. Furthermore, by 1913 the government's own ministry of agriculture had itself begun to lose confidence in the policy.

Table 3.1 Number of peasant households that opted to set up independent farms (out of an estimated total of 10–12 million households) 1907–14

1907	48,271
1908	508,344
1909	579,409
1910	342,245
1911	145,567
1912	122,314
1913	134,554
1914	97,877

Benefits of Stolypin's liaison with the *duma*

One notable feature of Stolypin's land policy was his effective working relations with the *duma*. The understanding which he developed with the Octobrists, the largest party in the third *duma* (see page 54), allowed him to pursue his reforms with little obstruction from the other deputies. His success here hinted at how much co-operation might have developed between government and progressive opinion had the tsarist regime been willing to trust its own ministers.

The industrial front

Although Witte was no longer a minister after 1906, his earlier work still influenced Russian industrial development and it is arguable that had he remained in charge he might have been able to avoid, or at least lessen, the impact of the recurrent recessions that occurred. The period from 1908 to 1914 saw an overall increase in industrial output of 8.5 per cent (Table 3.2).

Table 3.2 Economic growth in Russia 1908–14

	1908	1914
State revenues (in roubles)	2 billion	4 billion
Number of banks	1,146	2,393
Number of factories	22,600	24,900
Number of workers	2,500,000	2,900,000

Nevertheless, against the bright picture these figures paint has to be set the darker aspect. Few workers gained from the industrial and financial expansion. Weak trade unions and minimal legal protection left the workforce very much at the mercy of the employers. Little of the greater amount of money in circulation reached the pockets of the workers. Although the rate of inflation rose by 40 per cent between 1908 and 1914, the average industrial wage rose from 245 to only 264 roubles per month (seven per cent) in the same period. Of course, a national average does not tell the whole story. Some workers did better than others; for example, wages were 30 per cent higher in St Petersburg than in Moscow. Nonetheless, the large number of strikes in the pre-1914 years, culminating with a general strike in 1914, show the scale of the dissatisfaction with the conditions (see page 57).

Stolypin and Witte

It is helpful to regard the work of Witte and Stolypin as complementary: Witte was mainly concerned with the development of industry, Stolypin with the development of agriculture. This is not to suggest that the two men fully co-operated in a common policy. Witte was deeply jealous of Stolypin. Nevertheless, they did share a basic objective: the preservation of the tsarist system. Had the tsarist government and bureaucracy been willing to support Witte and Stolypin in their efforts to modernise the Russian economy, this might have prevented the build-up of the social and political tensions.

Resistance to reform

The economic policies of Witte and Stolypin and the introduction of the *duma* were important advances but they were not enough to alter the essentially reactionary character of the tsarist system. The government remained hostile towards reform. The tsar's resistance to change would have mattered less if the system had operated efficiently. But the tsarist autocracy was both oppressive and inefficient, thereby alienating the progressive elements in society, who could see no possibility of real advance in Russia as long as government and administration remained in the hands of incompetents. It was this that undermined the work of the few enlightened ministers, such as Witte and Stolypin, within the government. They were reformers but they were also loyalists. The irony was that they were not trusted by the representatives of the very system they were trying to preserve. By 1914, all the signs were that Imperial Russia was heading towards a major confrontation between intransigent tsardom and the forces of change.

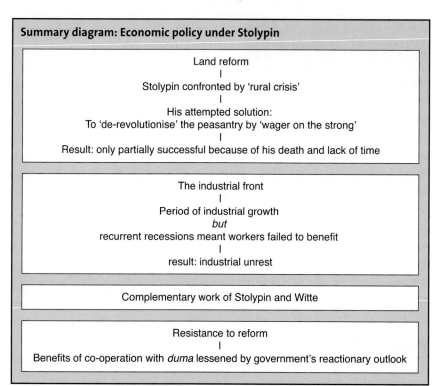

Summary diagram: Economic policy under Stolypin

Land reform
|
Stolypin confronted by 'rural crisis'
|
His attempted solution:
To 'de-revolutionise' the peasantry by 'wager on the strong'
|
Result: only partially successful because of his death and lack of time

The industrial front
|
Period of industrial growth
but
recurrent recessions meant workers failed to benefit
|
result: industrial unrest

Complementary work of Stolypin and Witte

Resistance to reform
|
Benefits of co-operation with *duma* lessened by government's reactionary outlook

2 The *dumas* 1906–14

▶ *How did the composition of the* dumas *change over the period 1906–14?*

The tsar's granting of a *duma* in the October Manifesto was the most striking of the concessions made to the liberals. It remained to be seen what role this new parliament, the first in Russian history, would play. There were four *dumas* in the years between the 1905 Revolution and the February Revolution of 1917 (see page 86). The four elections produced the results shown in Table 3.3.

Table 3.3 *Duma* election results

Party or group	First *duma* 1906	Second *duma* 1907	Third *duma* 1907–12	Fourth *duma* 1912–17
SDs (Mensheviks)	18	47	–	–
SDs (Bolsheviks)	–	–	19	15
SRs	–	37	–	–
Labourists	136	104	13	10
Kadets	182	91	54	53
Octobrists	17	42	154	95
Progressists	27	28	28	41
Rightists	8	10	147	154
National parties	60	93	26	22
Others	–	50	–	42
Total	448	502	441	432

The first *duma*, April–June 1906

The high hopes the liberals had held that the granting of the *duma* marked a real constitutional advance were dashed even before it first met. Having survived the challenge of the 1905 Revolution, the tsarist regime quickly recovered its confidence. Early in 1906, it successfully negotiated a substantial loan from France. This lessened the likelihood of the *dumas* being able to exercise a financial hold over the government.

A still greater limitation on the *duma*'s influence was the tsar's promulgation of the Fundamental Laws, which was timed to coincide with the opening of the *duma*. In addition to declaring that 'Supreme Autocratic Power belongs to the emperor of all Russia', the laws announced that the *duma* would be **bi-cameral**; one chamber would be an elected lower house, the other would be a state council, the majority of whose members would be appointed by the tsar.

The existence of a second chamber with the right of veto deprived the elected *duma* of any real power. Taken together with the declaration that no law could come into being without the tsar's approval, these restrictions made it clear that the tsarist regime had no intention of allowing the concessions it had made in 1905 to diminish its absolute authority. The tsar had made this clear during ministerial discussions preceding the issuing of the Fundamental Laws.

KEY TERMS

Labourists The Social Revolutionaries as a party officially boycotted the elections to the first *duma*, but stood as Labourists.

Progressists A party of businessmen who favoured moderate reform.

Rightists Not a single party; they represented a range of conservative views from right of centre to extreme reaction.

Bi-cameral A parliament made up of two chambers: an upper and a lower.

According to his statement in Source A, why was Nicholas II unwilling to consider any limitation on his power?

SOURCE A

Extract from the tsar's statement, April 1906, quoted in Marc Ferro, *Nicholas II: The Last of the Tsars*, Penguin, 1990, p. 107.

If I were convinced that Russia wanted me to abdicate my autocratic powers, I would do that, for the country's good. But I am not convinced this is so, and I do not believe that there is need to alter the nature of my supreme power. It is dangerous to change the way that power is formulated. I know, too, that if no change is made, this may give rise to agitation, to attacks. But where will these attacks come from? From so-called educated people, from the proletariat, from the Third Estate? Actually, I feel that eighty per cent of the people are with me.

Duma radicalism: the Vyborg appeal

The result was that the *duma* met in a mood of bitterness. The elections had returned an assembly that was dominated by the reformist parties, who immediately took a radical stance by voicing their anger at what they regarded as the government's reneging on its promises. They demanded that the rights and powers of the *duma* be increased. **Ivan Goremykin**, the chief minister, told them that their demands were 'inadmissible' and Nicholas II was reported as saying, 'Curse the *duma*. It is all Witte's doing.' After two months of bitter wrangling, the tsar ordered the *duma* to be dissolved.

In frustration, 200 Kadet and Labourist deputies reassembled at Vyborg in Finland, where they drew up an 'appeal', urging the people of Russia to defy their government in two main ways by:

- refusing to pay taxes
- disobeying conscription orders.

The rebellious Kadets who issued the appeal had made a serious tactical error. The response from the Russian people was not the widespread **passive disobedience** they had hoped for, but scattered violence. This provided the government with a ready excuse for retaliation. The tsar appointed Stolypin as chief minister to act as his strong man. The Vyborg group of deputies was arrested and debarred from re-election to the *duma*.

Repression under Stolypin

The crushing of the Vyborg group was the prelude to Stolypin's introduction of a policy of fierce repression, which he sustained until his assassination in 1911. **Martial law** was proclaimed and a network of military courts, with sweeping powers, was used to quell disturbances wherever they occurred. Between 1906 and 1911 there were over 2500 executions in Russia, a grim detail that, in a piece of black humour, led to the hangman's noose being nicknamed 'Stolypin's necktie'.

The Kadet failure in 1906 had serious long-term effects. Although the Kadet Party survived under the leadership of Milyukov, it never really recovered from

KEY FIGURE

Ivan Goremykin (1839–1917)

A committed monarchist and reactionary, he succeeded Witte as chief minister in 1906.

KEY TERMS

Passive disobedience Opposing government not by violent challenge but by refusing to obey particular laws.

Martial law The placing of the population under direct military authority.

SOURCE B

How effectively does the drawing in Source B depict the fate of the first *duma*?

THE DEATH OF THE FIRST-BORN.

**'Mother Russia weeping over the death of the first-born'.
A cartoon published in the British magazine *Punch* in August 1906 representing the failure of the first *duma*.**

its humiliation. The liberal cause had discredited itself, thus allowing both the left and the right to argue from their different standpoints that Russia's salvation could not be gained through moderate policies but only by revolution or extreme reaction.

The second *duma*, February–June 1907

The immediate result of the Vyborg fiasco was that, in the elections for the second *duma*, the Kadets lost half their seats. These were filled by the SDs and the SRs, who between them returned over 80 deputies. This made the new assembly strongly radical and anti-government. Indeed, the SRs proclaimed dramatically that it was 'the *duma* of the people's wrath'. However, since the right-wing parties had also increased their numbers, there was considerable disagreement within the *duma*, as well as between it and the government.

Whatever the internal divisions among the parties, the mood of the *duma* was undeniably hostile to the government. Stolypin, who, despite his stern repression of social disorder, was willing to work with the *duma* in introducing necessary reforms, found his land programme strenuously opposed. The tsar was particularly incensed when the *duma* directed a strong attack on the way the imperial army was organised and deployed. The SD and SR deputies were accused of engaging in subversion and Nicholas ordered that the assembly be dissolved. Deputies scuffled and shouted out in protest as the session was duly brought to an end.

The third *duma*, November 1907 to June 1912

Despite the **radicalism** of the first two *dumas*, the tsar made no attempt to dispense with the *duma* altogether. There were two main reasons for this:

- The first related to foreign policy. The tsar was keen to project an image of Russia as a democratic nation. He was advised by his foreign ministers, who at this time were in trade talks with France and Britain, that Russia's new commercial allies were greatly impressed by his creation of a representative national parliament.
- The second reason was that the *duma* had been rendered docile by the government's doctoring of the electoral system. Stolypin introduced new laws that restricted the vote to the propertied classes. The peasants and industrial workers lost the franchise. The consequence was that the third and fourth *dumas* were heavily dominated by the right-wing parties (as Table 3.3 on page 51 shows), a reversal of the position in the first two *dumas* in which the radical parties had held a large majority. Any criticisms of tsardom were now much more muted.

With the balance of the parties redressed in this way, Stolypin found the third *duma* more co-operative, which enabled him to pursue his land reforms without opposition from the deputies. This is not to say that the *duma* was entirely subservient. It exercised its right to question ministers and to discuss state finances. It also used its **committee system** to make important proposals for modernising the armed services. Among the bills it approved were social-reform measures that included setting up schools for the children of the poor and **national insurance** for industrial workers.

The fourth *duma*, November 1912 to August 1914

After 1917, it was usual for historians to follow the lead of the Bolsheviks in dismissing the later *dumas* as having been merely rubber stamps of government policy. However, modern scholars tend to be less dismissive. Although the fourth *duma* was less openly obstructive than the earlier ones had been, it still voiced criticism of the tsar's government. Interestingly, a Moscow *Okhrana* report in 1912 blamed the tension in Russia on the awkward and searching questions continually being asked in the *duma* about government policy.

🔑 KEY TERMS

Radicalism The desire to change society fundamentally – literally at its roots.

Committee system A process in which the *duma* deputies formed various subgroups to discuss and advise on particular issues.

National insurance A system of providing workers with state benefits, such as unemployment pay and medical treatment, in return for the workers contributing regularly to a central fund.

SOURCE C

From a Moscow *Okhrana* report in 1913, quoted in J.N. Westwood, *Endurance and Endeavour: Russian History 1812–1980*, Oxford University Press, 1985, p. 178.

People can be heard speaking of the government in the sharpest and most unbridled tones. Influenced by questions in the duma and the speeches which they called forth there, public tension is increasing still more. It is a long time since even the extreme left has spoken in such a way, since there have been references in the duma to 'the necessity of calling a Constituent Assembly and overthrowing the present system by the united strength of the proletariat'.

> According to Source C, what influence has the *duma* had in increasing social tension in Moscow in 1912?

Historians also emphasise the progressive work of the *duma* in providing the beginnings of state welfare and suggest that it was only the blindness of the tsarist government that prevented the *dumas* from making a greater contribution to the development of Russia. This, indeed, was the essence of the plea made by the *duma* chairman, Rodzianko, directly to the tsar in 1913, humbly requesting that the role of the *duma* should be clarified so that it could play a constructive role in Russian affairs.

SOURCE D

From a report by Rodzianko's of his audience of the tsar in 1913, quoted in Lionel Kochan, *Russia in Revolution*, Paladin, 1974, p. 171.

The members of the government either do not wish to execute your will, or do not take the trouble to understand it. Each minister has his own opinion. The cabinet is for the most part split into two parties, the state council form a third, the Duma a fourth, and your own will is unknown to the nation. This not government, it is anarchy.

> Read Source D. Why has the tsar's government descended into anarchy?

Summary diagram: The *dumas* 1906–14

	Character	Achievements
1st *duma* 1906	Dominated by reformist parties	Short lived – little achieved
2nd *duma* 1907	Clash between revolutionaries and right-wing parties	Dissolved in disorder – little achieved
3rd *duma* 1907–12	Election rigged by Stolypin to produce more co-operative deputies from moderate parties	Committees did achieve effective work in social reform
4th *duma* 1912–14	Dominated by right-wing parties again willing to co-operate	Social reform work continued, but prepared to criticise government

The debate on the role of the *dumas*
- Were they ever more than a talking shop?
- How valuable was their committee work?
- How significant were they as critics of tsardom?

Growing tensions in Russia 1911–14

▶ *Why was there mounting political and social strain during 1911–14?*

Urban unrest

Initially, during the great spurt (see page 16), the peasants who had left the land to work in the urban areas were prepared to accept their grim factory conditions because of the higher wages they received. However, recurrent recessions caused widespread unemployment. The authorities found themselves facing large numbers of rootless workers who had had their expectations of a better life dashed by harsh economic realities. The regular presence of thousands of disaffected workers on the streets of St Petersburg and Moscow played an important part in the growth of serious social unrest in Russia between 1911 and 1914.

Repression and disorder

Following Stolypin's assassination in 1911, the various ministers the tsar appointed were distinguished only by their ineptitude. Since they lacked political imagination, their only course was further repression. Between 1911 and 1914 the regime's terror tactics were both cause and effect of a dramatic increase in public disorder. The number of strikes listed as 'political' by the ministry of trade and industry rose from 24 in 1911 to 2401 in 1914, the year of a general strike. Trotsky's estimates put the number of political strikes even higher. This discrepancy was explained by the difficulty of distinguishing between a strike for better pay or conditions, and a strike as a political act of protest.

The Lena goldfields incident 1912

The Moscow *Okhrana* report (Source C, page 55) that had referred to the role of the *duma* in creating tension went on to cite the 'shooting of the Lena workers' as the major reason why the 'people can be heard speaking of the government in the sharpest and most unbridled tones'. The mention of the Lena workers was a reference to the notorious incident that occurred in 1912 in the Lena goldfields in Siberia. Demands from the miners there for better pay and conditions were resisted by the employers, who appealed to the police to arrest the strike leaders as criminals.

The issue thus became the much larger one of trade union rights in Russia. When the police moved into Lena, the strikers closed ranks and the situation rapidly deteriorated, resulting in troops firing on and killing or injuring a large number of miners. The *Okhrana* appeared to have acted as **agents provocateurs** in order to identify the organisers of the strike.

 **KEY TERM**

Agents provocateurs
Government agents who infiltrate opposition movements with the aim of stirring up trouble so that the ringleaders can be exposed.

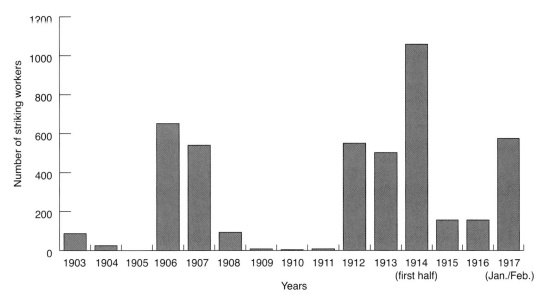

Figure 3.2 Trotsky's estimate of the numbers of workers striking for political reasons, 1903–17. (Source: Leon Trotsky, *The History of the Russian Revolution*, Sphere Books, 1967, p. 56.)

General strike 1914

Even the moderate liberal parties began to despair of the government's dealing effectively with the problems that confronted Russia. The Octobrist leader, Alexander Guchkov, told his party conference in 1913 that their attempts to achieve 'a peaceful, painless transition from the old condemned system to a new order' had failed. He warned that the blindness of the tsar's government was daily driving the Russian people closer to revolution. Guchkov's warning seemed to be closer to realisation in July 1914 when a general strike paralysed St Petersburg. Barricades were erected by the strikers which the police tried to break down; violence followed as the two sides clashed. Many of the progressive members of the *duma* openly supported the strikers. What finally prevented matters getting out of hand was Russia's entry into the First World War later that month.

Summary diagram: Growing tensions in Russia 1911–14

Urban unrest
Disaffected workers took to the streets
Strikes spread
Repression the government's only response to disorder

The Lena goldfields incident 1912
revealed
Worker militancy and government brutality

General strike 1914
Ended only by outbreak of war

Russia's foreign policy before 1914

 ▶ *By 1914, what factors had shaped Russia's attitude towards the outside world?*

Russia's foreign concerns

As an empire covering a huge land area, tsarist Russia had always been concerned for the security of its borders, but its major anxiety was in regard to its European frontiers. Russia believed that the greatest potential threat came from its neighbours in central and south-eastern Europe. Three particular developments in Europe in the second half of the nineteenth century had alarmed Russia:

- The growth of a united Germany. Russia feared that the unification of Germany in 1871 meant that central Europe was dominated by a powerful and ambitious nation, eager to expand eastwards.
- The formation of the Austro-Hungarian Empire in 1867. Russia was concerned that Austria would build on its new strength as a joint empire by an expansionist policy in south-east Europe.
- The decline of the Ottoman (Turkish) Empire. Russia's worry was that as Turkey weakened it would be increasingly challenged by aggressive national movements seeking independence from Turkish rule. This threatened Russian interests in the **Balkans**.

Russia and the Balkans

Two main considerations influenced Russia's attitude towards the Balkans:

- The first had a long tradition attached to it. As a predominantly Slav nation, Russia had always regarded it as its duty to protect the Slav Christian peoples of the Balkans from oppression by their Turkish Islamic masters.
- The second was a commercial concern. Seventy-five per cent of Russia's grain exports (which accounted for 40 per cent of its total foreign trade) were shipped through the Straits of the Dardanelles (see Figure 3.4). It was, therefore, necessary to ensure that the Straits did not come under the control of a hostile power capable of interrupting the passage of Russian ships from the Black Sea into the Mediterranean.

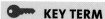 **KEY TERM**

Balkans The area of south-eastern Europe (fringed by Austria-Hungary to the north, the Black Sea to the east, Turkey to the south and the Aegean Sea to the west), which had largely been under Turkish control.

Figure 3.3 Russia and its neighbouring western states in 1914.

Russia's relations with Germany, France and Britain

In the quarter of a century before 1914, Russia's response to the shifts and turns of European diplomacy was consistently defensive. Russia was reluctant to take the diplomatic initiative, but was willing to enter into alliances that protected its western borders and possessions. In particular, Russia was concerned that its traditional control over Poland, a **buffer state** between Russia and Germany, should not be weakened.

 **KEY TERM**

Buffer state An area that lies between two states, providing protection for each against the other.

Figure 3.4 The Balkans in 1914.

The unified Germany that came into being in 1871 dominated the European scene for a generation. Chancellor **Otto von Bismarck** achieved this largely by developing an alliance system. In order to encourage the European powers to make agreements with Germany, he played on their fears of becoming isolated. All the major powers came to accept the need for a diplomacy that guaranteed that they would not be left friendless should war threaten. However, in 1890, Bismarck was dismissed by the new German Kaiser, William II, who adopted a more aggressive form of diplomacy that hardened international attitudes and led eventually to the splitting of Europe into two opposed, armed camps. William II showed every intention of joining with Austria in asserting German influence in the Balkans and the Near East. This frightened the Russian government into looking for agreements with other powers so as to counterbalance the Austro-German threat.

The Franco-Russian Convention 1892

To avoid isolation, Russia turned first to France. These two countries had not been on good terms, but a common fear of German aggression now outweighed their traditional dislike of each other. In the Franco-Russian Convention, signed in 1892, each partner promised to give military support to the other should it go to war with Germany. Economic co-operation also brought them closer. France was the major foreign investor in Russia's 'great spurt' in the 1890s (see page 17).

The Triple Entente 1907

The original alliance between France and Russia expanded into a **Triple Entente** with the inclusion of Britain in 1907. This, too, was something of a diplomatic revolution. Anglo-Russian relations had been strained for decades. Imperial rivalries in Asia and Britain's resistance to what it regarded as Russia's attempts to dominate the eastern Mediterranean had aroused mutual animosity. However, by the turn of the century, Germany had embarked on an expansive naval programme that Britain interpreted as a direct threat to its own security and to its empire. Britain's response was to form an understanding with Germany's major western and eastern neighbours, France and Russia. In the Anglo-French **Entente** of 1904, Britain and France had already agreed to abandon their old rivalry. It made diplomatic sense for Russia and Britain to do the same.

Consequently, in 1907 they agreed to settle their past differences by recognising each other's legitimate interests in Afghanistan, Persia and Tibet. No precise agreement was reached regarding military co-operation but there was a general understanding that such co-operation would follow in the event of war. A key experience that had helped to convince Russia of the wisdom of entering into foreign alliances had been its defeat in the 1904–5 war against Japan (see page 32). This strongly suggested that Russia's plans for eastward expansion had been misplaced. It redirected Russia's attention towards the west and made it keener still to form protective agreements with friendly European powers.

Russia's relations with Austria-Hungary

In 1908, Austria-Hungary made a startling move by annexing the Balkan state of Bosnia. When, Izvolski, the Russian foreign minister, protested, he was urged by his Austrian counterpart, Aehrenthal, to accept the takeover as a means of creating greater stability in the Balkan region. Izvolski eventually agreed, in return for Austria-Hungary's promise that it would acknowledge Russia's unrestricted right to the use of the Dardanelles Straits, and would persuade the other European powers to do the same. Russia kept its side of the bargain by recognising Austria-Hungary's takeover of Bosnia. The Austrians, however, did not honour their promise; they made no effort to encourage the international recognition of Russian rights in the Straits.

The question of Serbia

From this time onwards, relations between Russia and Austria-Hungary steadily deteriorated. A key issue dividing them was the position of Serbia. Bosnia contained many Serbs and its annexation by Austria-Hungary in 1908 aroused fierce Serbian nationalism. Russia, viewing itself as the special defender of

KEY TERMS

Triple Entente Not a formal alliance, but a declared willingness by three powers to co-operate.

Entente An agreement to remain on friendly terms.

Serbia and its Slav people, backed it in demanding compensation. Germany sided aggressively with Austria-Hungary and warned Russia not to interfere.

The crisis threatened for a time to spill over into war. However, in 1909 none of the countries involved felt ready to fight. Russia backed off from an open confrontation, while at the same time stating clearly that it regarded Germany and Austria-Hungary as the aggressors.

The Balkan Wars

Between 1909 and 1914 Russia continued to involve itself in the complexities of Balkan nationalist politics. The aim was to prevent Austria-Hungary from gaining a major advantage in the region. The tactic was to try to persuade the various nationalities in the region to form a coalition against Austria-Hungary. Russia had some success in this. Balkan nationalism led to a series of conflicts, known collectively as the Balkan Wars (1912–13). These were a confused mixture of anti-Turkish uprisings and squabbles between the Balkan states themselves over the division of the territories they had won from the Turks.

On balance, the outcome of these wars favoured Russian rather than Austro-Hungarian interests. Serbia had been doubled in size and felt itself more closely tied to Russia as an ally and protector. However, such gains as Russia had made were marginal. The international issues relating to Turkish decline and Balkan nationalism had not been resolved. The events of 1914 were to show how vulnerable Imperial Russia's status and security actually were.

Summary diagram: Russia's foreign policy before 1914

Russia's chief concerns
- The growth of a united Germany
- The formation of the Austro-Hungarian Empire
- The decline of the Ottoman (Turkish) Empire threatened Russian interests in the Balkans, where Russia saw itself as the defender of Slav nationalism

Consequences of Russia's concerns
Russia:
- drew away from Germany
- formed ententes with France and Britain
- competed with Austria-Hungary for influence in the Balkans

The Serbia question and the Balkan Wars heightened tension

Critical factors that made the Balkans a flashpoint
Russia's:
- role as champion of Slav culture
- commercial interests in the area

The tsar's position at the outbreak of war in 1914

▶ *How strong was the tsar's position at the outbreak of war in 1914?*

In 1914, despite the continuing social unrest, there was no reason to consider that tsardom would collapse within three years. Indeed, 1913 had witnessed the celebration of the tri-centenary of the Romanov dynasty. The pomp and pageantry that accompanied the occasion gave no hint of the trouble that was to come. While it is true that Nicholas II had poor political judgement and lacked a sense of realism, he had legitimate reasons in 1914 to regard himself as being in a strong position:

- Tsardom had emerged stronger, not weaker, from the 1905 Revolution. Despite defeat in the Russo-Japanese War, the tsar's troops had remained loyal and had suppressed internal troubles (see page 40). The three groups who had caused problems in 1905 (liberals, peasants and workers) had been placated or overcome.
- The October Manifesto had not been a relinquishing of power. This was clearly indicated by the tsar's issuing the Fundamental Laws, which reaffirmed his autocratic powers.
- The *dumas* never became a threat to the tsar's power in the way that some had feared. Nicholas let them remain as a manageable parliamentary experiment that impressed international onlookers. In any case, Stolypin had so neutered the *dumas* that by the time of the fourth *duma*, which outlived him, it had been reduced to nothing more dangerous than a talking shop.
- The liberals would not openly challenge the tsar even though, as their complaints in the *dumas* indicated, they had not been fully satisfied.
- The revolutionary parties were not considered, even by themselves, to be capable of mounting a successful assault on tsarist institutions or power. In 1914, they were on the fringe of the political scene. Indeed, most of the leading figures among them were in exile. Although they were to become prominent in 1917, it is reading history backwards to assume that they were poised to take power.
- Russia remained feared by the European nations. This was especially true for Germany, which regarded Russia as a great military power whose vast resources of labour made it a formidable force.
- The tsar was convinced that only a minority of industrial workers were opposed to his rule. His own estimate was that four-fifths of his people were dedicated and loyal. While it was undeniable Russia had great problems of economic and social disparity and poverty, these were perennial. As Witte remarked to the tsar, 'these we have always had'. Their persistence did not mean tsardom was doomed.

- Russia's potential for growth seemed enormous. While the Russian economy overall was some way behind its European rivals, it saw growth in the following areas:
  - Railways: the trans-Siberian railway was bringing Russia's distant provinces in touch with the centre. Migration and resettlement offered the prospect of Russia utilising its as yet untapped, plentiful, natural and human resources.
  - The economy in both the agricultural and industrial sectors had grown by six per cent by 1914. An interesting example of this was that Russia had become a major textile manufacturer, being fourth in world output behind the USA, Britain and Germany.

While it is arguable that Russia's main institutions, political, social and economic, were in crisis in pre-war Russia, that was also the case in many other countries. Crises are a constant in most nations – but crisis does not always entail collapse. Until war came to Russia in 1914, there was no clear sign that its problems were of a magnitude that would lead unavoidably to revolution. In 1914, Nicholas II's throne was not at risk.

These factors gave grounds for optimism and there were many sound reasons in 1914 to look to the future with confidence. One of the unanswerable 'ifs' of history is whether, had the destructive war of 1914–17 not intervened, Russia would have progressed towards becoming a modern industrial state capable of turning its nascent parliamentary system into a constitutional monarchy. But war did intervene, on an unimaginable scale, ending any hopes of Russia's evolving in an ordered manner into modernity.

Summary diagram: The tsar's position at the outbreak of war in 1914

Tsardom had been strengthened by outcome of 1905 Revolution

The October Manifesto had not weakened his authority

The *dumas* never became a threat

The liberals would not openly challenge the tsar

Revolutionary parties incapable of mounting a successful challenge

Russia remained feared by the European nations

Tsar convinced that only a minority of the people were opposed to his rule

Russia's potential for growth seemed enormous

These factors gave grounds for optimism rather than pessimism

Key debate

▶ *Was tsardom already doomed in 1914?*

An absorbing question which continues to engage historians is whether tsardom was already doomed by 1914. Armed with the knowledge that three years after 1914, Russia would witness the downfall of the tsar and the system he represented, they continue to ponder whether, without the turmoil of the war that began in 1914, tsardom could have dealt successfully with the crises confronting it and thus survived to lead Russia's transition into modern statehood. There is a sense in which the debate was started as long ago as 1911 when Lenin, destined to take power in 1917 (see page 118), prophesied that Europe, beginning with Russia, was about 'to overthrow the rule of the bourgeoisie and establish the communist order'.

The question of the Russian economy in 1914

There are those who regard Lenin as having been right, but premature. They suggest that, until the First World War intervened, Russia was in the process of developing into a modern industrial state. They cite the figures of increased industrial production, growth of the labour force and expansion of foreign investment. Other historians, while accepting these figures, argue that compared to developments in other countries, Russian growth was too limited to provide a genuine industrial base. They further stress that in 1914, four-fifths of the population were still peasants, a fact that undermines the claim that there had been significant industrial development.

In the end, no final answer can be given to the question as to how the economy would have developed had the war and the revolution not occurred. There are too many ifs and buts. The comment of Alex Nove, an acknowledged Russian authority on the subject, is particularly telling in this context. He says that there are convincing arguments on either side of the question as to whether Russia would have modernised.

EXTRACT I

Excerpt from Alex Nove, *An Economic History of the USSR*, Penguin, 1973, p. 17.

The question of whether Russia would have become a modern industrial state but for the war and the revolution is in essence a meaningless one. One may say that statistically the answer is in the affirmative. If the growth rates characteristic of the period 1890–1913 for industry and agriculture were simply projected over the succeeding 50 years, no doubt citizens would be leading a reasonable existence. However, this assumes that the imperial authorities would have successfully made the adjustment necessary to govern in an orderly manner a rapidly developing and changing society. But there must surely be a limit to the game of what-might-have-been.

The role of the tsar

The question turns on how the tsar's position in 1914 is assessed. US historian Leopold Haimson points to the strength of Nicholas II in 1914 even when he seemed to be assailed by problems.

EXTRACT 2

Excerpt from an article by Leopold Haimson, quoted in M. Cherniavsky, editor, _The Structure of Russian History_, Random House, 1970, p. 359.

No demonstrations, no public meetings, no collective petitions – no expressions of solidarity even comparable to those of bloody Sunday had evoked were now aroused. Thus in the last analysis, the most important source of the political impotence revealed by the Petersburg strike was precisely the one that made for its monstrous revolutionary explosiveness: the sense of isolation, of psychological distance, that separated the Petersburg workers from educated, privileged society.

Haimson is backed in this by Australian scholar David Christian.

EXTRACT 3

Excerpt from David Christian, _Imperial and Soviet Russia_, Macmillan, 1997, pp. 160–1.

Despite everything, traditions of loyalty to Tsarism survived among many sections of the population. These resurfaced immediately after the declaration of war, on 20 July 1914. In the first flush of enthusiasm the capital was renamed Petrograd instead of the Germanic St Petersburg. In the duma criticism of the government ceased. So did the demonstrations and strikes in the capital. Patriotic manifestations took their place.

Tsarist resistance to change

However, there is the added consideration that its blindness to the need for change made tsardom vulnerable to a major crisis. Despite some limited modifications of tsarist authority since 1906, Russia in 1914 was still essentially an autocratic state. A fundamental question remained unanswered in 1914. Was Russian capable or, indeed, willing to adopt the political and social changes necessary to become a modern state comparable with those of western Europe? The distinguished Marxist historian Christopher Hill had no doubt that the coming of war in 1914 simply exposed the underlying reality that the foundering tsarist system had no possibility of surviving in a modern age.

EXTRACT 4

Extract from Christopher Hill, *Lenin and the Russian Revolution*, Penguin, 1971, p. 19.

Social change came with the rapid industrial development of the last three decades of the nineteenth century. But this was almost entirely financed by foreign capital, and had little effect on the position of the native middle class. Dependent on the West alike for capital, technicians and political ideas, the Russian bourgeoisie had to invoke the protection of the tsarist state against their economically more powerful rivals. They had no thought of challenging the political dominance of the monarchy until, in the twentieth century, the regime again revealed, under the stress of modern war, its utter incompetence and corruption, its inability even to maintain order and financial stability.

This problem with which historians grapple in this key debate is often referred to as 'the tsarist crisis' or 'the institutional crisis', which has been neatly summarised in question form by Robert Service, the outstanding modern Western scholar of Russia, in Extract 5.

EXTRACT 5

From Robert Service, *Lenin: A Biography*, Macmillan, 2000, p. 4.

It was a race against time. Would the tsarist system sustain its energy and authority for a sufficient period to modernise society and the economy? Would the revolutionaries accommodate themselves to the changing realities and avoid the excesses of violent politics? And would the tsarist system make concessions to bring this about?

> **?** In what respects do the historians quoted in Extracts 1–5 agree or differ in their assessment of the strength of tsardom at the time of the outbreak of war in 1914?

Chapter summary

In the aftermath of the 1905 Revolution, the tsarist government followed two lines of policy in which Peter Stolypin as chief minister took the lead. A political conservative, he was determined that the peasants must not again become the threat they had been in 1905. His method for dealing with them was to construct an agricultural system that would provide them with security and create incentives for them to become increasingly productive. His 'wager on the strong' was an attempt to create a class of peasant proprietors, who would adopt progressive, profit-making methods, thus rewarding themselves and becoming a bulwark of support for the tsarist government. This policy was coupled with the sternest measures to suppress social disorder.

Stolypin followed the same approach in his relations with the *duma*. Wanting a quiescent parliament, he changed the critical character of the first two *dumas* by so manipulating membership qualifications that by the time of the fourth *duma* it had become dominated by the political right. Despite his best efforts, Russia at his death in 1911 was still a troubled land, as indicated by the unrest and industrial strikes of the period 1911–14. Meanwhile, troubles in the Balkans were threatening to draw Russia into an international crisis, which would test the strength of the tsar and tsardom. Whether it was war that brought down tsardom, or whether it was already doomed, is a question historians still debate.

Refresher questions

Use these questions to remind yourself of the key material covered in this chapter.

1 Why had a rural crisis developed in Russia by the first decade of the twentieth century?

2 How did Stolypin intend to de-revolutionise the peasantry?

3 What did Stolypin mean by the 'wager on the strong'?

4 Did Stolypin's land reforms have any realistic chance of success?

5 How strong had the Russian economy become by 1914?

6 Why was the first *duma* unsuccessful?

7 Why was the second *duma* even more critical of the government than the first?

8 Why was the third *duma* less hostile to the government?

9 Did the fourth *duma* serve any real purpose?

10 What was at issue in the Lena goldfields strike?

11 What factors drew Russia away from Germany but closer to France and Britain?

12 Why did Russia's relations with Austria-Hungary become increasingly strained?

 # Question practice

ESSAY QUESTIONS

1 'In their economic reforms, Witte and Stolypin were using different methods to achieve the same ends.' How far do you agree with this statement?

2 'The four *dumas* which sat between 1906 and 1914 talked much but did little.' How far do you agree with this statement?

3 'The tsar's government introduced major economic and political reforms in the period 1906–14.' How far do you agree with this statement?

4 How accurate is it to say that Russia's involvement in the First World War (in 1914) had a great impact on the lives of the peasants and workers?

SOURCE QUESTIONS

1 How far could the historian make use of Sources 1 and 2 together to investigate the ways in which the outbreak of war in July 1914 altered the position of Nicholas II as tsar of Russia? Explain your answer, using both sources, the information given about them and your own knowledge of the historical context.

2 How much weight do you give the evidence of Source 1 for an enquiry into the warnings given to Nicholas II about the possible consequences of war with Germany? Explain your answer, using the source, the information given about it and your own knowledge of the historical context.

3 Why is Source 2 valuable to the historian for an enquiry into the position and reputation of Nicholas II at the start of the war in 1914? Explain your answer, using the source, the information given about it and your own knowledge of the historical context.

SOURCE I

In February 1914, Peter Durnovo, a former minister of the interior, sent a memorandum to the tsar warning him of the dire consequences if Russia were to enter an unsuccessful war against Germany. Quoted in Thomas Riha, editor, *Readings in Russian Civilization*, University of Chicago Press, 1964, volume 2, p. 457.

In the event of defeat by Germany, social revolution in its extreme form is inevitable. It will start with all disasters being attributed to the government. In the legislative institutions a bitter campaign against the government will begin, which will result in revolutionary agitation throughout the country. There will immediately ensue Socialist slogans – which alone are capable of arousing and rallying the masses – first the complete reapportionment of land and then the reapportionment of all valuables and property. The defeated army, having lost its most dependable men during the war, and carried away for the most part by the tide of the general elemental desire of the peasants for land, will prove to be too demoralized to serve as a bulwark of law and order. The legislative institutions and the opposition intelligentsia parties, lacking real authority in the eyes of the people, will be powerless to stem the rising popular tide, which they themselves had aroused, and Russia will be flung into hopeless anarchy, the outcome of which cannot even be foreseen.

SOURCE 2

Mikhail Rodzianko, a member of the Octobrist Party and chairman of the fourth *duma*, describes how the outbreak of war in July 1914 affected Nicholas II's standing with his people. Quoted in David Christian, editor, *Imperial and Soviet Russia*, Macmillan, 1997, p. 161.

On the day of the Manifesto of the war with Germany a great crowd gathered before the Winter Palace. After a prayer for the granting of victory, the tsar spoke a few words ending with the solemn promise not to end the war while the enemy still occupied one inch of Russian soil. A loud 'hurrah' filled the palace and was taken up by an answering echo from the crowd on the square. After the prayer, the tsar came out onto the balcony to his people, the empress behind him. The huge crowd filled the square and the nearby streets, and when the tsar appeared it was as if an electric spark had run through the crowd, and an enormous 'hurrah' filled the air. Flags and placards with the inscription 'Long Live Russia and Slavdom' bowed to the ground, and the entire crowd fell to its knees as one man before the tsar. The tsar wanted to say something; he raised his hand; those in front began to sh-sh-sh; but the noise of the crowd, the unceasing 'hurrah', did not allow him to speak. He bowed his head and stood for some time overcome by the solemnity of this moment of the union of the tsar with his people.

CHAPTER 4

War and revolution 1914–17

At the outbreak of war, the Russian people rallied enthusiastically behind the tsar and his government, but, as the war progressed, poor military and political leadership led to mounting opposition. By 1917, continuous military failures and growing disorder revealed Nicholas's inability to handle crisis. Opposed by a rebellious *duma*, and despaired of by his high command, Nicholas chose to abdicate. In the power vacuum that followed, the remnants of the *duma* and the newly formed Petrograd soviet of soldiers and workers began to exercise a dual authority. This chapter examines four main themes:

★ Why Russia went to war in 1914

★ The impact of war on Russia

★ The growth of opposition to tsardom

★ The February Revolution 1917

The key debate on *page 71* of this chapter asks the question: Why was Russia drawn into war in 1914?

Key dates

1914	June 28	Assassination of Franz Ferdinand at Sarajevo	1917	Feb. 18	Strike began at Putilov factories in Petrograd
	July 28	Austria-Hungary declared war on Serbia		Feb. 23	International Women's Day
	July 30	Russian full mobilisation orders given			Widespread workers' demonstrations
	Aug. 1	Germany declared war on Russia		Feb. 25	General strike began
		Suspension of fourth *duma*		Feb. 27	Unofficial meeting of *duma*
1915	June–July	Fourth *duma* reconvened			First meeting of the Petrograd soviet
	June 25	Progressive Bloc formed in the *duma*		Feb. 28	Nicholas II prevented from returning to Petrograd
	Aug. 22	Nicholas II put himself in charge of the military		March 2	Provisional Government formed from the *duma* committee
1916	Dec. 1	Rasputin murdered			Tsar signed abdication decree
				March 4	Tsar's abdication publicly proclaimed

Why Russia went to war in 1914

 ▶ *Why was Russia drawn into war in 1914?*

Russia's anxieties in foreign affairs predisposed it to regard Germany and Austria-Hungary with deep suspicion (see page 58). When crises occurred, therefore, they were more likely to lead to conflict. But this is not to say that the tsarist government was looking for war in 1914. Russia's experience ten years earlier against Japan had made it wary of putting itself at risk again, and its foreign policy after 1905 had been essentially defensive. Russia had joined France and Britain in the Triple Entente as a means of safeguarding itself against the alliance of the **Central Powers**. However, the events that followed the assassination in June 1914 of Franz Ferdinand, the heir to the Austro-Hungarian throne, by **Serbian nationalists** made it virtually impossible for Russia to avoid being drawn into a European conflict.

A critical factor at this point was Russia's perception of itself as the protector of the Slav peoples of the Balkans. **Sazonov**, the tsar's foreign minister in 1914, claimed that 'Russia's sole and unchanging object was to see that those Serbian peoples should not fall under the influence of hostile powers.' He added that the basic aim of Russian policy was to obtain free access to the Mediterranean, and to be in a position to defend Russia's Black Sea coasts against the threat of the irruption of hostile naval forces through the **Bosphorus** (see the map on page 60).

A month after Franz Ferdinand's murder, Austria-Hungary, with German encouragement, declared war on Serbia. Russia still expected to be able to force the Austrians to withdraw, without itself having to go to war. Russia hoped that if it mobilised this would act as a deterrent to Austria. This was not unrealistic. Despite Russia's defeat by Japan, its armies were still regarded as formidable. German generals often spoke of 'the Russian steamroller', a reference to the immense reserves of manpower on which it was calculated that Russia could draw.

With tension building, Nicholas II made a personal move to avoid war with Germany. In July he exchanged a series of personal telegrams with his cousin, Kaiser William II, regretting the growing crisis in Russo-German relations and hoping that conflict could be avoided. But although these 'Willy–Nicky' exchanges, written in English, were friendly, there was a sense in which the two emperors were being carried along by events beyond their control.

Russia's mobilisation plans

It was at this stage that the great length of Russia's western frontier proved to be of momentous significance. The Russian military high command had two basic mobilisation schemes:

 **KEY TERMS**

Central Powers Germany, Austria-Hungary and Turkey.

Serbian nationalists Activists struggling for Serbia's independence from Austria-Hungary.

Bosphorus The narrow waterway linking the Black Sea with the Dardanelles.

 KEY FIGURE

Sergei Sazonov (1860–1927) Russian foreign minister from 1910 to 1916.

- Partial: based on plans for a limited campaign in the Balkans against Austria-Hungary.
- Full: based on plans for a full-scale war against both Germany and Austria-Hungary.

Both forms of mobilisation depended on detailed and precise railway timetabling aimed at transporting huge numbers of men and vast amounts of material. The complexity of the timetables meant that the adoption of one type of mobilisation ruled out the use of the other. Horse-drawn wagons and marching men can change direction quickly; trains cannot. Russia's fear in July 1914 was that if it mobilised only partially it would leave it defenceless should Austria's ally, Germany, strike at its Polish borders (see the map on page 59).

SOURCE A

? How does the cartoon in Source A illustrate Austrian and German fears of Russia's strength?

"THE STEAM-ROLLER."

Austria. "I SAY, YOU KNOW, YOU'RE EXCEEDING THE SPEED LIMIT!"

A British cartoon of 1914 showing Franz Joseph, the Austro-Hungarian emperor, fleeing from the chasing Russian 'steamroller'. In pre-1914 Germany and Austria-Hungary, the image of Russia as a steamroller that could crush their armies was a powerful and frightening one.

On the other hand, full mobilisation might well appear to Germany as a deliberate provocation. The German government did, indeed, warn Sazonov that if Russia mobilised Germany would have to do the same.

Germany's mobilisation plans

Here a vital fact intervened and made war unstoppable. Germany had no room for manoeuvre. According to German contingency plans, if Russia mobilised, Germany would have to go to war. There would no longer be a choice. The German 'Schlieffen Plan' was based on the concept of eliminating the danger to Germany of a two-front war against France and Russia by a lightning knockout blow against France. Speed was of the essence. Germany could not play a game of diplomatic bluff; it had to strike first.

When, therefore, on 30 July after a long hesitation, Nicholas chose to sign the Russian full mobilisation order, he had taken a more fateful decision than he realised. What had been intended as a diplomatic move that would leave Russia free to hold back from war was the step that precipitated war. On 31 July, Germany demanded that the Russians cease their mobilisation. On 1 August, having received no response, Germany declared war on Russia. Four days later Austria-Hungary did the same.

Key sequence of events

- 28 July 1914: Austria-Hungary declared war on Serbia.
- 30 July 1914: Tsar signed full Russian mobilisation order.
- 1 August 1914: Germany declared war on Russia.

Summary diagram: Why Russia went to war in 1914

Line-up of opposed alliances

Central Powers	Triple Entente
• Germany	• Russia
• Austria-Hungary	• France
• Turkey	• Britain

Events in Serbia
Austro-Hungarian ultimatum to Serbia, following Franz Ferdinand's assassination in June 1914, resisted by Russia

Germany backed Austria-Hungary

The crisis did not make war unavoidable but Russian and German mobilisation plans did

Mobilisation plans

Russia	Germany
Choice between partial or full mobilisation	Schlieffen Plan ruled that if it mobilised it went to war

Consequence
When tsar signed full mobilisation order, Germany had no choice but to declare war on Russia

2 The impact of war on Russia

▶ *How was Russian morale affected during the course of the war?*

Whatever the tsar's previous uncertainties may have been, once war was declared, he became wholly committed to it. By 1917 the war would prove to be the undoing of tsardom, but in 1914 the outbreak of hostilities greatly enhanced the tsar's position. Nicholas II became the symbol of the nation's resistance in its hour of need. Watching the great crowds cheering the tsar as he formally announced that Russia was at war, the French ambassador remarked: 'To those thousands the tsar really is the autocrat, the absolute master of their bodies and souls.' At a special session of the *duma*, all the deputies, save for the five Bolshevik representatives, fervently pledged themselves to the national struggle.

Setback for the Bolsheviks

It was the same story in all the warring countries. The socialist parties abandoned their policies and committed themselves to the national war effort. Lenin was bitter in his condemnation of 'these class traitors'. He called on all true revolutionaries 'to transform the imperialist war everywhere into a civil war'. But the prevailing mood in Russia and Europe was all against him.

The early stages of the war were dark days for Lenin's Bolsheviks. Vilified as traitors and German agents for their opposition to the war, they were forced to flee or go into hiding. Lenin, who was already in exile in Poland, made his way with Austrian help into neutral Switzerland. Had the war gone well for Russia, there is every reason to think that the Bolshevik Party would have disappeared as a political force. But the war did not go well for Russia, and the reason was only partly military.

Russia's problems

KEY TERM

Total war A struggle in which the whole nation, people, resources and institutions, are involved.

The basic explanation for Russia's decline and slide into revolution in 1917 was an economic one. Three years of **total war** were to prove too great a strain for the Russian economy to bear. War is a time when the character and structure of a society are put to the test in a particularly intense way. The longer the war lasts, the greater the test. During the years 1914–17, the political, social and economic institutions of Russia proved increasingly incapable of meeting the demands that war placed on them.

This does not prove that Russia was uniquely incompetent. The pressure of total war on all countries was immense and it should be remembered that of the six empires engaged in the First World War – Germany, Austria, Turkey, Russia, France and Britain – only the last two survived.

Differing estimates have been made of Russia's potential for growth in 1914. But however that is assessed, the fact remains that the demands of the 1914–17 war eventually proved too heavy for Russia to sustain. The impact of the war on Russia can be conveniently studied under a number of headings:

- inflation
- food and transport
- living conditions
- the army
- prohibition.

Inflation

Russia had achieved remarkable financial stability by 1914. Its currency was on the gold standard (see page 18) and it had the largest gold reserves of any European country. This happy position was destroyed by the war. Between 1914 and 1917, government spending rose from 4 million to 30 million roubles. Increased taxation at home and heavy borrowing from abroad were only partially successful in raising the capital Russia needed. The gold standard was abandoned, which allowed the government to put more notes into circulation. This was what is now known as **quantitative easing**. In the short term this enabled wages to be paid and commerce to continue, but in the long term it made money practically worthless. The result was severe inflation, which became particularly severe in 1916. In broad terms, between 1914 and 1916 average earnings doubled while the price of food and fuel quadrupled (see Table 4.1).

KEY TERM

Quantitative easing
Printing extra currency to meet the demand for ready money; a risky process since the money is not tied to an actual increase in genuine wealth.

Table 4.1 The economic consequences of war in Russia 1914–17

Inflation (to a base unit of 100 in July 1914)			
Prices		**Notes in circulation**	
July 1914	100	July 1914	100
January 1915	130	January 1915	146
January 1916	141	January 1916	199
January 1917	398	January 1917	336
The cost of the war			
1914		1,655 million roubles	
1915		8,818 million roubles	
1916		14,573 million roubles	
1917 (up to August)		13,603 million roubles	

Food and transport

Initially, many of the peasant farmers benefited from the war, since the demand for food and increased agricultural production enabled them to charge higher prices and make profits. During the first two years of the war, Russia's grain yield was higher than it had been between 1912 and 1914. It was not until 1916 that it began to fall. There were four main reasons for this:

Requisitioning State-authorised takeover of property or resources.

Petrograd For patriotic reasons, soon after the war began, the German name for the capital, St Petersburg, was changed to the Russian form of 'Petrograd'.

- Inflation made trading unprofitable, so the peasants stopped selling food and began hoarding their stocks.
- The **requisitioning** of horses and fertilisers by the military for the war effort made it difficult for peasants to sustain agricultural output.
- The army had first claim on the more limited amount of food being produced.
- The military also had priority in the use of the transport system. It commandeered the railways and the roads, with the result that food supplies to civilian areas became difficult to maintain.

Transport dislocation meant that food supplies could not be distributed effectively. Hunger bordering on famine became a constant reality for much of Russia. Shortages were at their worst in the towns and cities. **Petrograd** suffered particularly badly because of its remoteness from the food-producing regions and because of the large number of refugees who swelled its population and increased the demand on its dwindling resources. By early 1917, bread rationing meant that Petrograd's inhabitants were receiving less than a quarter of the amount that had been available in 1914.

It was the disruption of the transport system rather than the decline in food production that was the major cause of Russia's wartime shortages. The growth of the railways, from 20,000 to 70,000 km (13,000–44,000 miles) between 1881 and 1914 (see page 19), had been an impressive achievement, but it did not meet the demands of war. The attempt to transport millions of troops and masses of supplies to the war fronts created unbearable pressures. The signalling system on which the railway network depended broke down; blocked lines and steam trains stranded by engine breakdown or lack of coal became commonplace.

Less than two years after the war began, the Russian railway system had virtually collapsed. By 1916, some 575 stations were no longer capable of handling freight. A graphic example of the confusion was provided by Archangel, the northern port through which the bulk of the Allied aid to Russia passed. So great was the pile-up of undistributed goods that they sank into the ground beneath the weight of new supplies. Elsewhere there were frequent reports of food rotting in railway trucks that could not be moved. One of the tsar's wartime prime ministers later admitted: 'There were so many trucks blocking the lines that we had to tip some of them down the embankments to move the ones that arrived later':

- By 1916, Petrograd and Moscow were receiving only a third of their food and fuel requirements.
- Before the war, Moscow had received an average of 2200 wagons of grain per month; by February 1917 this figure had dropped to below 700.
- The figures for Petrograd told a similar story; in February 1917 the capital received only 300 wagonloads of grain instead of the 1000 it needed.

Living conditions

Unsurprisingly, the disruption to food supplies made living and working conditions increasingly difficult. An insight into the war's impact on Russia's workers was provided by an *Okhrana* report from the capital Petrograd, written in October 1916 and recording the statistics relating to workers' conditions.

SOURCE B

From an *Okhrana* report, October 1916, in G. Vernadsky, editor, *A Source Book for Russian History from Early Times to 1917*, volume 3, Yale University Press, 1973, pp. 867–68.

Daily income		
Type of worker	**pre-war wages**	**present [1916] wages**
Unskilled	1 to 1.25 roubles	2.5 to 3 roubles
Metalworker	2 to 2.5 roubles	4 to 5 roubles
Electrician	2 to 3 roubles	5 to 6 roubles
Expenses		
Item	**pre-war cost**	**present [1916] cost**
Monthly rent (for a shared room)	2 to 3 roubles	8 to 12 roubles
Dinner	0.15 to 0.2 roubles	1 to 1.2 roubles
Tea	0.07 roubles	0.35 roubles
Boots	5 to 6 roubles	20 to 30 roubles
Shirt	0.75 to 0.9 roubles	2.5 to 3 roubles

Even if we estimate the rise in earnings at 100 per cent, the prices of products have risen on the average, 300 per cent. The impossibility of even buying many food products and necessities, the time wasted standing idle in queues to receive goods, the increasing incidence of disease due to malnutrition and unsanitary living conditions (cold and dampness because of lack of coal and wood), and so forth, have made the workers as a whole, prepared for the wildest excesses of a 'hunger riot'.

If in the future grain continues to be hidden, the very fact of its disappearance will be sufficient to provoke in the capitals and in the other most populated centers of the empire the greatest disorders, attended by pogroms and endless street rioting.

> What picture of the workers' conditions emerges from Source B?

The army

A striking detail of the First World War is that Russia, in proportion to its population, put fewer than half the troops into the field than either Germany or France (see Table 4.2 on page 78).

Table 4.2 Numbers and percentages of the population mobilised

	1914	1918	Total population	% of population mobilised
Russia	5.3 million	15.3 million	180 million	8.8
Germany	3.8 million	14.0 million	68 million	20.5
France	3.8 million	7.9 million	39 million	19.9
Britain	0.6 million	5.7 million	45 million	12.7

Yet, in total numbers the Russian army was still a mighty force. It was by far the largest army of all the countries that fought in the war. Its crippling weakness, which denied it the military advantage that its sheer size should have given it, was lack of equipment. This was not a matter of Russia's military underspending. Indeed, until 1914 Russia led Europe in the amount and the proportions it spent on defence (see Figure 4.1).

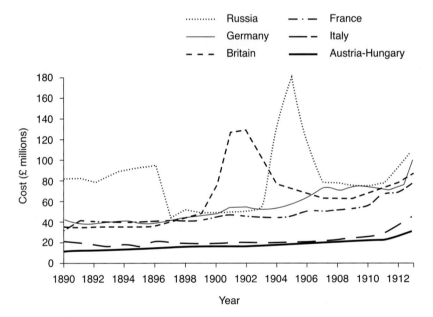

Figure 4.1 Graph showing the comparative defence expenditures of the European powers 1890–1913 (in £ million).

The problem was not the lack of resources but poor administration and lack of liaison between the government departments responsible for supplies. Despite its commandeering of the transport system, the military was as much a victim of the poor distribution of resources as the civilian population. In the first two years of the war the army managed to obtain its supply needs, but from 1916 serious shortages began to occur. Mikhail Rodzianko, the president of the *duma*, who undertook a special fact-finding study in 1916 of conditions in the army, reported to the *duma* on the widespread disorganisation and its dismal effects. He described as a 'great evil' the lack of direction and organisation by the government, which left Russia's gallant soldiers desperately short of food, ammunition and medical supplies.

Conscious, like Rodzianko, of the military situation, Alexander Naumov, minister of agriculture, made a similar visit to the front. Afterwards he wrote to the tsar attempting to impress on him the crying need for effective government direction (Source C).

SOURCE C

From a report by Alexander Naumov recording his meeting with Nicholas II, June 1916, quoted in Dominic Lieven, *Nicholas II*, Pimlico, 1993, p. 229.

I tried to tell His Majesty about the situation of the food supply … The Emperor kept interrupting me with questions that related not to the business side of my official journey but rather to everyday trivia that interested him … I must admit that this kind of attitude from the Emperor towards matters of fundamental national importance discouraged me greatly … I became clearly aware of a certain characteristic of the monarch which I attribute to general nervous exhaustion brought about by all the adversities attending his reign and the extraordinary complications he has encountered in governing the country since the outbreak of war in 1914.

What impression of the tsar as leader is conveyed in Source C?

The tsar's decision to become commander-in-chief, August 1915

The clear implication in Rodzianko's and Naumov's accounts was that the strong central leadership, which the war effort desperately needed, was not being provided. This was a view that became increasingly widespread and it was against the tsar that criticisms began to mount. Much of this resulted from a huge error of judgement Nicholas II had made. In August 1915, he had formally taken over the direct command of Russia's armed services. This was a momentous decision. The intention was to rally the nation around him as Tsar of Russia. But it also made him a hostage to fortune. Nicholas II was now personally responsible for Russia's performance in the war. If things went well he took the credit, but if they went badly he was to blame. Lack of success could no longer be blamed on his appointees.

Prohibition

Drink was not a trivial matter in Russia. The consumption of alcohol, particularly vodka, was an integral part of Russian social tradition. The primary purpose was not sensual enjoyment but a method of putting up with the grimness of life. It has been described as a Russian alternative to religion. Both provided a way of making life endurable. Periodically, tsarist governments had introduced anti-drink measures in order to control the disorder associated with drunkenness but these were not sustained for two reasons:

- taxes on vodka sales were a source of government revenue
- to deprive Russians of their drink was likely to cause more, not less, social unrest.

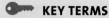

KEY TERMS

Prohibition The state's banning of the production and sale of alcohol.

Samogon Illicitly distilled vodka, the equivalent of 'moonshine' or 'hooch', Western forms of unlicensed alcohol.

According to Source D, how did drinkers try to obtain alcohol?

Nicholas II, however, in one of his major errors, took the moralistic and short-sighted decision at the very beginning of the war to introduce **prohibition**. His aim was to stimulate the war effort by removing a potent distraction from the people. What he had overlooked was that the government derived nearly a third of its revenue from the taxes on alcohol sales. The result was that at a critical point in its destinies, the Russian state had deprived itself of an irreplaceable source of income. By 1916, the damage being done was so evident that prohibition laws were repealed. But by then it was too late to recover what had been lost. Nor was it merely a matter of lost revenue. Prohibition had proved a social disaster. Since alcohol was no longer legally available, deprived drinkers turned to illegal ways of obtaining it. Production of **samogon** became a nationwide undercover industry, supplying towns and villages across Russia.

SOURCE D

D.N. Voronov, *O Samagone [Oh, Vodka]*, Izdatel'stro Z-oe, 1929, p. 6.

At first, instead of vodka, they tried to use various other substances containing alcohol – eau-de-cologne, varnish, or denatured alcohol. But these were hard to get hold of, they were expensive, and they were unpleasant tasting and obviously dangerous to the health of the consumers. Then people turned to domestic beers and braga *[a strong domestic beer], trying to make them as strong as possible, but these couldn't get you drunk enough. Finally … they learnt how to extract spirits by distilling fermented grains or sugary substances.*

Morale

The suffering that the food shortages and the dislocated transport system brought to both troops and civilians might have been more bearable had the news from the war front been encouraging, or had there been inspired leadership from the top. There were occasional military successes, such as those achieved on the south-western front in 1916 when a Russian offensive under General Brusilov killed or wounded half a million Austrian troops, and brought Austria-Hungary to the point of collapse. But the gains made were not followed up and were never enough to justify the appalling casualty lists. The enthusiasm and high morale of August 1914 had turned by 1916 into pessimism and defeatism. Ill-equipped and underfed, the 'peasants in uniform' who composed the Russian army began to desert in increasing numbers.

How broken were the Russian armies?

Care should be taken not to exaggerate the effect of the breakdown in morale. Modern research, such as that undertaken by E. Mawdsley and Norman Stone, has shown that the Russian army was not on the verge of collapse in 1917. Mutinies had occurred but these were not exclusive to Russia. The strains of war in 1917 produced mutinies in all the major armies, including the French and British. Stone dismisses the idea of a disintegrating Russian army as a Bolshevik 'fabrication'. With all its problems the Russian armies were still intact as a fighting force in 1917.

Stone also emphasises the vital role that Russia played as an ally of Britain and France in tying down the German army for over three years on the eastern front. An interesting detail, indicating how far Russia was from absolute collapse in 1916, is that in that year Russia managed to produce more shells than Germany. To quote these findings is not to deny the importance of Russia's military crises, but it is to recognise that historians have traditionally tended to overstate Russia's military weakness in 1917.

Summary diagram: The impact of war on Russia

Immediate effect
Enhanced the popularity and status of the tsar
Weakened the anti-war Bolsheviks

BUT
'Total war' created major problems for Russia

1. **Inflation** – value of money sharply declined, creating instability and high prices
2. **Food supplies** – dwindled as result of requisitioning and transport disruption – urban areas suffered acute shortages
3. **Transport system** – broke down under stress of war
4. **The army** – fought well but was undermined by poor organisation and lack of supplies
5. **Role of the tsar** – Nicholas II's fateful decision to become commander-in-chief made survival of tsardom dependent on military success
6. **Morale** – high at the start among army and civilians but was damaged by lengthening casualty lists at the front and declining supplies at home, particularly of prohibited vodka

---

 # The growth of opposition to tsardom

▶ *How did the war encourage the development of opposition to the tsar and his government?*

By 1916, the basic patriotism of the Russian people remained intact but among all-important sections of the population a common view had developed that the tsar was an inept political and military leader, incapable of providing the inspiration that the nation needed. It is significant that the first moves in the February Revolution in 1917, the event that led to the fall of tsardom, were not made by the revolutionary parties. The revolution was set in motion by those members of Russian society who, at the outbreak of the war in 1914, had been the tsar's strongest supporters, but who, by the winter of 1916, were too wearied by his incompetence to wish to save him or the barren system he represented.

The *duma* recalled

In August 1914 the *duma* had shown its total support for the tsar by voting for its own suspension for the duration of the war. But within a year Russia's poor military showing led to the *duma* demanding its own recall. Nicholas II bowed before the pressure and allowed the *duma* to reassemble in July 1915.

One major political mistake of the tsar and his ministers was their refusal to co-operate fully with the non-governmental organisations such as the **Union of *Zemstvos*** and the **Union of Municipal Councils**, which at the beginning of the war had been wholly willing to work with the government in the national war effort. These elected bodies formed a joint organisation, ***Zemgor***. The success of this organisation both highlighted the government's own failures and hinted that there might be a workable alternative to tsardom.

Formation of a 'Progressive Bloc'

A similar political blindness characterised the tsar's dismissal of the *duma*'s appeal to him to replace his ineffectual cabinet with 'a ministry of national confidence' whose members would be drawn from the *duma*. Nicholas II rejected this proposal, and in doing so destroyed the last opportunity he would have of retaining the support of the politically progressive parties. Milyukov, the Kadet leader, complained that the tsar and his advisers had 'brushed aside the hand that was offered them'.

Denied a direct voice in national policy, 236 of the 422 *duma* deputies formed themselves into a 'Progressive Bloc' composed of Kadets, Octobrists, Progressive Nationalists and the Party of Progressive Industrialists. The SRs did not formally join the bloc but voted with it in all the *duma* resolutions that criticised the government's handling of the war. Initially, the bloc did not directly challenge the tsar's authority, but tried to persuade him to make concessions. Nicholas, however, was not willing to listen to the bloc. It was part of that stubbornness that he mistook for firmness.

One of the bloc's leading members, **Vasily Shulgin**, pointed out despairingly how short-sighted the tsar was in viewing the bloc as an enemy, not a friend: 'The whole purpose of the Progressive Bloc was to prevent revolution so as to enable the government to finish the war.' The tragedy for the tsar was that as he and his government showed themselves increasingly incapable of running the war, the bloc, from having been a supporter, became a source of political resistance. It was another of tsardom's lost opportunities.

The government continued to shuffle its ministers in the hope of finding a successful team. In the year 1915–16, there were four prime ministers, three foreign secretaries, three ministers of defence and six interior ministers. It was all to no avail. None of them was up to the task. The description by the British ambassador in Petrograd of one of the premiers, Sturmer, might have been fairly applied to all the tsar's wartime ministers: 'Possessed of only a second-class

Nicholas II

1868	Born into the Romanov house
1894	Became tsar
	Married Alexandra, the German grand-daughter of Queen Victoria
1905	Granted the October Constitution
1906	Opened the first *duma*
1913	Led the celebrations of 300 years of Romanov rule
1914	Signed the general mobilisation order
1915	Became commander-in-chief of the Russian armed forces
1917	Advised by military high command and *duma* to stand down
	Abdicated on behalf of the Romanov dynasty
1918	Murdered with his family in Ekaterinburg

The character of Nicholas II is important in any analysis of revolutionary Russia. The evidence suggests that, though he was far from being as unintelligent as his detractors asserted, his limited imagination prevented him from fully grasping the nature of the events in which he was involved. As with many basically weak monarchs, when he attempted to be strong, he simply appeared obdurate. Pobedonostsev said of him, 'he only grasps the significance of a fact in isolation without its relationship to other facts', while Witte observed, 'His character is the source of all our misfortunes. His outstanding weakness is a lack of willpower.' **Alexander Kerensky** asserted, 'His mentality kept him wholly out of touch with his people. From his youth he had been trained to believe that his welfare and the welfare of Russia were one and the same thing.'

The tsar made a number of crucial errors in his handling of the war, the most significant being his decision in 1915 to take direct command of Russia's armed forces. This, in effect, tied the fate of the Romanov dynasty to the success or otherwise of Russia's armies. There are good grounds for arguing that the war had offered tsardom its last great opportunity to identify itself with the needs of modern Russia and so consolidate itself beyond challenge as the legitimate ruling system. That opportunity was squandered. In 1914 there had been a very genuine enthusiasm for the tsar as representative of the nation. Within three years that enthusiasm had wholly evaporated, even among dedicated tsarists. The fall of Nicholas was the result of his weak leadership rather than his savage oppression. He was not helped by his wife's German nationality or by court scandals, of which Rasputin's was the most notorious. But these would not by themselves have been sufficient to bring down a dynasty.

mind, and having no experience of statesmanship, he owed his appointment to the fact that he was a friend of **Rasputin** and enjoyed the support of the crowd of intriguers around the empress.'

The role of Rasputin

Gregory Efimovich Rasputin (1872–1916) was the individual on whom much of the hatred of the tsarist system came to be focused. By any measure his rise to prominence in Russia was an extraordinary story, but its true significance lay in the light it shed on the nature of tsarist government. Rasputin was a self-ordained holy man from the Russian steppes, who was notorious for his sexual depravity. This made him fascinating to certain women, who threw themselves at him. Many fashionable ladies in St Petersburg, including the wives of courtiers, boasted that they had slept with him. That Rasputin seldom washed or changed his clothes seemed to add to the attraction; in colloquial terms it is known as 'liking a bit of rough'.

 KEY FIGURE

Alexander Kerensky (1881–1970)

A lawyer and leading member of the SR Party, he was to be prime minister of the Provisional Government from July until its fall in October 1917.

 **KEY TERM**

Rasputin By an interesting coincidence, the word 'rasputin' in Russian also means lecher.

Rasputin's behaviour made him bitterly hated at the imperial court to which he was officially invited. Outraged husbands and officials detested this upstart from the steppes. But they could not get rid of him; he enjoyed royal favour. As early as 1907, Rasputin had gained himself a personal introduction to the tsar and his wife. The Empress Alexandra was desperate to cure her son, Alexei, the heir to the throne, of his **haemophilia**. Hearing that Rasputin had extraordinary gifts of healing, she invited him to court. Rasputin did, indeed, prove able to help Alexei, whose condition eased considerably when the *starets* was with him.

Rasputin did not, of course, have the magical or devilish powers that the more superstitious claimed for him, but he was a very good amateur psychologist. He realised that the prodding to which Alexei was invariably subjected when being examined by his doctors only made the boy more anxious and feverish. Rasputin's way was to speak calmly to him, stroking him gently so that he relaxed. This lowered Alexei's temperature and lessened his pain. It was not a cure but it was the most successful treatment he had ever had. Alexandra, a deeply religious woman, believed it was the work of God and that Rasputin was His instrument. She made the 'mad monk', as his enemies called him, her **confidant**.

Scandal inevitably followed. Alexandra's German nationality had made her suspect and unpopular since the outbreak of war, but she had tried to ride out the storm. She would hear no ill of 'our dear friend', as she called Rasputin in letters to Nicholas, and obliged the tsar to maintain him at court. Since Nicholas was away at military headquarters for long periods after 1915, it was no great exaggeration by opponents to assert that Alexandra and Rasputin effectively became the government of Russia. Even the staunchest supporters of tsardom found it difficult to defend a system that allowed a nation in the hour of its greatest trial to fall under the sway of the **'German woman'** and a debauched monk.

Alexandra was, indeed, German, having been born to the house of Hesse Darmstadt. However, after marrying Nicholas, she had made sincere efforts to make Russia her adopted country. She converted to the Orthodox Church, and endeavoured to learn and apply Russian customs and conventions. This counted for little after 1914, when, despite her undoubted commitment to the Russian cause, her enemies portrayed her as a German agent.

Death of Rasputin

In December 1916, in a mixture of spite, resentment and a genuine wish to save the monarchy, a group of aristocratic conspirators murdered Rasputin. His death was as bizarre as his life. Poisoned with arsenic, shot at point-blank range, battered over the head with a steel bar, he was still alive when he was thrown, trussed in a heavy curtain, into the River Neva. His post-mortem showed that he had water in lungs, evidence that he had still been breathing when finally sucked below the icy waters.

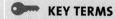

KEY TERMS

Haemophilia A genetic condition in which the blood does not clot, leaving the sufferer with painful bruising and internal bleeding, which can be life threatening.

Starets Russian for holy man, the name given to Rasputin by the impressionable peasants who believed he had superhuman powers.

Confidant A person in whom another places a special trust and to whom one confides intimate secrets.

'German woman' The disparaging term used by anti-tsarists to describe Empress Alexandra.

SOURCE E

„Самодержавіе"

How reliable is Source E as evidence for a historian researching the nature of the relationship between Rasputin and Alexandra?

One of the many pornographic postcards circulating in Petrograd in 1917. The word *samoderzhavie* means 'holding'. It is used here as a pun to suggest Raputin's hold on Russia as well as on the empress. Despite this cartoon and the rumours about Rasputin and Alexandra, it is unlikely that they were ever lovers in a physical sense.

Rasputin's importance

From time to time there have been various attempts to present Rasputin in a more sympathetic light, drawing attention, for example, to his achievement in reorganising the army's medical supplies system. In doing this, he showed the common sense and administrative skill that Russia so desperately needed and that his aristocratic superiors in government so markedly lacked. Ironically, it was his competence rather than his supposedly corrupting influence that infuriated many of those who wanted him out of the way. Yet, no matter how much the reactionaries in the court and government might rejoice at the death of the upstart, the truth was that by the beginning of 1917 it was too late to save tsardom. Rasputin's extraordinary life at court and his murder by courtiers were but symptoms of the fatal disease affecting the tsarist system.

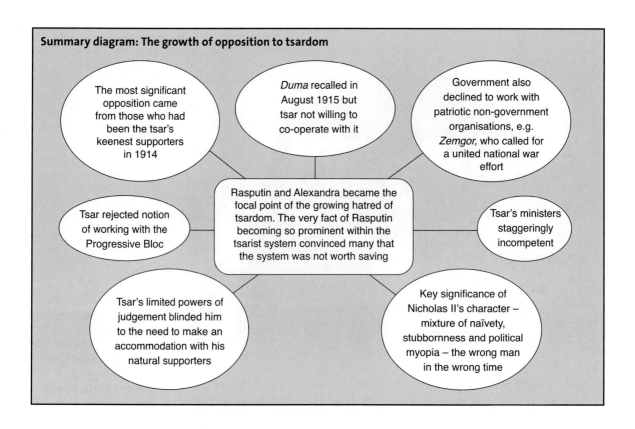

Summary diagram: The growth of opposition to tsardom

The most significant opposition came from those who had been the tsar's keenest supporters in 1914

Duma recalled in August 1915 but tsar not willing to co-operate with it

Government also declined to work with patriotic non-government organisations, e.g. *Zemgor*, who called for a united national war effort

Tsar rejected notion of working with the Progressive Bloc

Rasputin and Alexandra became the focal point of the growing hatred of tsardom. The very fact of Rasputin becoming so prominent within the tsarist system convinced many that the system was not worth saving

Tsar's ministers staggeringly incompetent

Tsar's limited powers of judgement blinded him to the need to make an accommodation with his natural supporters

Key significance of Nicholas II's character – mixture of naïvety, stubbornness and political myopia – the wrong man in the wrong time

4 The February Revolution

▶ *Were the events of February 1917 a revolution from below or a collapse at the top?*

In the year preceding February 1917, there had been a number of challenges to the tsar and his government. The Octobrists in the *duma* had frequently demanded the removal of unwanted ministers and generals. What made February 1917 different was the range of the opposition to the government and the speed with which events turned from a protest into a revolution. Rumours of the likelihood of serious public disturbances breaking out in Petrograd had been widespread since the beginning of the year. An *Okhrana* report of January 1917, reproduced in Source F, provides an illuminating summary of the situation.

SOURCE F

From an *Okhrana* report, January 1917, quoted in Lionel Kochan, *Russia in Revolution*, Paladin, 1974, p. 189.

The mass of industrial workers are quite ready to let themselves go to the wildest excesses of a hunger riot … The working masses, led in their actions and sympathies by the more conscious and already revolutionary-minded

What impression is given in Source F of the mood in Russia in early 1917?

elements, are violently hostile to the authorities and protest with all means and devices against a continuation of the war … Thus left wing – revolutionary – circles are firmly convinced that a revolution will begin very soon, that its undoubted forerunners have already appeared and that the government will at once show itself powerless in the struggles with the revolutionary masses, who will be all the more dangerous because they consist two-thirds of present soldiers … the internal source of Russian state life is at present threatened by the unrelenting approach of a grave shock.

On 14 February, Rodzianko, the *duma* president, warned the tsar that 'very serious outbreaks of unrest' were imminent. He added ominously, 'there is not one honest man left in your entourage; all the decent people have either been dismissed or left'. It was this desertion by those closest to the tsar that unwittingly set in motion what proved to be a revolution.

According to the **system of dating** in Imperial Russia, the revolution occupied the period from 18 February to 4 March 1917. A full-scale strike was started on 18 February by the employees at the Putilov steel works, the largest and most politically active factory in Petrograd. During the next five days, the Putilov strikers were joined on the streets by growing numbers of workers, who had been angered by rumours of a further cut in bread supplies. It is now known that these were merely rumours and that there was still enough bread to meet the capital's basic needs. However, in times of severe crisis rumour often has the same power as fact.

 **KEY TERM**

System of dating Until February 1918, Russia used the Julian calendar, which was 13 days behind the Gregorian calendar, the one used in most Western countries by this time. That is why different books may give different dates for the same event. This book uses the older dating for the events of 1917.

Key steps in the February Revolution

- 18 February: strike began at the Putilov factories in Petrograd.
- 23 February: International Women's Day, a demonstration organised by socialist groups to demand female equality.
- 25 February: a general strike began.
- 26 February: desertion of Petrograd garrison.
- 27 February: breakaway members of the *duma* formed a Provisional Committee. Petrograd soviet formed.
- 28 February: Nicholas II prevented from returning to Petrograd.
- 2 March: Provisional Committee declared itself a Provisional Government. Tsar signed abdication decree.
- 3 March: Provisional Government declared that a revolution had taken place.
- 4 March: tsar's abdication publicly proclaimed.

The course of events

It also happened that 23 February was International Women's Day. This brought thousands of women on to the streets to join the protesters in demanding food and an end to the war. By 25 February, Petrograd was paralysed by a city-wide strike. Factories were occupied and attempts by the authorities to disperse the workers were hampered by the growing sympathy among the police for the demonstrators. There was a great deal of confusion and little clear direction at the top. Events that were later seen as having had major political significance took place in an atmosphere in which political protests were indistinguishable from the general outcry against food shortages and the miseries brought by war.

SOURCE G

> What wartime conditions have led the women in Petrograd to make the protests expressed on their banners in Source G?

Some of the demonstrators at the 1917 International Women's Day. On the banner is written: 'As long as women are slaves, there will be no freedom. Long live equal rights for women'.

The breakdown of order

The tsar, at his military headquarters at Mogilev, 600 km (375 miles) from Petrograd, relied for news largely on the letters received from the tsarina, who was still in the capital. When he learned from her about the disturbances, Nicholas ordered the commander of the Petrograd garrison, General Khabalov, to restore order. Khabalov cabled back that, with the various contingents of the police and militia either fighting each other or joining the demonstrators, and his own garrison troops disobeying orders, the situation was uncontrollable.

Khabalov had earlier begged the government to declare martial law in Petrograd, which would have given him the power to use unlimited force against the demonstrators. But the breakdown of ordinary life in the capital meant that the martial law proclamation could not even be printed, let alone enforced. More serious still, by 26 February all but a few thousand of the original 150,000 Petrograd garrison troops had deserted. Desertions also seriously depleted a battalion of troops sent from the front under General Ivanov to reinforce the garrison.

Provisional Committee formed

Faced with this near-hopeless situation, Rodzianko on behalf of the *duma* informed the tsar that only a major concession on the government's part offered any hope of preserving the imperial power. Nicholas, again with that occasional stubbornness that he mistook for decisiveness, then ordered the *duma* to dissolve. It did so formally as an assembly, but a group of twelve members disobeyed the order and remained in session as a 'Provisional Committee'. This marked the first open unconstitutional defiance of the tsar. It was immediately followed by the boldest move so far, when Alexander Kerensky, a lawyer and a leading SR member in the *duma*, called for the tsar to stand down as head of state or be deposed.

Petrograd soviet formed

On that same day, 27 February, another event took place that was to prove as significant as the formation of the Provisional Committee. This was the first meeting of the 'Petrograd Soviet of Soldiers', Sailors' and Workers' Deputies', which gathered in the Tauride Palace, the same building that housed the Provisional Committee. The moving force behind the setting up of the soviet were the Mensheviks, who, under their local leader, **Alexander Shlyapnikov**, had grown in strength in Petrograd during the war.

These two self-appointed bodies – the Provisional Committee, representing the reformist elements of the old *duma*, and the soviet, speaking for the striking workers and rebellious troops – became the ***de facto*** government of Russia. This was the beginning of what Lenin later called the **Dual Authority**, an uneasy alliance that was to last until October. On 28 February, the soviet published the first edition of its newspaper *Izvestiya* (*The News*), in which it declared its determination 'to wipe out the old system completely' and to summon a constituent assembly, elected by **universal suffrage**.

The tsar abdicates

The remaining ministers in the tsar's cabinet were not prepared to face the growing storm. They used the pretext of an electricity failure in their government offices to abandon their responsibilities and to slip out of the capital. Rodzianko, who up to this point had struggled to remain loyal to the official government, then advised Nicholas that only his personal abdication could save the Russian monarchy. On 28 February, Nicholas decided to return to Petrograd, apparently in the belief that his personal presence would have a calming effect on the capital. However, the royal train was intercepted on its

 KEY FIGURE

Alexander Shlyapnikov (1885–1937)

Later became a Bolshevik, one of the few major revolutionaries to be in Petrograd during the February Revolution.

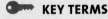 **KEY TERMS**

De facto 'By the very fact' – a term used to denote the real situation, as compared to what it should or might be in theory or in law.

Dual Authority Lenin first coined this term to describe the balance of power between the Provisional Government and the Petrograd soviet.

Universal suffrage An electoral system in which all adults have the right to vote.

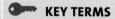

KEY TERMS

Stavka The high command of the Russian army.

Russian constituent assembly A full gathering of the elected representatives of the Russian people.

journey by mutinous troops who forced it to divert to Pskov, 300 km (190 miles) from Petrograd. It was at Pskov that a group of generals from ***stavka***, together with the representatives of the old *duma*, met the tsar to inform him that the seriousness of the situation in Petrograd made his return both futile and dangerous. They, too, advised abdication.

Nicholas tamely accepted the advice. His only concern was whether he should also renounce the throne on behalf of his son, Alexei. This he eventually decided to do. The decree of abdication that Nicholas signed on 2 March nominated his brother, the Grand Duke Michael, as the new tsar. However, Michael, unwilling to accept the poisoned chalice, refused the title on the pretext that it had not been offered to him by a **Russian constituent assembly**.

By default, the Provisional Committee, which had renamed itself the Provisional Government, thus found itself responsible for governing Russia. On 3 March, the new government officially informed the rest of the world of the revolution that had taken place. On the following day, Nicholas II's formal abdication was publicly announced. Thus it was that the house of Romanov, which only four years earlier in 1913 had celebrated its tri-centenary as a divinely appointed dynasty, came to an end not with a bang but a whimper.

The role of the Bolsheviks

Perhaps it would be more accurate to speak of the 'non-role'. The Bolsheviks, absent from the 1905 Revolution, were also missing when the February Revolution took place. Practically all their leaders were in exile. Lenin, who was himself in Switzerland at the time, had not been in Russia for over a decade. With so many of the leading Bolsheviks out of the country for so long before 1917, and given the difficulties of communication in wartime, their knowledge of the situation in Petrograd in 1917 was fragmentary and unreliable. It is small wonder, therefore, that the events of February took them by surprise. This is borne out by a statement of Lenin's to a group of students in Zurich in December 1916, only two months before the February Revolution. He told his audience of youthful Bolshevik sympathisers that although they might live to see the proletarian revolution, he, at the age of 46, did not expect to do so.

The role of Petrograd

One remarkable feature of the Revolution was that it had been overwhelmingly the affair of one city, Petrograd. Another was the willingness of the rest of Russia to accept it. As Trotsky observed in Source H.

? According to Source H, how significant does Trotsky consider Petrograd's role to have been in the February Revolution?

SOURCE H

Excerpt from Leon Trotsky, *The History of the Russian Revolution*, Pluto Press, 1985, p. 158.

It would be no exaggeration to say that Petrograd achieved the February Revolution. The rest of the country adhered to it. There was no struggle anywhere except in Petrograd. Nowhere in the country were there any groups of the population, any parties, institutions, or military units ready to put up a fight for the old regime. Neither at the front nor at the rear was there a brigade or regiment prepared to do battle for Nicholas II. The revolution was carried out upon the initiative and by the strength of one city, constituting approximately 1/75 of the population of the country.

The character of the February Revolution

The February Revolution was not quite the bloodless affair that some of the liberal newspapers in Petrograd claimed. Modern estimates suggest that between 1500 and 2000 people were killed or wounded in the disturbances. But, by the scale of the casualties regularly suffered by Russian armies in the war, this figure was small, which further supported Trotsky's contention that the nation was unwilling to fight to save the old regime.

It is difficult to see the events of 18 February to 3 March as an overthrow of the Russian monarchy. What does stand out is the lack of direction and leadership at the top, and the unwillingness at the moment of crisis of the tsarist generals and politicians to fight to save the system. Tsardom collapsed from within. Revolutionary pressure from outside had no direct effect. It should be re-emphasised that it was among tsardom's hitherto most committed supporters that the earliest rejection of the tsar occurred. It was the highest-ranking officers who first intimated to Nicholas that he should stand down. It was the aristocratic members of the *duma* who took the lead in refusing to disband on the tsar's orders. It was when the army and the police told Nicholas that they were unable to carry out his command to keep the populace in order that his position became finally hopeless.

The strikes and demonstrations in Petrograd in February 1917 did not in themselves cause the revolution. It was the defection of the tsar's previous supporters at the moment of crisis, compounded by Nicholas II's own failure to resist, that brought about the fall of the Romanov dynasty. Lenin once observed that a true revolution can occur only when certain preconditions exist; one essential is that the ruling power loses the will to survive. Some time before he formally abdicated, Nicholas had given up the fight. It was not the fact but the speed and completeness of the collapse of tsardom in February 1917 that was so remarkable.

The importance of the war 1914–17

What destroyed tsardom was the length of the war. A short war, even if unsuccessful, might have been bearable, as Russia's defeat by Japan twelve years earlier had shown. But the cumulative effect of a prolonged struggle proved overwhelming:

- deaths and casualties by the million
- soaring inflation

- a dislocated communications system
- hunger and deprivation
- a series of increasingly bewildered and ineffectual ministries under an incompetent tsar.

These were the lot of the Russian people between 1914 and 1917. The consequence was a loss of morale and a sense of hopelessness that fatally undermined the once-potent myth of the tsar's God-given authority. By 1917 the tsarist system had forfeited its claim to the loyalty of the Russian people.

Summary diagram: The February Revolution 1917

Background
A general unrest and anger in Petrograd, but this was not led or directed
|
The revolution began as a challenge not by revolutionaries but by traditional supporters of tsardom

Course
Strikes in major factories
|
International Women's Day protest became a riot for bread
|
Disorder spread throughout the city
|
Police and garrison troops declared the situation uncontrollable
|
12 rebellious *duma* members created the Provisional Committee
|
Mensheviks set up the Petrograd soviet
|
Nicholas tried to return to Petrograd but was prevented by mutinous troops
|
Army high command advised tsar to abdicate
|
Nicholas tamely abdicated
|
Dual authority became *de facto* government

Character
Not a revolution from below
|
Bolsheviks played no part
|
Revolution started by tsardom's traditional supporters
|
A failure of leadership and nerve at the top
|
A revolution of one city – Petrograd
|
Not the result of a social or political movement but a consequence of war
|
An institutional crisis?

Key debate

▶ *Why was there a February Revolution?*

The February Revolution was the first in a series of events in 1917 that changed the character of Russia and impacted on the whole world. Because of its importance, its causes have been debated by historians ever since.

An appropriate starting point is the view of the Russian revolutionary Leon Trotsky. In his classic account, *The History of the Russian Revolution* (1931), he laid down what was to become the received Bolshevik interpretation that dominated the thinking of the Soviet Union throughout its existence. Trotsky's premise was 'that the revolution was begun from below' by workers who had been educated in revolutionary ways by Lenin and the Bolsheviks. He added, however, that while the Bolshevik teaching had guaranteed the victory of the uprising, circumstances had not allowed the Bolsheviks to lead the revolution itself at this point. That would come later.

Trotsky's view was accepted and expanded in 1935 by a pro-Soviet, US writer W.H. Chamberlin, in *The Russian Revolution 1917–1921* (1935). He described the collapse of tsardom in February 1917 as 'leaderless and spontaneous', and stressed that 'no one, even among the revolutionary leaders, realized that the strikes and bread riots which broke out in Petrograd on February 23 would culminate in the overthrow of the government four days later'.

Another writer with basic sympathy for the Soviet Union was the celebrated British historian E.H. Carr, who also accepted Trotsky's interpretation.

EXTRACT 1

From E.H. Carr, *The Bolshevik Revolution*, Penguin, 1973, p. 81.

The February revolution of 1917 which overthrew the Romanov dynasty was the spontaneous outbreak of a multitude exasperated by the privations of the war and by manifest inequality in the distribution of burdens. It was welcomed and utilized by a broad stratum of the bourgeoisie and the official class, which had lost confidence in the autocratic system of government and especially in the persons of the Tsar and of his advisers; it was from this section of the population that the first Provisional Government was drawn. The revolutionary parties played no part in the making of the revolution. They did not expect it, and were at first nonplussed by it. The creation at the moment of the revolution of a Petrograd Soviet of Workers Deputies was a spontaneous act of groups of workers without central direction.

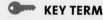 **KEY TERM**

Émigré One who fled from Russia after the Revolution, from fear or a desire to plan a counter-strike against the Bolsheviks.

However, George Katkov, a Russian *émigré* and stern critic of the Soviet Union, resurrected the notion that the February Revolution, far from being a spontaneous people's rising, was the work of conspirators in the pay of German agents eager to knock Russia out of the war.

EXTRACT 2

From G. Katkov, *Russia 1917: The February Revolution*, Prentice-Hall, 1967, p. 422.

The belief that German agents were behind it is as old as the events themselves – indeed older, for the Russian government had suspected and indeed known of the German wartime influence on the labour movement in Russia long before the Petrograd rising. We know now for certain that from the very beginning of the war the German government consistently pursued in Russia a Revolutionierungspolitik *[a strategy aimed at creating revolution], an essential element of which was the support of an economic strike movement capable, so it was hoped, of gradually escalating into a political revolution. The German government expended considerable sums on fostering the [Russian] strike movement.*

Richard Pipes, a Polish–American scholar, whose first-hand experience of the USSR made him a formidable critic of Soviet-style history, rejects the idea that February was a revolt by a bitter, war-weary people. His contention is that Russians wanted the war not to end but to be fought more effectively until victory was gained. What ultimately doomed the tsar was his abandonment by Russia's military and political establishment.

EXTRACT 3

From Richard Pipes, *Three Whys of the Russian Revolution*, Pimlico, 1998, pp. 28–9.

Having studied in minute detail the massive information regarding the steps leading up to the abdication of Nicholas II, I have not the slightest doubt that he faced no popular pressures to abdicate; the pressure stemmed exclusively from the ranks of politicians and generals who thought the Crown's removal essential to victory. The fact that the tsar's abdication had the opposite effect of that intended tells nothing of his motives in so doing.

[The tsar's] power, however dazzling its external glitter, was internally weak and quite unable to cope effectively with the strains – political, economic, and psychological – which the war brought in its wake. In my opinion, the principal causes of the downfall in 1917 were political and not economic or social … In 1917, you had intellectuals gathered in political parties that had well formulated programs for drastic change.

Australian historian David Christian also believes that the roles of the established class around the tsar were vital but he lays weight on the character of Nicholas II as being the decisive factor.

EXTRACT 4

From David Christian, *Imperial and Soviet Russia*, Macmillan, 1997, p. 176.

The February Revolution could have been avoided. There remained, even in 1916, a willingness within the upper classes to rally around the tsar, if only he could bring himself to create a genuinely constitutional government. If the tsar had been willing to accept the demands of the Progressive Bloc, this would have greatly narrowed the gulf within the ruling group. The Progressive Bloc, whose members dominated much of the Russian press would have swung the media behind the government and behind the war effort. When discontent did break out, the demonstrators would have faced a united ruling class. But Nicholas was incapable of seeing this alternative. By February 1917, he had alienated the only groups in the empire who might have been able to rescue him.

How do the historians quoted or referred to differ in their explanation of the February Revolution?

While not dismissing the importance of individuals and groups in the events of February 1917, many historians now interpret the rising as the climax of an 'institutional crisis' in Russia. What they mean by this is that what produced the 1917 crisis in Russia was the failure of its *institutions* – its political, social and economic systems – to cope with the problems it faced. Norman Stone is a leading proponent of this concept. His essential argument is that Russia's institutions were too backward to cope with the problems which Russia's attempts to modernise had brought: this was made patent by the war of 1914–17, which created economic chaos. 'But', Stone adds, 'economic backwardness did not alone make for revolution. The economic chaos came more from a contest between the old and the new in the Russian economy. There was a crisis, not of decline but rather of growth.'

It was an outstanding feature of the major wars of the twentieth century that they put immense pressures on the nations that fought them. The war that Russia entered in 1914 intensified all the problems from which it had traditionally suffered. Russia's institutional crisis showed up the tsarist system as being politically as well as economically bankrupt. While this line of thought does not absolve the tsar and his ministers from all responsibility for the collapse of Imperial Russia, it does lessen their blame. If the institutions of which they were a part were inadequate to meet the challenges, then no matter what efforts they might have made, the problems would have overwhelmed them.

Chapter summary

Tsar Nicholas II had never been more revered than when Russia went to war on 1 August 1914. The nation rallied behind him as the embodiment of Russian pride. But within three years all the goodwill had dissipated. By taking personal command of the Russian armies, he tied his dynasty's fate to the outcome of the war. Poorly led and equipped, his troops fought valiantly but unavailingly. An almost continuous series of military defeats created a deep disillusion to add to the privations of wartime. The tsar's political incompetence was even more marked than his military shortcomings. He appeared to let government slip into the hands of his unpopular German wife and her confidant, Rasputin, an uncouth upstart whom the court detested.

Unwilling to extend authority to the Progressive Bloc, Nicholas continued to rely on blundering ministers. The result was that when serious disorder occurred in Petrograd early in 1917, he had no one to whom he could turn. His officials and his high command advised him that abdication was the only way of preventing civil war. He duly abdicated, an event whose deeper causes have become the subject of continuous historical debate.

Refresher questions

Use these questions to remind yourself of the key material covered in this chapter.

1 How did Russia respond to the demands of war?

2 How was Russia's financial position damaged by the war?

3 How did the war disrupt the supply of food?

4 Why did the Russian transport system prove inadequate in wartime?

5 How well did the organisation of the Russian army adapt to the needs of war?

6 How did Nicholas respond to the war?

7 Why did Rasputin prove such an influential figure in the build-up to revolution?

8 Were the events of February 1917 a collapse at the top or a revolution from below?

9 Were the events of February really a revolution?

10 Did the February Revolution come from above or below?

Question practice

ESSAY QUESTIONS

1 'It was Nicholas II's decision in 1915 to become commander-in-chief of the imperial armies that led to the weakening of his position as tsar.' How far do you agree with this statement?

2 To what extent was the development of opposition in the *duma* to the tsarist government between 1914 and 1916 the result of Nicholas II's policies and actions?

3 Was popular discontent over food shortages the main reason for the collapse of the tsarist regime in 1917?

4 'The February rising in 1917 was a revolution without revolutionaries.' How far do you agree with this statement?

SOURCE QUESTION

1 How far could the historian make use of Sources 1 and 2 together to investigate the growing unrest in Petrograd in late 1916? Explain your answer, using both sources, the information given about them and your own knowledge of the historical context.

SOURCE 1

From a Petrograd *Okhrana* report, October 1916. Here, the report describes the threatening atmosphere and increasing tensions created by rising prices and food shortages in the capital. Quoted in G. Vernadsky, editor, *A Source Book for Russian History from Early Times to 1917*, volume 3, Yale University Press, 1973, pp. 867–8.

Despite the great increase in wages, the economic condition of the masses is worse than terrible. Even if we estimate the rise in earnings at 100 per cent, the prices of products have risen on the average, 300 per cent. The impossibility of even buying many food products and necessities, the time waste standing idle in queues to receive goods, the increasing incidence of disease due to malnutrition and unsanitary living conditions (cold and dampness because of lack of coal and wood), and so forth, have made the workers as a whole, prepared for the wildest excesses of a 'hunger riot'.

If, in the future, grain continues to be hidden, the very fact of its disappearance will be sufficient to provoke in the capitals and in the other most populated centers of the empire the greatest disorders, attended by pogroms and endless street rioting. The mood of anxiety, growing daily more intense, is spreading to ever wider sections of the populace. Never have we observed such nervousness as there is now. The slightest incident is enough to provoke the biggest brawl. This is especially noticeable in the vicinity of shops, stores, banks, and similar institutions, where 'misunderstandings' occur almost daily.

SOURCE 2

From a speech made by Paul Milyukov, the leader of the liberal Kadet Party, to the fourth *duma* on 1 November 1916. Here, Milyukov criticises the tsar's government. Quoted in G. Vernadsky, editor, *A Source Book for Russian History*, volume 3, Yale University Press, 1972, p. 870.

This present government has sunk beneath the level on which it stood during normal times in Russian life. And now the gulf between us and that government has grown wider and become impassable. Today we are aware that with this government we cannot legislate, and we cannot, with this government, lead Russia to victory. We are telling this government, as the declaration of the [Progressive Bloc] stated: We shall fight you, we shall fight you with all legitimate means until you go.

When the Duma declares again and again that the home front must be organized for a successful war and the government continues to insist that to organize the country means to organize a revolution, and consciously chooses chaos and disorganization – is this stupidity or treason? We have many reasons for being discontented with the government. But all these reasons boil down to one general one: the incompetence and evil intentions of the present government. We shall fight until we get a responsible government. Cabinet members must agree unanimously as to the most urgent tasks. They must agree and be prepared to implement the programme of the Duma majority. They must rely on this majority, not just in the implementation of this programme, but in all their actions.

CHAPTER 5

1917: From Provisional Government to October Revolution

The fall of the Romanovs was followed by an eight-month period in which the Provisional Government, initially in co-operation with the Petrograd soviet, struggled to resolve Russia's major problems: food shortages, disruption on the land and the continuing war with Germany. Troubles deepened as the Russian armies failed to achieve a significant victory. Led by Lenin, often from exile, the Bolsheviks strove to exploit the government's difficulties. After a thwarted attempt to seize power in July, they were again in a position in October to challenge for power. Kerensky's government, deprived by desertion of military support, caved in and fled. Carried to power in this bloodless way, Lenin proceeded to claim authority in the name of the soviets and establish a Bolshevik government. This chapter examines these developments under the following themes:

★ The Dual Authority

★ The return of the Bolsheviks

★ The Provisional Government and its problems

★ The October Revolution

★ Reasons for Bolshevik success

The key debate on *page 123* of this chapter asks the question: What was the true character of the October Revolution?

Key dates

1917	Feb. 28	Provisional Government claimed authority	1917	Sept. 25	Bolsheviks gained majority in Petrograd soviet
	March 1	Petrograd soviet issued Soviet Order Number 1		Oct. 9	Petrograd soviet set up Military Revolutionary Committee
	March 12	Bolsheviks began to return to Petrograd		Oct. 23	Bolsheviks rose against Kerensky's government
	April 3	Lenin returned to Petrograd		Oct. 24–25	Bolsheviks took control of Petrograd
	April 4	Lenin issued his *April Theses*		Oct. 25–26	Kerensky fled from Petrograd
	July 3–6	Failure of the Bolshevik 'July Days' uprising		Oct. 26	Bolsheviks established *Sovnarkom*, with Lenin as chairman
	July 8	Kerensky became prime minister		Oct. 27	Lenin informed the Congress of Soviets that the Bolsheviks had taken power in their name
	Sept. 1	Kornilov's abortive march on Petrograd			

The Dual Authority

▶ *What were the basic weaknesses of the Provisional Government?*

The Provisional Government, led by **Prince Lvov**, which picked up the reins of authority after the tsar's abdication (see page 89), was really the old *duma* in a new form. When Paul Milyukov, the foreign minister, read out the list of ministers in the newly formed government, someone in the listening crowd called out, 'Who appointed you lot, then?' Milyukov replied, 'We were appointed by the revolution itself.'

In that exchange were expressed the two crippling weaknesses of the Provisional Government throughout the eight months of its existence:

- It was not an elected body, having come into being as a rebellious committee of the old *duma*, refusing to disband at the tsar's order. As a consequence, it lacked legitimate authority and had no constitutional claim on the loyalty of the Russian people. Lacking this, it would be judged entirely on how well it dealt with the nation's problems.
- Its authority was limited by its unofficial partnership with the Petrograd soviet. It was not that the soviet was initially hostile. Indeed, at first, there was considerable co-operation between them. Some individuals were members of both bodies. For example, **Alexander Kerensky**, the SR leader, was for a time chairman of the soviet as well as a minister in the Provisional Government.

Role of the Petrograd soviet

The soviet did not set out to be an alternative government. It regarded its role as supervisory, checking that the interests of the soldiers and workers were fully understood by the new government. However, in the uncertain times that followed the February Revolution, the Provisional Government often seemed unsure of its own authority. This uncertainty tended to give the soviet greater prominence.

In addition, there was the impressive fact that in the aftermath of the February Revolution, soviets were rapidly set up in all the major cities and towns of Russia. Yet, although the soviets were to play an increasingly important role in the development of the revolution, in the early stages the Bolsheviks did not dominate them. The soviets were not, therefore, necessarily opposed to the Provisional Government. It was significant, however, that even before the Bolshevik influence became dominant, the ability of the Petrograd soviet to restrict the Provisional Government's authority had been clearly revealed. In one of its first moves as an organisation it had issued its 'Soviet Order Number 1', which declared that, in military matters, the orders of the Provisional Government were to be obeyed 'only when they do not contradict the orders and decrees of the soviet.'

 KEY FIGURE

Prince Lvov (1861–1925)
A prominent landowner and progressive reformer, he headed the Provisional Government from March to July 1917.

SOURCE A

An overflowing meeting of the Petrograd soviet in March 1917. Huge numbers of soldiers and workers, sometimes as many 3000, attended the early meetings. By the autumn, this had dropped to a few hundred but the Bolsheviks kept up their numbers, which gave them a disproportionate influence in the soviet.

? Study Source A. Why was the presence of the Bolsheviks in Petrograd soviet meetings so politically important between March and October 1917?

Importance of Soviet Order Number 1

What the order meant was that the decrees of the Provisional Government were not binding unless they were approved by the Petrograd soviet. History shows that unless a government has control of its army it does not hold real power. Order Number 1 made it clear that the Provisional Government did not have such power. It had, therefore, to compromise with the soviet. Between February and April 1917 this arrangement worked reasonably well; there were no serious disputes between the two bodies in the 'Dual Authority'.

Early political co-operation

An important factor promoting co-operation was the widespread elation in Petrograd in the weeks following the February Revolution. Excitement was in the air; people on the streets greeted each other with enthusiasm as if a new era had dawned. This encouraged a genuine feeling across all the political groups that Russia had entered a period of real freedom. For a time co-operation between opposing parties became much easier to achieve.

There was also a general acceptance that the new liberty that had come with the collapse of tsardom should not be allowed to slip into **anarchy**. This created a willingness to maintain state authority at the centre of affairs. Furthermore, at the beginning, both the Provisional Government and the soviet contained a wide range of political representation. In the first meetings of the soviet, moderate socialists had a bigger influence than the SRs or SDs. In addition, all parties, apart from the Bolsheviks and the **monarchists**, were represented in the Provisional Government during its early weeks. As the year wore on and the problems mounted, the Provisional Government moved increasingly to the right and the soviet to the left. But before that shift occurred there had been considerable harmony.

A further fact was that the socialist parties, not being as extreme as the Bolsheviks, who were not yet in a position to influence matters, were reluctant to demand too much, too soon. They judged that their relative weakness limited how far they could go and that they had to rely on the administrators from the old regime. **Nicolai Sukhanov**, a leading Menshevik member of the Petrograd soviet, later defined this attitude: 'the Soviet democracy had to entrust the power to the propertied classes, its class enemy, without whose participation it could not now master the technique of administration in the desperate conditions of disintegration'.

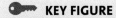

KEY FIGURE

Nicolai Sukhanov (1882–1940)

An SD activist who wrote an insider's account of 1917; he was tried under Stalin and shot.

Early achievements of the Provisional Government

The fruits of the early harmony between the soviet and the government were shown in a set of progressive measures adopted by the Provisional Government:

- amnesty for political prisoners
- trade unions legally recognised
- an eight-hour day for industrial workers
- replacement of the tsarist police with a **people's militia**
- granting of full civil and religious freedoms
- preparations made for the election of a constituent assembly.

KEY TERM

People's militia A new set of volunteer law-enforcement officers drawn from ordinary people.

Noticeably, however, these changes did not touch on the critical issues of the war and the land. It would be these that would destroy the always tenuous partnership of the Dual Authority, and it would be Lenin who would begin the process of destruction.

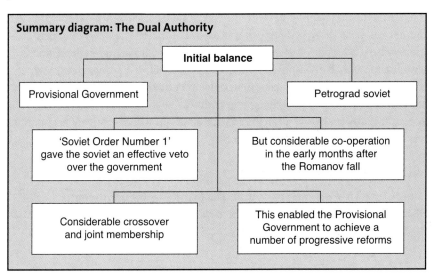

Summary diagram: The Dual Authority

Initial balance

Provisional Government — Petrograd soviet

'Soviet Order Number 1' gave the soviet an effective veto over the government

But considerable co-operation in the early months after the Romanov fall

Considerable crossover and joint membership

This enabled the Provisional Government to achieve a number of progressive reforms

2 The return of the Bolsheviks

▶ *What impact did Lenin's return have on the situation in Petrograd?*

The impact of Stalin and Kamenev

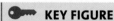

KEY FIGURE

Lev Kamenev (1883–1936)
Held various key positions under Lenin between 1917 and 1924.

Once the exiled Bolsheviks learned of Nicholas II's abdication they rushed back to Petrograd. Those, like Stalin, who had been in Siberia were the first to return in March. Stalin's reappearance was significant. Because of their standing in the party, he and his fellow returnee, **Lev Kamenev**, became the leading voices among the Petrograd Bolsheviks. Initially, this duo took an anti-Lenin line. Lenin, who did not reach Petrograd until nearly a month later, still tried to direct things from exile. In his 'Letters from Afar', he urged that the war Russia was fighting should be turned into a class war; Bolsheviks should infiltrate the armies of the warring nations and encourage the soldiers to turn their weapons against their officers as the first step towards overthrowing their governments. Lenin also instructed the Bolsheviks not to co-operate with the Provisional Government or with the other parties.

Stalin and Kamenev ignored Lenin's instructions. On the war issue, they argued that the best policy was to press for international negotiations to be started. Stalin wrote to the Bolsheviks in Petrograd telling them to 'put pressure on the Provisional Government to announce its willingness to start peace talks at once'. On the question of the Bolsheviks' relations with the Provisional Government, Kamenev insisted that circumstances made co-operation with it essential, at least for the time being, since the government was 'genuinely struggling against the remnants of the old regime'.

As to the other parties, Kamenev believed that co-operation with them made perfect sense. He backed a proposal that it was 'possible and desirable' for the Bolsheviks to restore links with the Mensheviks. Clearly at this juncture, there was a wide divergence of view between Lenin and the other two men. Interestingly, Kamenev appears to have been the major partner in his relations with Stalin, who later admitted that, in the period before Lenin arrived, Kamenev dominated Bolshevik discussions in Petrograd. What Kamenev was advancing and what Stalin went along with was what is often referred to as **accommodationism**. It was an approach that Lenin would totally reject once he was back in Petrograd.

KEY TERM

Accommodationism
The idea that the Bolsheviks should co-operate with the Provisional Government and work with the other revolutionary and reforming parties.

Lenin's return in April 1917

Lenin arrived in Petrograd on 3 April. The manner of his return from Switzerland was a remarkable story in itself. His wife, Krupskaya, recorded it, as described in Source B.

SOURCE B

From K. K. Krupskaya, *Reminiscences of Lenin*, Lawrence & Wishart, 1959, pp. 336–67.

The moment the news of the February Revolution was received, Ilyich [Lenin] was all eagerness to get back to Russia. As there were no legal ways of travelling, illegal ways would have to be used. But what ways? From the moment the news of the Revolution was received, Ilyich had no sleep. His nights were spent building the most improbable plans. Naturally the Germans gave us permission to travel through Germany in the belief that Revolution was a disaster to a country, and that by allowing emigrant internationalists [Russian revolutionaries in exile] to return to their country they were helping to spread the Revolution in Russia. The Bolsheviks, for their part, considered it their duty to bring about a victorious proletarian revolution. They did not care what the German bourgeois government thought about it.

> According to Krupskaya in Source B, in what way did the attitudes of the Bolsheviks and the Germans coincide?

Krupskaya's account is instructive. In the hope that the tsar's fall would be the prelude to the collapse of the Russian armies, the German government arranged for Lenin to return to Russia in a sealed train across occupied Europe. British historian Norman Stone waggishly referred to it as 'the first no-smoking train in history', Lenin being a fanatical anti-smoker.

Since the outbreak of war in 1914, Lenin's opponents had continually accused him of being in the pay of the German government. Their charge had weight. Between 1914 and 1917, the German foreign office gave regular financial support to Lenin and the Bolsheviks, in the hope that if they achieved their revolutionary aims they would pull Russia out of the war. As Krupskaya observed, Lenin did not really care what the attitude of the Germans was. It just so happened that, for quite different reasons, what they wanted – the withdrawal of the Russian armies from the war – was precisely what he wanted. However, it made no difference to anti-Bolsheviks that the German reasons were military and Lenin's were political. They considered the German government and the Bolshevik Party to be co-operating in a common cause, the defeat of Russia.

Lenin's impact

There is no doubting the great significance of Lenin's return to Petrograd in April 1917. A German official likened it to the transporting of a deadly virus in a test-tube. Once safely arrived in Russia, the test-tube was broken, releasing the lethal germ to infect the Russian body politic. It was an apt simile. Up to the time of Lenin's arrival, the Bolsheviks, led by Kamenev and Stalin, had accepted the formation of the Dual Authority as part of a genuine revolution. They had been willing to work with the other reformist parties. Lenin changed all that. In his speech on his arrival at Petrograd's Finland Station on 3 April, he declared that the events of February, far from giving Russia political freedom, had created a **parliamentary-bourgeois republic**. He scorned the Provisional Government and called for its overthrow in a genuine revolution.

 KEY TERM

Parliamentary-bourgeois republic Lenin's contemptuous term for the Provisional Government, which he dismissed as an unrepresentative mockery that had simply replaced the rule of the tsar with the rule of the reactionary *duma*.

V.I. Lenin

1870	Lenin born as Vladimir Ilyich Ulyanov to a minor aristocratic family of Jewish ancestry
1897	Exiled to Siberia, took the alias Lenin
1900	Joined the SD Party
1903	Led the Bolshevik breakaway movement in the SDs
1906–17	In exile abroad
1917	Returned to Petrograd to lead the Bolsheviks in the October Revolution
1917–22	Led the Bolsheviks in consolidating their hold on Russia
1921	Introduced the New Economic Policy
1924	Died after being incapacitated for two years by strokes

A natural contrarian, Lenin was confirmed in his hatred of tsardom by the execution of his brother in 1887 for an attempted assassination of the tsar. On the authorities' list of 'dangerous persons' from the age of seventeen, Lenin became a powerful revolutionary writer. In 1903, he led the Bolsheviks in a breakaway movement from the Marxist SD party which he had joined five years earlier.

Convinced of the correctness of his theories, Lenin survived the failure of the 1905 revolution. Having been in exile for most of the period 1906–17, he returned to Petrograd in April 1917 following the February Revolution. After a desperate six months of preparation, during which the Bolsheviks were almost destroyed, Lenin was the inspiration behind the successful coup in October which saw his party take power from the ineffectual Provisional Government.

Over the next five years, Lenin, against great odds, proceeded to create a new Soviet state, overcoming his internal opponents in a savage civil war and resisting the attempts of a number of foreign powers to crush Bolshevism. He showed ruthless determination in transforming Russia into a Communist state. Thwarted in his plans to develop a socialist economy, Lenin was forced to return to capitalist methods in his New Economic Policy (NEP) in 1921. Already weakened by an attempt on his life in 1918, he suffered a number of strokes which from 1922 left him increasingly incapable of direct government. Having given no clear indication as to who should follow him as leader, he left the way open for a power struggle over the succession. At his death in 1924, Lenin bequeathed the Soviet state a legacy of totalitarianism, economic experimentation and Soviet hostility towards the outside world.

The *April Theses*

On the following day, Lenin issued his *April Theses*, in which he spelt out future Bolshevik policy. To the bewilderment of those Bolsheviks who had been in Petrograd since February and expected to be congratulated for their efforts in working with the other revolutionary groups, Lenin condemned all that had happened since the fall of the tsar. He insisted that, since the Bolsheviks were the only truly revolutionary proletarian party, they must:

- abandon co-operation with all other parties
- work for a true revolution entirely by their own efforts
- overthrow the Provisional Government, which was simply the old, class-ridden *duma* in a new garb
- struggle, not to extend freedom to all classes, but to transfer power to the workers
- demand that authority pass to the soviets.

Lenin had ulterior motives in demanding the soviets take over government. Although he rejected much of what the soviets had done, he saw them as a power base. Circumstances had made them an essential part of the structure of post-tsarist government. Lenin calculated that the soviets – the Petrograd soviet in particular – offered his small Bolshevik Party the means by which it could obtain power in the name of the proletariat. By infiltrating and dominating the soviets, the Bolshevik Party would be in a position to take over the state.

The essence of Lenin's argument was summed up in two provocative Bolshevik slogans that he coined: 'Peace, Bread and Land' and 'All Power to the Soviets'. But these were more than slogans. They were Lenin's way of presenting in simple, dramatic headings the basic problems confronting Russia:

- 'peace' – the continuing war with Germany
- 'bread' – the chronic food shortage
- 'land' – the disruption in the countryside.

Lenin asserted that as long as the Provisional Government stayed in power these problems could not be solved because the ministers governed only in the interests of their own class. They had no wish to end the war, which brought them profits, or supply food to the Russian people, whom they despised, or reform the land-holding system, which guaranteed their property rights and privileges. That is why Lenin demanded 'All Power to the Soviets'. The current ministers must be swept aside and replaced with a government of the soviets. Only then would the people's needs be addressed.

Lenin's analysis was shrewd and prophetic; the Provisional Government's failure to deal with the three principal issues he had identified would lead to its eventual downfall.

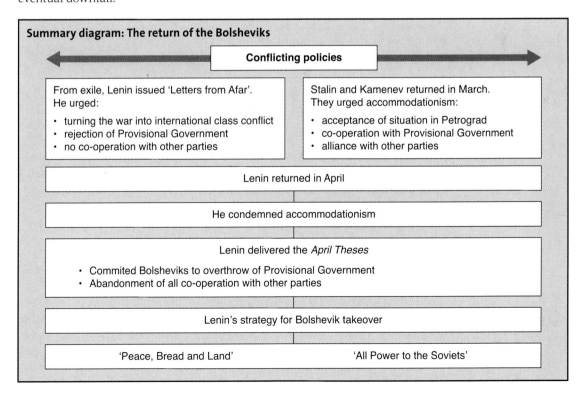

Summary diagram: The return of the Bolsheviks

Conflicting policies

From exile, Lenin issued 'Letters from Afar'. He urged:
- turning the war into international class conflict
- rejection of Provisional Government
- no co-operation with other parties

Stalin and Kamenev returned in March. They urged accommodationism:
- acceptance of situation in Petrograd
- co-operation with Provisional Government
- alliance with other parties

Lenin returned in April

He condemned accommodationism

Lenin delivered the *April Theses*
- Commited Bolsheviks to overthrow of Provisional Government
- Abandonment of all co-operation with other parties

Lenin's strategy for Bolshevik takeover

'Peace, Bread and Land'   'All Power to the Soviets'

The Provisional Government and its problems

▶ *What particular difficulties beset the Provisional Government?*

The war

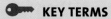
From the outset, the Provisional Government was in a troubled position. The main problem was the war. For the Provisional Government after February 1917 there was no choice but to fight on. The reason was not idealistic but financial. Unless it did so, it would no longer receive the supplies and **war-credits** from the Western allies on which it had come to rely. Tsardom had left Russia virtually bankrupt. No government could have carried on without large injections of capital from abroad. Foreign bankers were among the first to visit Russia after Nicholas's abdication to ensure that the new regime would carry on the war.

The strain that this obligation imposed on the Provisional Government finally proved unsustainable. Its preoccupation with the war prevented it from dealing with Russia's social and economic problems. This was a paradox: in order to survive, the Provisional Government had to keep Russia in the war, but in doing so it destroyed its own chances of survival.

Ministerial crisis

The question of the war brought about the Milyukov crisis, the first serious rift between the Petrograd soviet and the Provisional Government. On 14 March, the soviet had issued an 'Address to the people of the whole world', calling for 'peace without annexations or **indemnities**'. The government declared that it accepted the address, but this appeared meaningless when it became known that Milyukov, the foreign minister, had made a pledge to the Allies that Russia would fight on until Germany was defeated.

Late in April, a series of violent demonstrations occurred in Petrograd directed against Milyukov. These produced a ministerial crisis. Milyukov and Guchkov, the war minister, resigned early in May. These resignations were an illustration of the divisions within the government as well as of the outside pressures it faced. In the reshuffled cabinet, Alexander Kerensky become the war minister and places were found for leading Mensheviks and SRs.

It was hoped that this apparent leftward shift of the Provisional Government would ease its relationship with the soviet. But the opposite happened. The socialists in the government tended to become isolated from the soviet. This was because in joining the government they had to enter into coalition with the Kadets, which opened them to the charge that they were compromising with the bourgeoisie. Lenin wrote of 'those despicable socialists who have sold out to the government'.

Emergence of Kerensky

Some individuals within the Provisional Government had misgivings about continuing the war, but at no time did the government as a body contemplate withdrawing from it. This would have mattered less had the Russian armies been successful, but the military situation continued to deteriorate, eroding the support the government had initially enjoyed.

Lvov stayed as nominal head of the government but it was Kerensky who became the major influence. As war minister, he campaigned for Russia to embrace the conflict with Germany as a crusade to save the revolution, requiring the total dedication of the nation. He made a number of personal visits to the front to deliver passionate speeches to the troops, appealing to them to be prepared to lay down their lives for Russia: 'Forward to the battle for freedom. I summon you not to a feast but death.'

Government troubles increase

The attempt to turn the war into a national crusade took no account of the real situation. The truth was that Russia had gone beyond the point where it could fight a successful war. Yet Kerensky persisted. In June, a major offensive was launched on the south-western front. It failed badly. With their already low morale further weakened by Bolshevik agitators, who encouraged them to disobey orders, the Russian forces were no match for the Austrians, who easily repulsed them and inflicted heavy losses. Whole Russian regiments mutinied or deserted. **General Kornilov**, the commander on the south-western front, called on the Provisional Government to halt the offensive and direct its energies to crushing the **political subversives** at home. This appeal for a tougher policy was taken up by the government. Early in July, Lvov stood down as prime minister, to be replaced by Kerensky. Kornilov became commander-in-chief.

Kronstadt

The government's troubles were deepened by events on the island of Kronstadt, the naval base situated 30 km (18 miles) west of Petrograd in the Bay of Finland. Sailors and workers there defied the central authorities by setting up their own separate government. Such developments tempted a number of revolutionaries in Petrograd into thinking that the opportunity had come for them to bring down the Provisional Government. The attempt to do so became known as the 'July Days'.

The July Days

By the summer of 1917 it seemed that the government was no longer in control of events. The most ominous signs were:

- the spread of soviets
- worker control of the factories
- widespread seizure of land by the peasants
- internal government disputes.

 KEY FIGURE

General Kornilov (1870–1918)
Distinguished by his bravery as a soldier, he was a fierce patriot who hated Russia's revolutionaries.

 KEY TERM

Political subversives
Kornilov's term for the SDs and SRs in Russia.

National minorities

An especially pressing problem was that a number of Russia's ethnic peoples had exploited the Provisional Government's difficulties by setting up their own national minority governments and claiming independence of central control. The most notable example of a breakaway government was Ukraine. It was this that helped to provoke the July Days crisis. Ukraine in southern Russia contained the largest number of non-Russian people (23 million) in the empire. It was also the nation's largest food-producing region and, therefore, vital to the Russian state. When the Kadet ministers in the government learned in late June that a Provisional Government deputation had offered independence to Ukraine, they resigned, protesting that only an all-Russian constituent assembly could properly decide such matters.

This ministerial clash coincided with large-scale street demonstrations in Petrograd. Public protests were not uncommon; they had been almost a daily occurrence since February. But, in the atmosphere created by the news of the failure of the south-western offensive and the government's mounting problems, the demonstrations of early July turned into a direct challenge to the Provisional Government.

Failure of the uprising

The uprising itself was a confused, disorderly affair. In the course of the three days the demonstrators fell out among themselves; those members of the soviet who seemed reluctant to make a real bid for power were physically attacked. The disunity made it relatively easy for the Provisional Government to crush the rising. Troops loyal to the government were rushed from the front. They duly scattered the demonstrators and restored order.

It is not entirely clear who started the rising of 3–6 July. A month before, at the first **All-Russian Congress of Soviets**, Lenin had declared that the Bolshevik Party was ready to take power, but the delegates had regarded this as a general intention rather than a specific plan. There were also a number of SRs and other non-Bolshevik revolutionaries in the soviet who, for some time, had been demanding that the Petrograd soviet take over from the Provisional Government.

Trotsky later referred to the July Days as a 'semi-insurrection' and argued that it had been begun by the Mensheviks and SRs. In saying this, he was trying to absolve the Bolsheviks from the blame of having started a rising that failed. The explanation offered afterwards by the Bolsheviks was that they had come heroically to the aid of the workers of Petrograd and their comrades-in-arms, the sailors of Kronstadt, who had risen spontaneously against the government. The opposite point of view was put at the time by **Nikolei Chkheidze**, who argued that the Bolsheviks, having been behind the rising from the beginning, then tried to disclaim responsibility for its failure.

KEY TERM

All-Russian Congress of Soviets A gathering of representatives from all the soviets formed in Russia since February 1917.

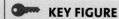

KEY FIGURE

Nikolei Chkheidze (1864–1926)

The Menshevik chairman of the Petrograd soviet.

SOURCE C

Anti-government protesters scattering under rifle-fire during the suppression of the July Days.

What evidence does Source C provide regarding the Provisional Government's response to the July Days?

The consequences of the July Days

While the origins of the July Days may have been uncertain, the results were not. The failed uprising revealed a number of important facts:

- The opposition movement was disunited.
- The Bolsheviks were still far from being the dominant revolutionary party.
- The Provisional Government still had sufficient strength to put down an armed insurrection.

This last revelation did much to raise the spirits of the Provisional Government and brought particular credit to Kerensky as war minister. Two days after the rising had been crushed, he became prime minister. He immediately put the Bolsheviks under pressure. *Pravda* was closed down and many of the Bolshevik leaders, including Trotsky and Kamenev, were arrested. Lenin fled to Finland. Kerensky also launched a propaganda campaign in which Lenin and his party were branded as traitors and agents in the pay of the German high command. A fortnight after the July Days, the Bolshevik Party appeared to have been broken as a political force in Russia. What enabled the Bolsheviks to survive, as the next two sections show, were the critical misjudgements by the Provisional Government over the land question and the Kornilov Affair.

SOURCE D

Photo of Lenin clean-shaven and bewigged, in hiding in Petrograd 1917. Throughout the period April–October 1917, Lenin went in constant fear of being arrested and executed by the Provisional Government. He adopted various disguises, kept continually on the move and frequently fled to Finland. Yet, oddly, as Kerensky later regretfully admitted, the authorities made little concerted effort to capture their chief opponent. This raises the interesting question of whether Lenin exaggerated, or the government underestimated, his powers of disruption.

? Why did Lenin regard it necessary to disguise himself as shown in Source D?

The land question

The Provisional Government had misread the public attitude towards the war. It similarly failed to appreciate the common view on the land question. Land shortage was a chronic problem in Russia. It had been a chief cause of peasant unrest since the emancipation of the serfs in 1861 (see page 46). The February Revolution had led the peasants to believe that they would soon benefit from a major land redistribution, which the government would introduce after taking over the landowners' estates. When the government made no such moves, the peasants in many parts of Russia took the law into their own hands and seized the property of local landlords. Disturbances in the countryside occurred daily throughout 1917 in what amounted to a national peasants' revolt.

The Provisional Government had no real answer to the land problem. While it was true that it had set up a Land Commission with the ultimate aim of redistributing land, this body made little progress in handling a massive task. It was doubtful, moreover, whether the government's heart was ever really in land reform. The majority of its members came from the landed and propertied classes. They were unlikely to be enthusiasts for a policy that would threaten their own interests. They had supported the February Revolution as a political change, not as a social upheaval. They were quite willing for the estates of the fallen monarchy to go to the peasants, but they had no intention of losing their own possessions in a state land grab. This had been the strength of Lenin's assertion in the *April Theses* that tsardom had been replaced not by a revolutionary but by a bourgeois regime.

The Bolshevik position on the land question

Interestingly, the land issue was equally difficult for the Bolsheviks. They simply did not have a land policy. As a Marxist party, they had dismissed the peasantry as, in Trotsky's words, 'the pack horse' of history, lacking true revolutionary initiative. By definition, the proletarian revolution was an affair of the industrial working class. Lenin, on his return in April, had declared that it would be pointless for the Bolsheviks, the party of the workers, to make an alliance with the backward peasantry. However, faced with the fact of peasant land-seizures throughout Russia, Lenin was quite prepared to make a tactical adjustment. Appreciating that it was impossible to ignore the disruptive behaviour of four-fifths of the Russian population, he asserted that the special circumstances of post-tsarist Russia had produced a situation in which the peasants were acting as a truly revolutionary force. This adaptation of Marxist theory thus allowed Lenin to add the Russian peasants to the proletarian cause.

Lacking a land policy of his own, Lenin simply stole one from the SRs. 'Land to the Peasants', a slogan lifted straight from the SR programme, became the new Bolshevik catchphrase. What this meant in mid-1917 was that the Bolsheviks recognised the peasant land-seizures as perfectly legitimate. This produced a considerable swing to the Bolsheviks in the countryside. It had the further effect of splitting the SRs, a significant number of whom began to align themselves with the Bolsheviks. Known as **Left SRs**, they sided with the Bolshevik Party on all major issues.

The Kornilov Affair

In August, Kerensky's government became involved in the Kornilov Affair, a crisis that undermined the gains it had made from its handling of the July Days, and allowed the Bolsheviks to recover from their humiliation. Parts of the story have been obscured by the conflicting descriptions later given by some of the participants, but there was little doubt as to the intentions of the chief figure in the episode, General Kornilov, the new commander-in-chief.

Kornilov was the type of army officer who had never accepted the February Revolution. He believed that before Russia could fulfil its national duty of defeating Germany, it must first destroy the socialist enemies within. 'It's time', he said, 'to hang the German supporters and spies, with Lenin at their head, and to disperse the soviet.' By late August, the advance of German forces deeper into Russia began to threaten Petrograd itself. Large numbers of refugees and deserters flocked into the city, heightening the tension there and increasing the disorder. Kornilov declared that Russia and the government

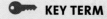 **KEY TERM**

Left SRs Social revolutionaries who sided with the Bolsheviks in their recognition of the legitimacy of the peasant land-seizures and in their demand that Russia withdraw from the war.

stood in grave danger of a socialist-inspired insurrection. He informed Kerensky that he intended to bring his loyal troops to Petrograd to save the Provisional Government from being overthrown.

Accounts tend to diverge at this point in their description of Kerensky's response. Those who believe that he was involved in a plot with Kornilov to destroy the soviet and set up a dictatorship argue that Kerensky had at first fully supported this move. It was only afterwards, when he realised that Kornilov also intended to remove the Provisional Government and impose military rule, that he turned against him.

Other commentators, sympathetic to Kerensky, maintain that he had not plotted with Kornilov and that his actions had been wholly consistent. They also emphasise that a special Commission of Enquiry into the affair in 1917 cleared Kerensky of any complicity. But, however the question of collusion is decided, it was certainly the case that Kerensky publicly condemned Kornilov's advance. He ordered him to surrender his post and placed Petrograd under martial law. Kornilov reacted by sending an open telegram.

SOURCE E

Extract from Kornilov's appeal, 26 August 1917, quoted in Richard Pipes, *The Russian Revolution*, Collins Harvill, 1990, p. 460.

People of Russia! Our great motherland is dying. The moment of death is near. I, General Kornilov, declare that the Provisional Government, under pressure from the Bolshevik majority in the Soviet, acts in full accord with the plans of the German General Staff, and concurrently with the imminent landings of the enemy forces on the coast of Riga, destroys the army and convulses the country from within.

I, General Kornilov, declare to each and all that I personally desire nothing but to save Great Russia. I swear to lead the people through victory over the enemy to the Constituent Assembly, where it will decide its own destiny and choose its new political system.

> ? According to Kornilov in Source E, what role are the Bolsheviks currently playing in Russia?

Kerensky's response

Fearful that Kornilov would attack, Kerensky called on all loyal citizens to take up arms to defend the city. The Bolsheviks were released from prison or came out of hiding to collect the weapons issued by the Provisional Government to all who were willing to fight. By this strange twist in the story of 1917, the Bolsheviks found themselves being given arms by the very government they were pledged to overthrow.

In the event, the weapons were not needed against Kornilov. The railway workers refused to operate the trains to bring Kornilov's army to Petrograd. When he learned of this and of a mass workers' militia formed to oppose him, Kornilov abandoned the advance and allowed himself to be arrested. He was to die early in April 1918, killed by a stray shell at the start of the Russian civil war (see page 141).

Bolshevik gains

It was the Bolsheviks who benefited most from the failure of the attempted coup. They had been able to present themselves as defenders of Petrograd and the revolution, thereby diverting attention away from their failure in the July Days. What further boosted the Bolsheviks was that, despite the obvious readiness of the people of Petrograd to defend their city, this could not be read as a sign of their belief in the Provisional Government. Indeed, the episode had damaged the Provisional Government by revealing its political weakness and showing how vulnerable it was to military threat. Kerensky later admitted that the Kornilov Affair had been 'the prelude to the October Revolution'.

Summary diagram: The Provisional Government and its problems	
The war Government obliged to continue the war in order to maintain loans from the Allies Caused first serious split between Soviet and Provisional Government Prevented resources being spent on other needs Kerensky emerged as committed supporter of the war	**National minorities question** Caused ministerial crisis which led to the July Days, which saw the near extinction of Bolsheviks
The land question Provisional Government not genuinely committed to land reform Enabled Bolsheviks to steal a march and gain peasant support	**The Kornilov Affair** Provisional Government survived but gravely weakened Bolsheviks began recovery The prelude to the October Revolution

4 The October Revolution

▶ *What factors put the Bolsheviks in a position to bid for power by October 1917?*

The political shift in Petrograd

The measure of the Bolsheviks' recovery from the July Days and of their gains from the Kornilov Affair was soon apparent. By the middle of September they had gained a majority in both the Petrograd and Moscow soviets. However, this should be seen not as indicating a large swing of opinion in their favour, but rather as a reflection of the changing character of the soviets.

In the first few months after the February Revolution the meetings of the soviets had been fully attended. Over 3000 deputies had packed into the Petrograd soviet at the Tauride Palace. But as the months passed enthusiasm waned. By the autumn of 1917 attendance was often down to a few hundred. This was a major advantage to the Bolsheviks. Their political dedication meant that they continued to turn up in force while the members of the other parties attended only occasionally. The result was that the Bolshevik Party exerted an influence out of proportion to its numbers. This was especially the case in regard to the composition of the various soviet subcommittees.

Broadly what happened in Petrograd following the Kornilov Affair was that the Petrograd soviet moved to the left while the Provisional Government shifted to the right. This made some form of clash between the two bodies increasingly likely. Lenin put it as a matter of stark choice: 'Either a soviet government or Kornilovism. There is no middle course.'

Lenin's strategy

From his exile in Finland, Lenin constantly appealed to his party to prepare for the immediate overthrow of Kerensky's government. He claimed that his earlier prediction had proved wholly correct: the Provisional Government, incapable of solving the war and land questions, was becoming increasingly reactionary. This left the soviet as the only hope of true revolutionaries. He further argued that the Bolsheviks could not wait; they must seize the moment while the government was at its most vulnerable. In a sentence that was to become part of Bolshevik legend, Lenin wrote on 12 September: 'History will not forgive us if we do not assume power.'

Lenin's sense of urgency arose from his concern over two events that were due to take place in the autumn, and which he calculated would seriously limit the Bolsheviks' freedom of action:

- the meeting of the All-Russian Congress of Soviets in late October
- the elections for the Constituent Assembly in November.

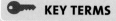 **KEY TERMS**

Fait accompli An established situation that cannot be changed.

Progressives Those who believed in parliamentary government for Russia.

Lenin was convinced that the Bolsheviks would have to take power before these events occurred. If, under the banner 'All Power to the Soviets', the Bolsheviks could topple the Provisional Government before the Congress of Soviets met, they could then present their new authority as a ***fait accompli*** which the Congress would have no reason to reject.

The elections to the Constituent Assembly presented a different problem. The assembly was the body on which all **progressives** and reformers had set their hopes. Once it came into being, its moral authority would be difficult to challenge. Lenin told his party that, since it was impossible to forecast how successfully the Bolsheviks would perform in the elections, they would have to be in power before the results were announced. This would provide them with the authority to undermine the results should they go against them.

The 'pre-parliament'

At the same time as Lenin pressed this policy on his party, Kerensky tried to make his government less exposed by announcing plans for the creation of a 'pre-parliament'. This was to be a body with authority to advise the government. Drawn from a variety of parties and thus representative of a range of political opinion, it was intended to fill the interim before the Constituent Assembly came into being. Lenin immediately condemned the pre-parliament as a manoeuvre not to broaden the government's base but to strengthen its grip on power. Acting on his orders, the Bolshevik members of the soviet who were entitled to attend the pre-parliament first derided it loudly and then walked out.

Lenin urges a rising

Emboldened by the Bolshevik's success in undermining the pre-parliament, Lenin began urging his party to prepare to overthrow the Provisional Government. Despite the passionate conviction with which Lenin put his arguments to his colleagues, there were Bolsheviks on the Central Committee of the party who doubted the wisdom of striking against the Provisional Government at this point.

In an effort to enforce his will, Lenin slipped back into Petrograd on 7 October. His personal presence stiffened Bolshevik resolve, but did not produce total unity. During the next two weeks he spent exhausting hours at a series of Central Committee meetings trying to convince the waverers. On 10 October, the Central Committee pledged itself to an armed insurrection, but failed to agree on a specific date. In the end, by another quirk of fate, it was Kerensky and the government, not the Bolsheviks, who initiated the actual rising.

Kerensky makes the first move

Rumours of an imminent Bolshevik coup had been circulating in Petrograd for some weeks, but it was not until an article, written by two members of the Bolshevik Central Committee, appeared in a journal that the authorities felt they had sure proof. The writers of the article, **Grigor Zinoviev** and Lev Kamenev, argued that it would be a mistake to attempt to overthrow the government in the current circumstances.

Kerensky interpreted this as indicating that a date had already been set. Rather than wait to be caught off guard, he ordered a pre-emptive attack on the Bolsheviks. On 23 October, the Bolshevik newspapers, *Pravda* and *Izvestiya*, were closed down by government troops and an attempted round-up of the leading Bolsheviks began. The Bolsheviks no longer had a choice; Lenin ordered the planned insurrection to begin.

 KEY FIGURE

Grigor Zinoviev (1883–1936)

A close colleague of Lenin since the formation of the Bolshevik Party in 1903.

> ## Key steps in the Bolshevik revolution 1917
> - September 25: Bolsheviks gained a majority in the Petrograd soviet.
> - October 12: Petrograd soviet set up the Military Revolutionary Committee (MRC).
> - October 23: Kerensky moved to close down *Pravda* and *Izvestiya*. Lenin instructed the Bolsheviks to begin the rising against Kerensky's government.
> - October 24: first session of the Congress of Soviets.
> - October 24–25: Bolsheviks took control of Petrograd.
> - October 25–26: Kerensky fled from Petrograd after failing to raise troops. Bolsheviks seized the Winter Palace.
> - October 26: Bolsheviks established *Sovnarkom*.
> - October 27: Lenin claimed power in the name of Congress of Soviets.

Trotsky's role

That the Bolsheviks had a plan at all was the work not of Lenin but of Trotsky. While it was Lenin who was undoubtedly the great influence behind the October rising, it was Trotsky who actually organised it. The key to Trotsky's success in this was his chairmanship of the Petrograd soviet, to which he had been elected in September. On 9 October the soviet set up the Military Revolutionary Committee (MRC) to organise the defence of Petrograd against a possible German attack or another Kornilov-type assault from within Russia. It proved a critical decision. Realising that, if the Bolsheviks could control the MRC, they would control Petrograd, Trotsky used his influence to have himself accepted as one of the **troika** appointed to run the MRC. This meant that he had at his disposal the only effective military force in Petrograd. Moreover, it was a legitimate force since theoretically it acted on the authority of the soviet. Trotsky was now in a position to draft the plans for the overthrow of the Provisional Government. When Lenin gave the order for the uprising to begin, it was Trotsky who directed the **Red Guards** in their seizure of the key vantage points in Petrograd, such as the bridges and the telegraph offices.

Collapse of the Provisional Government

In the three days (25–27 October) that it took for the city to fall under Bolshevik control there was remarkably little fighting. There were only six deaths during the whole episode and these were all Red Guards, most probably accidentally shot by their own side. The simple fact was that the Provisional Government had hardly any military forces on which to call. The Petrograd garrison that had turned out to defend the government on previous occasions did not come to its aid now. The truth was that desertions had reduced the garrison to a few loyal officer-cadets, a small group of **Cossacks** and a unit known as the **Amazons**.

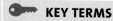

KEY TERMS

Troika A three-person team.

Red Guards Despite the Bolshevik legend that these were the crack forces of the revolution, the Red Guards, some 10,000 in number, were largely made up of elderly men recruited from the workers in the factories.

Cossacks The remnants of the élite cavalry regiment of the tsars.

Amazons A special corps of female soldiers recruited by Kerensky to show the patriotism of Russia's women in the anti-German struggle.

When the Red Guards approached the Winter Palace, which housed the Provisional Government, they expected stiff resistance, but there was none. A black-and-white film of the dramatic, death-defying storming of the palace gates often appears in television documentaries about the October Revolution. This is very misleading since there was no such event. What modern programme makers invariably use are the powerful images from the feature film *October*, made in 1927 on the tenth anniversary by the celebrated Bolshevik film director Sergei Eisenstein.

The Bolshevik forces did not need to storm the gates; there was nobody defending them. The Winter Palace was a vast building many times larger than London's Buckingham Palace. The Red Guards simply entered through the back doors. This was enough to make the defenders give up. The Cossacks declined to fight and made off when confronted by the Red Guards. After that, it did not take much pressure to persuade the cadets and the Amazons that it was better for them to lay down their arms and go home rather than die in a futile struggle.

The sounding of its guns in a prearranged signal by the pro-soviet crew of the cruiser *Aurora*, moored in the River Neva, convinced the remaining members of the government that their position was hopeless. As many as were able escaped unnoticed out of the building. Kerensky, having earlier left the city in a

SOURCE F

A contingent of Amazons under instruction in 1917. Kerensky had specially recruited these female soldiers, also known as 'the Women's Battalion of Death', as an example of the fighting spirit of the Russian people.

Look at Source F. From where would the Amazons in this photo likely to have been recruited?

?

vain effort to raise loyal troops, fled to the US embassy. He later slipped out of Petrograd, disguised as a female nurse, and made his way to the USA, where he eventually became a professor of history.

The Bolsheviks take power

The Bolsheviks did not seize power; it fell into their hands. The speed and ease with which it had happened surprised even Lenin. In the early hours of 27 October, he said to Trotsky, 'from being on the run to supreme power makes one dizzy'. He then rolled himself up in a large fur coat, lay down on the floor, and went to sleep.

On the following evening, the All-Russian Congress of Soviets began their first session. They had barely completed the opening formalities when the chairman, who happened to be Lev Kamenev, the Bolshevik who had originally opposed the rising, informed the delegates that they were now the supreme authority in Russia; the Petrograd soviet had seized power in their name and had formed a new government. Kamenev then read out to the bewildered delegates the list of fourteen names of the new government they had supposedly just appointed. The fourteen were all Bolsheviks or left SRs. At the head of the list of **Commissars** who made up the new *Sovnarkom* was the name of the chief minister – Vladimir Ilyich Lenin.

The SRs and the Mensheviks walked out, protesting that it was not a taking of power by the soviets but a Bolshevik coup. Trotsky jeered after them that they and their kind had 'consigned themselves to the garbage heap of history'. Lenin then announced to the Bolshevik and the Left SR delegates who had remained that they would now proceed 'to construct the towering edifice of socialist society'.

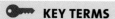

KEY TERMS

Commissars Russian for ministers; Lenin chose the word because he said 'it reeked of blood'.

Sovnarkom Russian for government or cabinet.

Summary diagram: The October Revolution

Political left	Political centre	Political right
• Petrograd soviet • By October moved to the left and dominated by Trotsky	• Dual Authority	• Provisional Government • By October moved to the right and deserted by socialists • Kerensky left without allies

The building blocks of revolution

• Soviet Order No. 1 • Peace, Bread and Land • July Days	• Lenin's return • Failure of Summer Offensive • Kornilov Affair	• *April Theses* • 'All Power to the Soviets' • Trotsky and the MRC

Reasons for Bolshevik success

▶ *Why was there so little resistance to the Bolshevik coup in October 1917?*

Trotsky later said that there were two principal factors that explained the Bolshevik success in October 1917:

- the failure of the Petrograd garrison to resist
- the existence of the Military Revolutionary Committee (MRC).

Trotsky claimed that the soviet decision to create the MRC had sounded the death-knell for the Provisional Government. The Bolsheviks' control of the MRC gave them 'three-quarters if not nine-tenths' of their victory in the October Revolution. Since Trotsky was a major player in the drama played out in October 1917, his views demand respect. But his analysis was largely concerned with the immediate events of October. The success of the coup had as much to do with government weakness as Bolshevik strength, a weakness that was in-built into the Provisional Government from the start.

Provisional Government weaknesses

The collapse of tsardom had left a power vacuum. Although the Provisional Government held office between February and October 1917, it never held power. It lacked the ruthlessness which the desperate situation demanded. Furthermore, from the first, its authority was weakened by the existence of the Petrograd soviet. Unable to fight the war successfully and unwilling to introduce the reforms that might have given it popular support, the Provisional Government tottered towards collapse. When it was challenged in October 1917 by the Bolsheviks, who themselves had been on the point of political extinction in July, it was friendless. It gave in with scarcely a show of resistance.

The failure of the Provisional Government to rally effective military support in its hour of need followed from its political failure over the previous eight months. It was not that the Provisional Government was bitterly rejected by the Russian people. It was more a matter of its inability to arouse genuine enthusiasm. Kerensky's government had come nowhere near to solving Russia's problems. Its support had evaporated. Economically incompetent and militarily incapable, the Provisional Government was not considered worth struggling to save. In October 1917, the Bolsheviks were pushing against an already open door.

An important consideration is that the Provisional Government had never been meant to last. As its very title suggested, it was intended to be an interim government. Along with its partner in the Dual Authority, the Petrograd soviet, its role was to provide a caretaker administration until an All-Russian Constituent Assembly was formed after the autumn election. The assembly was the ultimate dream of all liberals and democrats; it would be the first fully elected, nationwide, democratic parliament in Russia. All parties, including the Bolsheviks, were committed to it.

As a consequence, the Provisional Government was always open to the charge that as an unelected, self-appointed body it had no right to exercise the authority that properly belonged to the Constituent Assembly alone. Such limited strength as the Provisional Government had came from its claim to be the representative of the February Revolution. Lenin had made it his task to undermine that claim.

The weakness of the non-Bolshevik parties

An obvious question is why none of the other parties was able to mount a serious challenge to the Bolsheviks for the leadership of the revolution between February and October. One answer is that they had all accepted February as a genuine revolution. Consequently, it made sense for them to co-operate with the Provisional Government, which claimed to represent the progressive forces in Russia. The result was that the supposedly revolutionary parties, such as the SRs, were prepared to enter into coalition with the Kadets, the dominant party in the government, and await the convening of the Constituent Assembly. This gave the Bolsheviks a powerful propaganda weapon, which Lenin exploited. He charged the socialists with having sold out to the bourgeoisie.

Another explanation is that the other parties were weakened by their support for the war. None of them opposed the continuation of the struggle against Germany with the consistency that Lenin's Bolsheviks did after April 1917. The non-Bolshevik parties regarded it as Russia's duty to defeat the enemy. The SRs, the Mensheviks and, indeed, some individual Bolsheviks believed wholeheartedly in a revolutionary war against bourgeois Germany. On the left of the Menshevik Party there was a vociferous wing of international revolutionaries who saw the war as the ideal opportunity for beginning the worldwide class struggle.

The Menshevik position

As committed Marxists, the Mensheviks had good reason for co-operating with the Provisional Government rather than opposing it. They saw the February Revolution as marking a critical stage in the class war, when the bourgeoisie had overthrown the old feudal forces represented by the tsar. This stage of the dialectic, as Marx had argued, was the necessary prelude to the revolution of the proletariat. However, the Mensheviks judged that since Russia did not yet possess a proletariat large enough to be a truly revolutionary force, it was their immediate task to align themselves with the other parties and work for the consolidation of the bourgeois revolution. When this had been achieved the Mensheviks could then turn to the ultimate objective of a proletarian rising. One of the interesting paradoxes of the Russian Revolution is that, in strictly theoretical terms, the Mensheviks were always better, that is to say more consistent, Marxists than were Lenin and his Bolsheviks.

Bolshevik ruthlessness

A key factor was that none of the contending parties was as determined as the Bolsheviks to exploit the crises facing Russia in 1917. **Tsereteli**, a prominent Menshevik, admitted: 'Everything we did at that time was a vain effort to hold back a destructive elemental flood with a handful of insignificant chips.' Struve, a liberal émigré, observed: 'Only Bolshevism was logical about revolution and true to its essence, and therefore in the revolution it conquered.' Milyukov, the Kadet leader, shared Struve's view of the Bolsheviks: 'They knew where they were going, and they went in the direction which they had chosen once and for all toward a goal which came nearer with every new, unsuccessful, experiment of compromise.'

Lenin's Bolsheviks were a new breed of politician: utterly self-confident, scornful of all other parties and ideas. This drive and utter conviction came from the belief that they were an unstoppable force of history. As Trotsky put it: 'The party in the last analysis is always right, because the party is the only historical instrument given to the proletariat to resolve its fundamental tasks.' The ruthlessness of the Bolsheviks did not guarantee their success, but it did mean that no other party could hope to gain or hold power unless it was able to overcome the challenge of these dedicated revolutionaries. In the event, none of the other parties was ever in a position to do this.

The role of mutual misunderstanding

An irony of the pre-October situation was that both the Provisional Government and the Bolsheviks overestimated each other's power, each delaying their moves against the other for fear of overplaying their hand. Historians have often wondered why the Provisional Government did not make a more sustained effort to destroy the Bolsheviks politically. It is true that some arrests were made, but the government's efforts at suppression were half-hearted.

One reason for this, odd though it seems in retrospect, is that Kerensky's government was more frightened of an attack from the right than from the left. Fear of a tsarist reaction against the revolution preoccupied the thoughts of many in the government. For much of 1917, Kornilov was regarded as a bigger threat than Lenin. This was not entirely unrealistic. The Bolsheviks were not militarily strong. Sukhanov, a Menshevik eyewitness of the events of 1917, calculated that so limited was Bolshevik strength at the time of the October rising that 'a good detachment of 500 men would have been enough to liquidate **Smolny** and everybody in it'. Trotsky agreed, but asked mockingly where the Provisional Government would find 500 good men to fight for it.

For their part, the Bolsheviks similarly miscalculated the strength and determination of the Provisional Government. Lenin expected to be summarily shot if ever the government's agents found him. This was why he was either

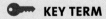

KEY FIGURE

Iraklii Tseretelli (1882–1959)

A Georgian revolutionary and a leading member of the Petrograd soviet before its domination by the Bolsheviks.

KEY TERM

Smolny The Bolshevik headquarters in Petrograd, housed in what had been a young ladies' finishing school.

incognito or absent altogether from Petrograd for long periods during the critical months between the two revolutions of 1917.

Lenin's importance

It says much for Lenin's forcefulness as leader that despite his frequent absences from Petrograd between February and October he continued to dominate the actions of the Bolshevik Party. Trotsky later made an interesting assessment of the part played by Lenin in the October Revolution: 'Had I not been present in 1917 in Petersburg, the October Revolution would still have taken place – on the condition that Lenin was present and in command. If neither Lenin nor I had been present in Petersburg, there would have been no October Revolution.' However, most historians are now careful not to overstate Lenin's power to dictate events in 1917. In the standard Bolshevik version of what happened, Lenin was portrayed as having fulfilled his plans for revolution along the lines he had laid down in such writings as his 1902 pamphlet, *What Is To Be Done?* This had visualised the development of a tightly knit, disciplined Bolshevik Party that would seize power in the name of the masses at the opportune moment (see page 26). Yet, the structure and authority of his party in 1917 were markedly different from Lenin's 1902 model. The evidence of the many disputes within the Bolshevik ranks over policy between February and October 1917 and well into 1918 suggests that they were by no means as disciplined or centrally controlled as the party later claimed them to have been.

Part of the reason for this was that the composition of the party had changed in ways that Lenin and the Central Committee had not planned. After the February Revolution there had been a large increase in membership, which the Central Committee had not wanted but which, in the heady but politically confused situation following the fall of tsardom, they seemed unable to prevent. The figures indicate the remarkable transformation that the Bolshevik Party underwent in 1917 (see Table 5.1).

Table 5.1 Membership of the Bolshevik Party in 1917

February	24,000
April	100,000
October	340,000 (60,000 in Petrograd)

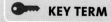

KEY TERM

Radicalisation A movement towards more sweeping or revolutionary ideas.

Modern commentators view this influx of party members as an aspect of the general **radicalisation** of Russian politics that occurred as the Provisional Government got into increasing difficulties. What had helped to prepare the ground for the successful Bolshevik coup in October was the growth in the Petrograd factories of workers' committees that, while not necessarily pro-Bolshevik, were certainly not pro-government. One result of the anti-government agitation of these committees was that, when the open challenge to the Provisional Government came in October, Kerensky's desperate appeal for support from the people of Petrograd went unheeded.

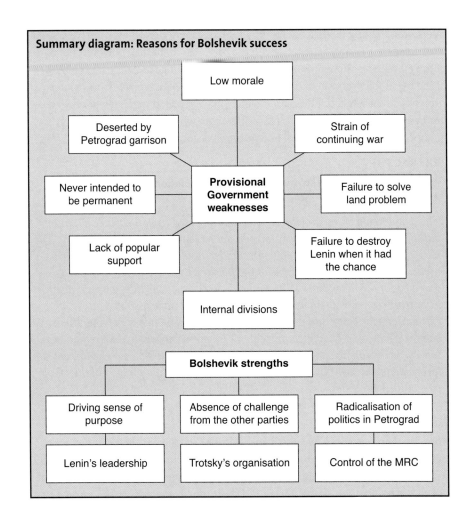

Summary diagram: Reasons for Bolshevik success

Low morale

Deserted by Petrograd garrison

Strain of continuing war

Never intended to be permanent

Provisional Government weaknesses

Failure to solve land problem

Lack of popular support

Failure to destroy Lenin when it had the chance

Internal divisions

Bolshevik strengths

Driving sense of purpose

Absence of challenge from the other parties

Radicalisation of politics in Petrograd

Lenin's leadership

Trotsky's organisation

Control of the MRC

⑥ Key debate

▶ *What was the true character of the October Revolution?*

Since 1917, there has been continuous debate and disagreement over the October Revolution. The official version maintained by the Soviet Communist Party was that Lenin, backed by the Russian people, had led his Bolshevik Party to power and had then gone on to create a workers' state. Critics, however, have challenged this interpretation as an oversimplification and a distortion. The following indicates some of the major contributions to the debate.

The received Soviet view

Although he was later disgraced in Stalin's time, Leon Trotsky provided the historical analysis that became the official interpretation of events. According to this, Lenin, having developed a tightly knit, disciplined Bolshevik Party, steered it to victory in October when it seized the opportunity to take power in the name of the masses. Lenin had thus led the party in fulfilling the Marxist prophecy of the inevitable triumph of the proletariat over the bourgeoisie. Trotsky later contended that while the Russian Revolution was indeed inevitable it needed Lenin's particular dynamism to make it happen when it did. Lenin was a great historical force; he was the vital link in the dialectical chain.

EXTRACT 1

From Leon Trotsky, *The History of the Russian Revolution*, Pluto Press, 1977, pp. 343–4.

The dictatorship of the proletariat was to be inferred from the whole situation, but it had still to be established. It could not be established without a party. The party could fulfil its mission only after understanding it. For that Lenin was needed. Until his arrival, not one of the Bolshevik leaders dared to make a diagnosis of the revolution. Without Lenin the crisis, which the opportunistic leadership was inevitably bound to produce, would have assumed an extraordinarily sharp and protracted character … The role of personality arises before us here on a truly gigantic scale. It is necessary only to understand that role correctly, taking personality as a link in the historic chain … Lenin was not an accidental element in the historical development, but a product of the whole past of Russian history.

A number of Western sympathisers accepted the Soviet line in its essentials. Prominent among these was the British Marxist scholar Eric Hobsbawm, who in the 1990s described Lenin's essential achievement in 1917 as having been to convince 'the hesitant elements in his party that power would escape them … if not seized by planned action during the short time it was within their grasp'.

Opposition to the received view

Other historians, mainly those on the right, challenged the notion that Lenin led a popular movement to success in October. Richard Pipes argued that Lenin headed a minority-party coup in October that violently wrenched the revolution away from its popular roots.

EXTRACT 2

From Richard Pipes, *Three Whys of Revolution*, Pimlico, 1998, pp. 60–1.

[W]hat occurred in October 1917 was a classical coup d'état *accomplished without mass support. It was a surreptitious seizure of the nerve centre of the modern state, carried out under false slogans in order to neutralize the population at large, the true purpose of which was revealed only after the new claimants were firmly in the saddle.*

The population at large offered little resistance at a time when resistance would have made all the difference because it believed that the new regime could not last. The so-called Soviet government was seen as made up of crazy utopians who would be swept from the scene as suddenly as they had appeared. When Bolshevik policies began to affect adversely the interests of workers and peasants they rebelled

While Pipes differs in points of detail and emphasis from Robert Service, the major authority on Lenin, what the two historians share is a **non-determinist approach**. They concur in suggesting that in 1917 Russia nothing was preordained, nothing absolutely had to happen the way it did. Politics was crucial. Things occurred the way they did because of the decisions made by the participants. Lenin was pivotal. Service stresses that at the time of the actual October takeover Lenin acted essentially practically, giving little attention to ideology or theory.

KEY TERM

Non-determinist approach Rejection of the idea that history follows a fixed, inevitable course.

EXTRACT 3

From Robert Service, *Lenin*, Macmillan, 2000, p. 315.

Not once did Lenin mention Marxism in his various speeches of 25–27 October. He referred to 'socialism' only very fleetingly. Nor did he explain that his immediate objective was the establishment of a class-based dictatorship and that ultimately he aimed at the realisation of a communist, classless society. He was keeping his political cards close to his chest. He was a party boss and wanted Bolshevism to be attractive to those workers, soldiers, peasants and intellectuals who had not yet supported it. And so terms such as dictatorship, terror, civil war and revolutionary war were again quietly shelved … His emphasis was skewed more sharply in favour of a revolution from below … His wish was for the Bolsheviks to appear as a party that would facilitate the making of Revolution by and for the people.

The 'unfinished' revolution

This theory is associated particularly with the later followers of Trotsky. It argues that a genuine workers' revolution had indeed occurred in 1917, but it had then been betrayed by Lenin's successors. According to this school of thought, which was powerfully represented in the West by such writers as Isaac Deutscher and Adam Ulam, the initial revolutionary achievement of the workers was perverted by the deadening rule of Stalin. That was why Lenin's October Revolution was 'unfinished'.

The 'optimist' view

An extension of the 'unfinished' theory is the 'optimistic' notion advanced by Russian émigré historians, such as George Katkov. The optimism lay in their claim that Imperial Russia had been successfully transforming itself into a modern, democratic, industrial society, until it was weakened by the First World War. However, at that point, Lenin's Bolsheviks, who were in the pay of the German government, had unscrupulously exploited the nation's difficulties to seize power in an illegal coup which diverted Russia from the path of progress.

The 'pessimist' view

In the 1960s, Leopold Haimson, a US scholar, had a major impact on studies of the revolution. He suggested that, far from moving towards modernisation, Imperial Russia by 1914 was heading towards revolutionary turmoil, even before war came. Hence the term 'pessimist'. He argued that Russia was suffering an 'institutional crisis'; an unbridgeable gap had developed between the reactionary tsarist establishment and the progressive professional classes and urban workers So great was the divide that violent revolution was the unavoidable outcome. Lenin and the Bolsheviks exploited the crisis, but they did not create the revolution; it was created for them.

Revisionism

Certain modern commentators, often termed revisionists, veered back towards the notion that the 1917 October Revolution may have indeed been at base a popular movement. The grounds for this argument were that in 1917 a radicalisation of Russian politics had occurred as a result of the mistakes made by the Provisional Government. Angry soldiers and frustrated workers began to agitate against Kerensky's government, which became friendless. In October 1917, the Bolsheviks did not seize power; they simply picked it up.

1917 as a cultural revolution

An interesting line of interpretation has developed among revisionist historians, involving less concentration on individuals and a greater emphasis on the broad social shifts occurring in late Imperial Russia. The claim is not that Lenin and the Bolsheviks were unimportant but that they were representatives rather than initiators of the revolutionary movement associated with them. In simplified form the argument is that late tsarist society was undergoing a profound cultural revolution, brought about by modernisation. Although Russian conservatives tried to resist change, change was occurring nonetheless; industrialisation and contact with Western countries fundamentally altered the character of society to the point where it fractured.

So, although Lenin and the Bolsheviks were a minority, fringe party working to take power, their real significance was that, without knowing it, they represented a deeper driving force for change within society. This view is expressed by US historian Robert C. Williams.

EXTRACT 4

From Robert C. Williams, 'The Bolsheviks' in Anna Geifman, editor, *Russia and the Last Tsar: Opposition and Subversion 1894–1917*, Blackwell, 1999, p. 49.

Over the course of the twentieth century Bolshevism has ceased to mean the Marxist ideology of one individual, Lenin, and has come to mean the cultural transformation of an entire society. Bolshevism before 1917 appears in retrospect more internally divided and disputatious, more popular and less conspiratorial, linked more with society and less with ideology, than imagined.

Of all the political parties of imperial Russia, Bolshevism may have seemed the most unlikely to seize power in 1917. Yet a deeper and more extensive knowledge of Russian society and culture has made it possible for historians to discover roots of social support and cultural resonance in a movement previously associated with raw power political power. We now know that Bolshevism was more supported from below by workers and peasants, and more embedded in the deep structure of Russian culture than we thought.

> How far do the historians quoted in Extracts 1–4 differ or agree in their interpretation of the Russian Revolution?

The view of the 'cultural revolutionists' has not won universal acceptance among historians, although it has added another dimension to the ongoing debate about one of modern history's most controversial issues.

Chapter summary

The February Revolution was followed by the establishment of a Dual Authority, which saw initial co-operation between the Provisional Government and the Petrograd soviet. This harmony had broken down by the summer months and, prompted by Lenin, who had returned in April to demand the end of the Bolsheviks' co-operation with the other parties, his party began to consider rising against the government. An attempt to do so in July proved premature and brought the Bolsheviks to the verge of destruction. They were saved only by the government's mishandling of the Kornilov Affair, which enabled them to act as defenders of Petrograd against tsarist reaction.

Unable to deal with the major problems facing Russia – disastrous war losses, food shortages and a rebellious peasantry – Kerensky's government by the autumn had forfeited popular support. To avoid arrest, Lenin was only intermittently in Petrograd but, such was his influence from afar, that by late October he had persuaded his followers to strike against the government. Trotsky, in the name of the soviet, whose chairman and military chief he had become, organised the October Revolution which overthrew a barely resistant government.

Refresher questions

Use these questions to remind yourself of the key material covered in this chapter.

1 Why was there so little initial political conflict between the Provisional Government and the Petrograd soviet?

2 What did Stalin and Kamenev think Bolshevik policy should be after the February Revolution?

3 What was the essential argument in Lenin's *April Theses*?

4 How were the Bolsheviks able to survive their failure in the July Days?

5 How real a threat was the Kornilov Affair to the Provisional Government?

6 Why was land such a contentious issue in revolutionary Russia?

7 Why did the Provisional Government continue the war against Germany?

8 Why was it the Bolsheviks, and not any of the other parties, who took power in October 1917?

9 In what ways did the Bolsheviks and the Provisional Government overestimate each other's strength?

10 What roles did Lenin and Trotsky play in the October rising?

 Question practice

ESSAY QUESTIONS

1 How accurate is it to say that the return of Lenin to Petrograd in April 1917 fundamentally changed the political situation in Petrograd?

2 To what extent did the character and composition of the Petrograd soviet change between February and October 1917?

3 How far were the problems faced by the Provisional Government in 1917 a consequence of the continuing war with Germany?

4 'The weakness of the Provisional Government, not the strength of the revolutionaries, explains why the Bolsheviks were able to take power in October 1917.' How far do you agree with this statement?

SOURCE QUESTIONS

1 How far could the historian make use of Sources 1 and 2 together to investigate the disputes within the Bolshevik party regarding an insurrection against the Provisional Government? Explain your answer, using both sources, the information given about them and your own knowledge of the historical context.

2 Why is Source 1 valuable to the historian for an enquiry into Lenin's attitude towards a rising against the Provisional Government in 1917? Explain your answer using the source, the information given about it and your own knowledge of the historical context.

3 How much weight do you give the evidence of Sources 1 and 2 for an enquiry into the disagreements among the Bolsheviks over the timing of a rising against the Provisional Government in 1917? Explain your answer using both sources, the information given about them and your own knowledge of the historical context.

SOURCE 1

Lenin's letter to the Central Petrograd Committee and to Bolshevik members of the Petrograd soviet, 1 October 1917. Here, anxious that events might overtake the Bolsheviks, Lenin urges an immediate rising. Quoted in V.I. Lenin, *Selected Works*, Progress Publishers, 1971, p. 361.

Without losing a single moment [we must] organise a headquarters of the insurgent detachments, distribute our forces, move the reliable regiments to the most important points, surround the Alexandrinsky Theatre, occupy the Peter and Paul fortress, arrest the General Staff and the government, and move against the officer cadets – those detachments which would rather die than allow the enemy to approach the strategic points of the city. We must mobilise the armed workers and call them to fight the last desperate fight, occupy the telegraph and the telephone exchange and connect it by telephone with all the factories, all the regiments, all the points of armed fighting, etc.

Of course, this is all by way of example, only to illustrate the fact that at the present moment it is impossible to remain loyal to Marxism, to remain loyal to the revolution unless insurrection is treated as an art.

SOURCE 2

From an article of 11 October 1917, written by leading Bolsheviks, Lev Kamenev and Grigor Zinoviev, in which they caution against the Bolsheviks' attempting an armed rising. Quoted in Martin McCauley, *The Russian Revolution & the Soviet State 1917–21: Documents*, Macmillan, 1984, p. 115.

A current is forming and growing in workers' groups which see the only way out in an immediate declaration of an armed uprising. Now all the timescales have coincided so that if one is to speak of such an uprising, one has plainly to fix a date and moreover for the immediate future. This question is already being debated in one form or another in all the periodical press, in workers' meetings and is occupying the minds of a wide circle of party workers. We, in our turn, regard it as our duty and our right to speak out on this question with full frankness.

We are most profoundly convinced that to declare at once an armed uprising would mean to stake not only the fate of our party, but also the fate of the Russian and international revolution. There is no doubt that there are such historical situations that an oppressed class has to acknowledge that it is better to join battle and lose than to surrender without a fight. Is the Russian working class in such a position now?
No, and a thousand times no.

CHAPTER 6

The Bolshevik consolidation of power 1917–24

The successful Bolshevik uprising of October 1917 marked the beginning rather than the end of the Russian Revolution. The big test was whether the Bolsheviks could retain their power and build on it. Their successful efforts to do so are studied in this chapter under the following headings:

★ The Bolsheviks in power

★ The dissolution of the Constituent Assembly

★ The Treaty of Brest-Litovsk 1918

★ The Russian Civil War 1918–20

★ The foreign interventions 1918–20

★ Lenin's methods for imposing control 1917–21

★ War Communism 1918–21

★ The Kronstadt Rising 1921

★ The New Economic Policy

Key dates

1917		November Decrees on Land and Workers' Control	1918	Sept.	Red Terror
1918–20		Russian Civil War and foreign interventions	1919	March	Comintern established
					Bolshevik Party renamed the Communist Party
1918–21		War Communism	1920	April	Invading Red Army driven from Poland
1918	Jan.	Bolsheviks forcibly dissolved the Constituent Assembly	1921	March	Kronstadt Rising
		Red Army established			Introduction of New Economic Policy
	March	Treaty of Brest-Litovsk	1921–4		NEP leads to economic recovery
	June	Decree on Nationalisation	1924	Jan.	Death of Lenin
	July	Forced grain requisitions began			
		Murder of tsar and his family			

1 The Bolsheviks in power

▶ *How did the Bolsheviks tackle the problems confronting them after they had taken power in 1917?*

Problems

In power, the Bolsheviks under Lenin faced huge difficulties in trying to consolidate their hold over what had been the tsarist empire. These can be identified as four basic questions:

- Could the Bolsheviks survive at all?
- If so, could they extend their control over the whole of Russia?
- Could they negotiate an end to the war?
- Could they bring economic stability to Russia?

The traditional Soviet view was that after the Bolsheviks had taken power under Lenin they transformed old Russia into a socialist society by following a set of measured, planned reforms that had been previously prepared. Few historians now accept that was what happened. Lenin's policy is now seen as having been a **pragmatic** adjustment to the harsh realities of the situation.

From the beginning, the Bolshevik regime was engaged in a desperate struggle for survival. In their government of Russia, the Bolsheviks were working from hand to mouth. They had few plans to help them. This was because before 1917 they had spent their time in preparing for revolution. They had given little thought to the details of how affairs would be organised once this had been achieved. It had always been a Marxist belief that after the triumph of the proletariat the state would 'wither away'. Trotsky had expressed this simple faith at the time of his appointment in October 1917 as **commissar for foreign affairs** when he said 'all we need to do is issue a few decrees, then shut up shop and go home'. But circumstances were not to allow such a relaxed approach to government.

The distribution of power

Lenin claimed that the October Revolution had been the taking of power by the soviets. In fact, it had been a seizure of power by the Bolshevik Party. Nevertheless, Lenin persisted with the notion that *Sovnarkom* had been appointed to govern by the Congress of Soviets. According to this view, the distribution of power in revolutionary Russia took the form of a pyramid, with *Sovnarkom* at the top, drawing its authority from the Russian people who expressed their will through the soviets at the base (see Figure 6.1 on page 132).

The reality was altogether different. Traditional forms of government had broken down in 1917 with the fall of tsardom and the overthrow of the Provisional Government. This meant that the Bolsheviks ruled *de facto*, not **de jure**. To put

KEY TERMS

Pragmatic An approach in which policies are changed according to circumstance rather than in accordance with a fixed theory.

Commissar for foreign affairs Equivalent to the secretary of state in the USA or the foreign secretary in the UK.

De jure By legitimate legal right.

Figure 6.1 The distribution of power in revolutionary Russia.

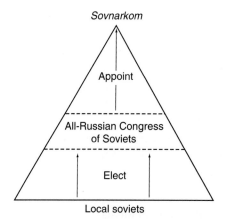

it another way, they were in a position to make up their own rules. And since not all the soviets were dominated by the Bolsheviks, who in any case were a minority party, Lenin had no intention of letting true democracy get in the way. The notion that it was the soviets who had taken power and now ruled was simply a convenient cover. From the beginning, whatever the claims may have been about soviets' being in authority, it was in fact the Bolsheviks who held power. The key body here was the Central Committee of the Bolshevik Party. It was this organisation, under Lenin's direction, that provided the members of the government. In a sense, *Sovnarkom* was a wing of the Bolshevik Party.

In theory, the Central Committee derived its authority from the All-Russian Congress of the Bolshevik Party, whose locally elected representatives voted on policy. In practice, the congress and the local parties did as they were told. This was in keeping with Lenin's demand that the Bolshevik Party operate according to the principle of democratic centralism (see page 28), a formula that guaranteed that power was exercised from the top down, rather than the bottom up.

The Bolsheviks' early measures

In Bolshevik theory, the October Revolution had marked the victory of the proletariat over the bourgeoisie, of socialism over capitalism. But theory was of little immediate assistance in the circumstances of late 1917. A hard road lay ahead if the Bolsheviks were truly to transform the Russian economy.

Before the October Revolution, Lenin had written powerfully against landlords and grasping capitalists, but he had produced little by way of a coherent plan for their replacement. It is understandable, therefore, that his policy after taking power in 1917 was a pragmatic one. He argued that the change from a bourgeois to a proletarian economy could not be achieved overnight. The Bolshevik government would continue to use the existing structures until the transition had been completed and a fully fledged socialist system could be adopted. This transitional stage was referred to as state capitalism.

Lenin explained to his colleagues that 'for the present we shall have to adopt the old bourgeois method and agree to pay higher salaries for the "services" of the biggest bourgeois specialists. All who are familiar with the situation see the necessity of such a measure.' Lenin was aware that there were many Bolsheviks who wanted the immediate introduction of a sweeping revolutionary policy, but he pointed out that the new regime simply did not possess the power to impose this. Its authority did not run much beyond Petrograd and Moscow. Until the Bolsheviks could exercise a much wider political and military control, their policies would have to fit the prevailing circumstances. The war against Germany and Austria had brought Russia to the point of economic collapse.

Immediate difficulties

- The shortage of raw materials and investment capital had reduced industrial production to two-thirds of its 1914 level.
- Inflation had rocketed.
- The transport system was broken.
- Hunger gripped large areas of Russia – grain supplies were over 13 million tonnes short of the nation's needs.
- Within a few months of the October Revolution, the food crisis had been further deepened by the ceding to Germany of Ukraine, Russia's richest grain-producing region (see page 108).

All Lenin's economic policies from 1917 onwards can be seen as attempts to deal with these problems, the most pressing being whether Russia could produce enough to feed itself. Lenin was a realist on the peasant question. Although he considered that the future lay with the industrial workers, he was very conscious that the peasantry, who made up the mass of the population, were the food producers. The primary consideration, therefore, was how best the peasants could be persuaded or forced to provide adequate food supplies for the nation. Immediately after coming to power, the new government introduced two measures that are usually regarded as having initiated Bolshevik economic policy. These were the 'Decree on Land' and the 'Decree on Workers' Control', both issued in November 1917. However, these were not so much new departures as formal recognitions of what had already taken place.

The 'Decree on Land'

The key article of this measure is given in Source A.

SOURCE A

From the 'Decree on Land', November 1917, on webpage http://www.marxists.org/archive/lenin/works/1917/oct/25-26/26d.htm.

Private ownership of land shall be abolished forever; land shall not be sold, purchased, leased, mortgaged, or otherwise alienated. All land, whether state, crown, monastery, church, factory, private, public, peasant, etc., shall be confiscated without compensation and become the property of the whole people, and pass into the use of all those who cultivate it.

What restrictions on land-holding does Source A specify?

Rather than being a new move, the decree gave Bolshevik approval to what had been happening in the countryside since the February Revolution: in many areas the peasants had overthrown their landlords and occupied their property. Lenin had earlier accepted this when he had adopted the slogan 'Land to the Peasants' (see page 111).

The 'Decree on Workers' Control'

This measure was also largely concerned with authorising what had already occurred. During 1917, a large number of factories had been taken over by the workers. However, the workers' committees that were then formed seldom ran the factories efficiently. The result was a serious fall in industrial output. The decree accepted the workers' takeover, but at the same time it instructed the workers' committees to maintain 'the strictest order and discipline' in the workplace.

Passing decrees was one thing, enforcing them another. A particular problem for the government was that not all the workers' committees were dominated by Bolsheviks. Until the party gained greater control at shop-floor level it would be difficult for the central government to impose itself on the factories. Nevertheless, the government pressed on with its plans for establishing the framework of state direction of the economy, even if effective central control was some way off. In December, *Vesenkha* was set up 'to take charge of all existing institutions for the regulation of economic life'.

Initially, *Vesenkha* was unable to exercise the full authority granted to it. However, it did preside over a number of important developments:

* The banks and the railways were nationalised.
* Foreign debts were cancelled (see page 151).
* The transport system was made less chaotic.

These were important practical achievements, which suggested how effective centralised control might become should the Bolshevik regime be able to gain full power.

Creation of the *Cheka* 1917

While some Bolsheviks may have found the initial pace of revolutionary change too slow for their liking, there was no doubting that Lenin was determined to impose absolute Bolshevik rule by the suppressing of all political opposition. A development that gave the Bolsheviks muscle in dealing with their opponents was the creation in the weeks following the October coup of the **Cheka**.

In essense, the *Cheka* was a better organised and more efficient form of the *Okhrana*, the tsarist secret police, at whose hands nearly every Bolshevik activist had suffered. Its express purpose was to destroy '**counter-revolution** and sabotage', terms that were so elastic they could be stretched to cover anything of which the Bolsheviks disapproved (see page 156).

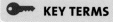
KEY TERMS

Vesenkha Supreme Council of the National Economy.

Cheka All-Russian Extraordinary Commission for Fighting Counter-Revolution, Sabotage and Speculation.

Counter-revolution A term used by the Bolsheviks to cover any action of which they disapproved by branding it as reactionary.

Summary diagram: The Bolsheviks in power

Problems confronting the Bolsheviks

- Bolsheviks controlled only Petrograd and Moscow
- Low industrial production
- High inflation
- Severe food shortages
- Occupation by Germany

Measures to tackle problems

1. **Economic**
   Adoption of state capitalism – a compromise measure to achieve the transition to a socialist economy
   Decree on Land – abolished private property – recognised peasant takeovers
   Decree on Workers' Control – an attempt to assert government authority over the factories which had been seized by workers
   Vesenkha – body to oversee economic development

2. **Political**
   Cheka – special state police to crush counter-revolution and impose Bolshevik rule

The dissolution of the Constituent Assembly

▶ *What does this event reveal about Lenin's attitude towards the exercise of power?*

As a revolutionary, Lenin had never worried greatly about how many people supported the Bolsheviks. Mere numbers did not concern him. He had no faith in democratic elections, which he dismissed as tricks by which the bourgeoisie kept itself in power. His primary objective was not to win mass support, but to create a party capable of seizing power when the opportune moment came. This was why he had refused to join a broad-front opposition movement before 1917 and why he had consistently opposed any form of co-operation with the Provisional Government.

After the successful October coup in 1917, Lenin was even more determined not to allow elections to undermine the Bolsheviks' newly won power. However, there was an immediate concern. The October events had come too late to prevent the elections to the All-Russian Constituent Assembly from going ahead in November as planned. When the results came through by the end of the year they did not make comfortable reading for the Bolsheviks:

- They had been outvoted by nearly two to one by the Social Revolutionaries (SRs).
- They had won only 24 per cent of the total vote.
- They had gained barely a quarter of the seats in the assembly.

Table 6.1 Results of the election for the Constituent Assembly, November 1917

Party	Votes	Seats
SRs	17,490,000	370
Bolsheviks	9,844,000	175
National minority groups	8,257,000	99
Left SRs (pro-Bolshevik)	2,861,000	40
Kadets	1,986,000	17
Mensheviks	1,248,000	16
Total	41,686,000	717

Lenin's motives for destroying the assembly

Lenin had originally supported the idea of a Constituent Assembly, not out of idealism but for purely expedient reasons; it offered a way of further weakening the authority of the Provisional Government. Now, however, with his party in power, he had no need of an assembly. Furthermore, since it was overwhelmingly non-Bolshevik it would almost certainly make life difficult for his government. One possibility was that he could have tried to work with the new assembly. But that was not how Lenin operated. He was not a democrat; he did not deal in compromise. He was a revolutionary who believed that the only way to govern was not by compromise but by crushing opposition. Hence, his response to the Constituent Assembly, when it gathered in January 1918, was simple and ruthless. After only one day's session, it was dissolved at gunpoint by the Red Guards. A few members tried to protest, but, with rifles trained on their heads, their resistance soon evaporated. It was a bitter end to the dreams of liberals and reformers. There would not be another democratic body in Russia until after the collapse of Soviet communism over 70 years later.

Lenin's act of violence in January 1918 has to be viewed in context. The Bolsheviks' hold on power was precarious. Indeed, the prospects of Bolshevik survival at all seemed slim. There was strong and widespread opposition to them inside the country. Moreover, Russia was still at war with Germany, which meant that the Allies, France and Britain, were all set to interfere should the new Russian government make a separate peace. In such an atmosphere, the Bolsheviks were not prepared to consider power sharing.

Lenin justified the Bolshevik action by arguing that the original reason for electing an assembly, the establishing of an all-Russian representative body, had already been achieved by the creation of a Soviet government in October 1917. The people's will had expressed itself in the October Revolution. The Constituent Assembly was, therefore, superfluous. More than that, it was corrupt. The elections, he asserted, had been rigged by the SRs and the Kadets; consequently, the results did not truly reflect the wishes of the Russian people. In such circumstances, Lenin declared, to hand over power to the Constituent Assembly would be 'to compromise with the malignant bourgeoisie. Nothing in the world will induce us to surrender the Soviet power.'

Commenting on Lenin's attitude, Trotsky noted that Lenin was always ready to back his theories with force by using 'sharpshooters'. He recorded a remark Lenin had made to him in private: 'The dissolution of the Constituent Assembly by the Soviet Government means a complete and frank liquidation of the idea of democracy by the idea of dictatorship.'

Reactions to the crushing of the assembly

Lenin's ruthlessness caused unease among some of his own supporters. **Maxim Gorky**, one of the Bolshevik Party's leading intellectuals, likened it to Bloody Sunday 1905 (see page 36).

SOURCE B

Excerpt from an article by Maxim Gorky, 22 January 1918, quoted in David Shub, *Lenin*, Penguin, 1976, p. 328.

The best Russians have lived for almost 100 years with the idea of a Constituent Assembly as a political organ which could provide Russian democracy as a whole with the possibility of freely expressing its will. On the altar of this sacred idea rivers of blood have been spilled – and now the 'people's commissars' have ordered the shooting of this democracy which had manifested itself in honour of this idea.

Many foreign communists were appalled by Lenin's behaviour. Rosa Luxemburg, a German socialist, condemned 'the elimination of democracy' in Russia. She complained bitterly that the 'remedy' provided by Lenin and Trotsky was 'worse than the disease it is supposed to cure'. Such criticisms did not move Lenin. As he saw it, the desperately vulnerable position the Bolsheviks were in – attempting to impose themselves on Russia while surrounded by enemies on all sides – demanded the sternest of measures. Nor was he short of theory to justify his actions. The concept of democratic centralism, which required the absolute obedience of party members to the leaders, perfectly fitted the situation in which the Bolsheviks found themselves.

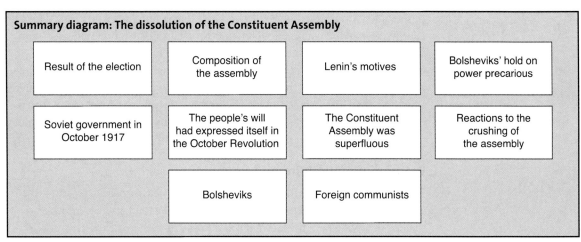

Summary diagram: The dissolution of the Constituent Assembly

Result of the election	Composition of the assembly	Lenin's motives	Bolsheviks' hold on power precarious
Soviet government in October 1917	The people's will had expressed itself in the October Revolution	The Constituent Assembly was superfluous	Reactions to the crushing of the assembly
	Bolsheviks	Foreign communists	

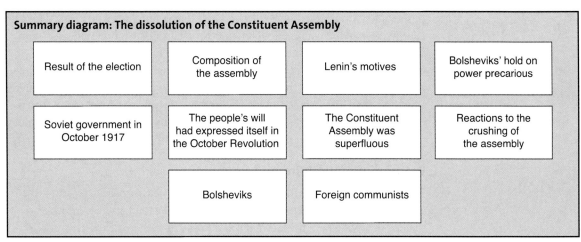

KEY FIGURE

Maxim Gorky (1868–1936)

Internationally celebrated Russian social and political commentator.

According to his description in Source B, why is Gorky outraged by the Bolsheviks' dissolution of the assembly?

The Treaty of Brest-Litovsk 1918

▶ *Why were the Bolsheviks willing to accept the humiliation of Russia in the Treaty of Brest-Litovsk?*

Lenin and Trotsky were united in their suppression of the Constituent Assembly. However, there was a marked difference of attitude between them over the issue of the war with Germany. Both wanted it ended but they disagreed on how this could best be achieved. Lenin wanted an immediate peace; Trotsky wanted a delay.

Lenin's view

Lenin's thinking ran along the following lines. Russia's military exhaustion made it impossible for it to fight on successfully. If Germany eventually won the war on both fronts it would retain the Russian territory it now possessed. But if Germany lost the war against the Western Allies, Russia would regain its occupied lands. In the first eventuality, Russia would not be worse off; in the second it would actually gain. It was, therefore, pointless for Bolshevik Russia to continue to fight.

An interesting aspect of Lenin's readiness to make peace with Germany was that it was not wholly ideological. Between 1914 and 1917 the German foreign office had given substantial amounts of money to Lenin and the Bolsheviks in the hope that if they succeeded in their revolution they would pull Russia out of the war (see page 103). Germany continued to finance Lenin even after the October Revolution and the armistice of December 1917. A settlement with Germany was therefore very much in Lenin's interests since it was the best guarantee against the drying up of this lucrative source of Bolshevik revenue.

Trotsky's view

Trotsky took a middle position between Lenin, who wanted a peace immediately, and those Bolsheviks and Left Revolutionaries who pressed for the continuation of the war as a revolutionary crusade against imperialist Germany. Trotsky shared Lenin's view that Bolshevik Russia had no realistic chance of successfully continuing the military struggle against Germany. However, in the hope that within a short time the German armies would collapse on the western front and revolution would follow in Germany, Trotsky was determined to make the peace talks a protracted affair. He wanted to buy time for Bolshevik agitators to exploit the mutinies in the Austro-German armies.

Bolshevik tactics at Brest-Litovsk

Buying time, for which Trotsky coined the slogan 'neither peace, nor war', was intended to confuse and infuriate the German delegation at Brest-Litovsk, the Polish town where the Germans and Russians gathered to discuss peace terms. Trotsky showed his contempt for what he called 'bourgeois propriety' by consistently flouting the traditional etiquette of European diplomacy. He would yawn loudly while German representatives were speaking and start private conversations with his Bolshevik colleagues rather than listen to what was being said. When he did join in the formal negotiations, he would ignore the point under discussion and launch into revolutionary speeches praising the October coup in Russia and calling on Germany to overthrow its corrupt bourgeois government. Germany's chief negotiator, Field-Marshal Hindenburg, complained that Trotsky and Lenin 'behaved more like victors than vanquished'.

What Hindenburg had failed to grasp was that Trotsky and Lenin did indeed see themselves as victors – potential if not actual. They were not perturbed by the thought of national defeat. Their conviction was that time and history were on their side. They believed that a great international political victory was imminent. It is important to remember that Lenin and Trotsky were **international revolutionaries**. They had only a limited loyalty towards Russia as a nation. Their first concern was to spread the proletarian revolution. This readiness to subordinate Russian national interests explains why, to the dismay of most Russians and many Bolsheviks, the Soviet delegation at Brest-Litovsk was eventually willing to sign a devastating peace treaty as soon as it became clear that the exasperated Germans were seriously considering marching to Petrograd to overthrow Lenin's government.

Trotsky's outlook as an international revolutionary did not prevent him from scoring a sharp nationalist propaganda point. Before signing the treaty on 3 March 1918, Sokolnikov, the Soviet representative, declared, under instructions from Trotsky, that it was not a freely negotiated settlement but a German **Diktat** imposed on a helpless Russia. Backing was given to this claim by the terms of the treaty, which could hardly have been more humiliating for Russia:

- A huge slice of territory, amounting to a third of European Russia, stretching from the Baltic to the Black Sea and including Ukraine, Russia's major grain source, was ceded to Germany or its allies.
- The land lost by Russia – about a million square kilometres (625,000 square miles) – contained a population of 45 million.
- Russia was required to pay 3 billion roubles in war **reparations**.

Lenin's reasons for signing the treaty

Aware that the signing of the treaty would be resented by many Bolsheviks, who were still pressing for a revolutionary struggle against Germany, Lenin stressed that his policy was the only realistic one: 'Russia can offer no physical resistance because she is materially exhausted by three years of war.' He acknowledged that there were Russians willing to fight on in a great cause. But they were, he said, 'romanticists' who did not understand the situation. Wars were not won by idealism alone; resources and technical skills were needed. The plain truth

KEY TERMS

International revolutionaries Marxists who were willing to sacrifice mere national interests in the cause of the worldwide rising of the workers.

Diktat A settlement imposed on a weaker nation by a stronger one.

Reparations Payment of war costs by the loser to the victor.

was that Bolshevik Russia did not yet have these in sufficient quantity to match Germany. Therefore, 'the Russian revolution must sign the peace to obtain a breathing space to recuperate for the struggle'.

Lenin added that he expected that Russia would soon be in a position to reclaim its lost territories, since in the aftermath of the war a violent conflict would soon develop among the capitalist powers. The main struggle would be between 'English and German **finance capital**'. In Lenin's view, the First World War had been caused by the rivalry between the imperialist powers, France, Germany and Britain, competing for the dwindling markets in which to invest their surplus capital. His rallying cry was, therefore, 'Let the Revolution utilise this struggle for its own ends.' Lenin's argument was a powerful one, yet he still experienced great difficulty in convincing his colleagues. The matter was debated bitterly in the Central Committee. In the end, Lenin gained his way by a majority of only one in a crucial committee division.

A profound issue lay at the base of Bolshevik disagreements. Lenin and Trotsky were primarily international revolutionaries. They expected workers' risings, based on the Russian model, to sweep across Europe. Purely national conflicts would soon be superseded by the international class struggle of the workers. Lenin and Trotsky regarded the crippling terms of the Treaty of Brest-Litovsk as of small account when set against the great sweep of world revolution.

The 'Left Communists'

Not all Bolsheviks shared this vision. A number, known as Left Communists, condemned the signing of the Treaty at Brest-Litovsk. They were those Bolsheviks who were convinced that their first task was to consolidate the October Revolution by driving the German imperialist armies from Russia. In the end, after days of wrangling, it was only Lenin's insistence on the absolute need for party loyalty in a time of crisis that persuaded them reluctantly to accept the treaty. Even then, serious opposition to Lenin's leadership might well have persisted had not the turn of military events in Western Europe saved the day.

What eventually destroyed the argument of the Left Communists was the collapse of Germany's western front in August 1918, followed by the almost total withdrawal of German forces from Russia. Lenin's gamble that circumstances would soon make the Treaty of Brest-Litovsk meaningless had paid off. It strengthened his hold over the party and provided the opportunity to expel the Left SRs from the government and to outlaw them politically.

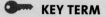 **KEY TERM**

Finance capital The resource used by stronger countries to exploit weaker ones. By investing heavily in another country, a stronger power made that country dependent on it.

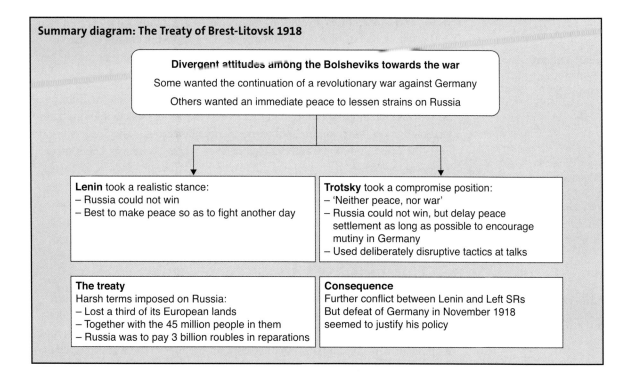

Summary diagram: The Treaty of Brest-Litovsk 1918

Divergent attitudes among the Bolsheviks towards the war

Some wanted the continuation of a revolutionary war against Germany

Others wanted an immediate peace to lessen strains on Russia

Lenin took a realistic stance:
– Russia could not win
– Best to make peace so as to fight another day

Trotsky took a compromise position:
– 'Neither peace, nor war'
– Russia could not win, but delay peace settlement as long as possible to encourage mutiny in Germany
– Used deliberately disruptive tactics at talks

The treaty
Harsh terms imposed on Russia:
– Lost a third of its European lands
– Together with the 45 million people in them
– Russia was to pay 3 billion roubles in reparations

Consequence
Further conflict between Lenin and Left SRs
But defeat of Germany in November 1918 seemed to justify his policy

 # The Russian Civil War 1918–20

▶ *How far was Lenin personally responsible for the Civil War?*

The Bolsheviks' crushing of the Constituent Assembly in January 1918, followed by their outlawing of all other parties, showed that they were not prepared to share power. This bid for absolute authority made civil war highly likely, given that the Bolsheviks had only a limited grip on Russia in their early years in power. They were bound to face military opposition from their wide range of opponents who were not prepared to accept being subjected to the absolute rule of a minority party.

Modern research strongly suggests that Lenin truly wanted a destructive civil war. Although it involved obvious dangers to the Bolsheviks, Lenin was convinced that his forces could win and in the process wipe out all their opponents, military and political. Better to have a short, brutal struggle than face many years of being harassed and challenged by the anti-Bolsheviks, who were a large majority in Russia, as the Constituent Assembly election results had shown (see page 136). Lenin feared that, had the Bolsheviks chosen to co-operate in a coalition of all the revolutionary parties in 1918, it would have had two consequences:

KEY TERMS

Popular mandate The authority to govern granted by a majority of the people through elections.

Reds The Bolsheviks and their supporters.

Whites The Bolsheviks' opponents, including monarchists looking for a tsarist restoration, and those parties who had been outlawed or suppressed by the new regime.

Greens Groups from the national minorities, struggling for independence from central Russian control.

- A successful counter-revolution would be easier to mount since the non-Bolshevik socialist parties would have had a **popular mandate** to govern.
- The Bolsheviks would have been unable to dominate government since they were very much a minority compared with the SRs.

It was the second consequence that Lenin refused to contemplate. As Dominic Lieven, an outstanding modern scholar, observes: 'Some Bolsheviks would have accepted a socialist coalition but Lenin was not one of them. The Bolshevik leader rejected this course and pursued policies, which, as he well knew, made civil war inevitable.'

Reds, Whites and Greens

The conflict that began in the summer of 1918 was not just a matter of the Bolsheviks (**Reds**) facing their political enemies (**Whites**) in military struggle. From the start the Civil War was a more complex affair. It involved yet another colour – the **Greens**.

The Bolsheviks presented the struggle as a class war, but it was never simply this. The sheer size of Russia often meant that local or regional considerations predominated over larger issues. A number of Russia's national minorities, most significantly the Ukrainians and the Georgians, fought in the war primarily to establish their independence from Russia. These national forces became known as the Greens. The best known of the Green leaders was Makhno, a one-time Bolshevik, who organised a guerrilla resistance to the Reds in Ukraine.

It was ironic that, although most of the leading Bolsheviks were non-Russian, their rule was seen by many as yet another attempt to reassert Russian authority over the rest of the country – the very situation that had prevailed under the tsars. An additional complication was that, as in all civil wars, the disruption provided a cover for settling old scores and pursuing personal vendettas, and it was not uncommon for villages or families to be divided against each other.

A war about food

On occasion, the fighting was simply a desperate struggle for food. Famine provided the backdrop to the Civil War. The breakdown in food supplies that had occurred during the war against Germany persisted. Until this was remedied whole areas of Russia remained hungry. The failure of the new regime to end hunger was a factor in the forming of the initial military opposition to the Bolsheviks in 1918. In addition to the problems of a fractured transport system, Lenin's government was faced with the loss to Germany of Russia's main wheat-supply area, Ukraine. In March 1918, the month in which the Treaty of Brest-Litovsk was signed, the bread ration in Petrograd reached its lowest ever allocation of 50 grams per day. Hunger forced many workers out of the major industrial cities. By June 1918, the workforce in Petrograd had shrunk by 60 per cent and the overall population had declined from 3 million to 2 million. A visitor to the city at this time spoke of 'entering a metropolis of cold, of hunger, of hatred, of endurance'. The Bolshevik boast that October 1917 had established worker-control of Russian industry meant little now that the workers were deserting the factories in growing numbers

Challenge from the SRs

The desperate circumstances encouraged open challenges to the Bolsheviks from both left and right. The SRs, who had been driven from the government following their refusal to accept the Brest-Litovsk settlement, attempted an anti-Bolshevik coup in **Moscow**. The Civil War could be said, therefore, to have begun not as a counter-revolution but as an effort by one set of revolutionaries to take power from another. In that sense it was an attempted act of revenge by a majority party, the SRs, against a minority party, the Bolsheviks, for having usurped the authority that they claimed was properly theirs. In their bitterness at being denied any say in government, the SRs joined the Whites in their struggle against Lenin's Reds.

KEY TERM

Moscow In 1918, for security reasons, Moscow replaced Petrograd as the capital of Soviet Russia.

Attempted assassination of Lenin

The SRs' military rising in Moscow failed, but their terrorism came closer to success. Lenin narrowly survived two attempts on his life, in July and August 1918. The second attempt, by Dora Kaplan, an SR fanatic, left him with a bullet lodged in his neck, an injury that contributed to his death six years later.

The Czech Legion

Armed resistance to the Bolsheviks had occurred sporadically in various parts of Russia since October 1917. What gave focus to this struggle was the behaviour in the summer of 1918 of one of the foreign armies still in Russia. There were 40,000 Czechoslovak troops who had volunteered to fight on the Russian side in the First World War as a means of gaining independence from Austria-Hungary. They found themselves isolated after the Treaty of Brest-Litovsk. They reformed themselves into the Czech Legion and decided to make the long journey eastwards to Vladivostok. Their aim was eventually to rejoin the Allies on the western front in the hope of winning international support for the formation of an independent Czechoslovak state. The Bolsheviks resented the presence of this well-equipped foreign army making its way arrogantly across Russia. Local soviets began to challenge the Czech Legion and fierce fighting accompanied its progress along the trans-Siberian railway.

Armed resistance spreads

All this encouraged the Whites, and all the revolutionary and liberal groups who had been outlawed by the Bolsheviks, to come out openly against Lenin's regime:

- The SRs organised a number of uprisings in central Russia and established an anti-Bolshevik Volga 'Republic' at Samara.

KEY FIGURES

General Denikin (1872–1947)

An ex-tsarist general who had supported Kornilov in 1917.

Admiral Kolchak (1873–1920)

Former commander of the Russian Black Sea fleet.

General Yudenich (1862–1933)

An ex-tsarist general who had distinguished himself in the Russo-Japanese War.

General Wrangel (1878–1928)

A decorated tsarist commander in the First World War.

- A White 'Volunteer Army', led by **General Denikin**, had already been formed in the Caucasus region of southern Russia from tsarist loyalists and outlawed Kadets.
- In Siberia, the presence of the Czech Legion encouraged the formation of a White army under **Admiral Kolchak**, the self-proclaimed 'Supreme Ruler of the Russian State'.
- In Estonia, **General Yudenich** began to form a White army of resistance.
- In the Caucasus and Ukraine, **General Wrangel** led an effective though short-lived White resistance.
- White units appeared in many regions elsewhere. The speed with which they arose indicated just how limited Bolshevik control was outside the cities of western Russia.

The patchwork of political, regional and national loyalties inside Russia made the Civil War a confused affair. It is best understood as a story of the Bolsheviks' resisting attacks on four main fronts, and then taking the initiative and driving back their attackers until they eventually withdrew or surrendered. The White generals, Denikin, Kolchak, Wrangel and Yudenich, did not co-ordinate their strategy and their isolated efforts were repulsed by the Red Army, which was able to deal with the White attacks separately and overcome them. Unlike the First World War, the Russian Civil War was a war of movement, mainly dictated by the layout of Russia's railway system. It was because the Bolsheviks were largely successful in their desperate fight to maintain control of the railways that they were able to keep themselves supplied, while denying the Whites the same benefit.

SOURCE C

? How does Source C help to explain why the presence of the Czech Legion in Russia was such a problem for the Bolsheviks?

Well armed and supplied, the troops of the Czech Legion aboard an armoured train in 1918.

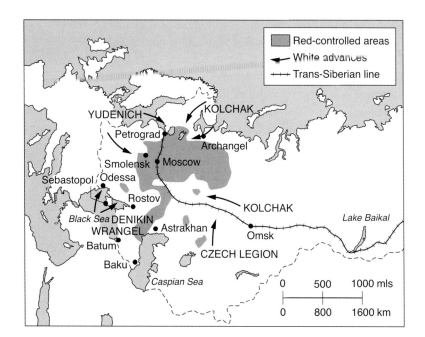

Figure 6.2 Areas involved in the Russian Civil War 1918–20. The names of the principal White opponents are in capitals.

Reasons for Bolshevik victory

The reasons for the final victory of the Reds in the Civil War are not difficult to determine.

White weaknesses

The Whites were hampered by a number of problems:

- The various White armies fought as separate detachments.
- Apart from their obvious desire to overthrow the Bolsheviks, they were not bound together by a single aim.
- They were unwilling to sacrifice their individual interests in order to form a united anti-Bolshevik front. This allowed the Reds to pick off the White armies separately.
- In the rare cases in which the Whites did consider combining, they were too widely scattered geographically to be able to bring sufficient pressure to bear on the enemy.
- The Whites were too reliant on supplies from abroad, which seldom arrived in sufficient quantities, in the right places, at the right time.
- The Whites lacked leaders of the quality of Trotsky.

Red strengths

The Reds, in contrast, had a number of overwhelming advantages:

- They remained in control of a concentrated central area of western Russia, which they were able to defend by maintaining their inner communication and supply lines.

- The two major cities, Petrograd and Moscow, the administrative centres of Russia, remained in their hands throughout the war, as did most of the railway network.
- The Reds also possessed a key advantage in that the areas where they had their strongest hold were the industrial centres of Russia. This gave them access to munitions and resources denied to the Whites.
- The dependence of the Whites on supplies from abroad appeared to prove the Red accusation that they were in league with the foreign interventionists (see page 150). The Civil War had produced a paradoxical situation in which the Reds were able to stand as champions of the Russian nation as well as proletarian revolutionaries.
- The Red Army was brilliantly organised and led by Trotsky.

Trotsky's role

Trotsky's strategy was simple and direct:

- To defend the Red Army's internal lines of communication.
- To deny the Whites the opportunity to concentrate large forces in any one location.
- To prevent the Whites maintaining regular supplies.

The basis of this strategy was control of Russia's railways. Trotsky viewed the function of the railways as equivalent to that of the cavalry in former times. They were the means of transporting troops swiftly and in large numbers to the critical areas of defence or attack. That was why the decisive confrontations between Reds and Whites took place near rail junctions and depots. Trotsky's broad strategy was successful. Once the Reds had established an effective defence of their main region around Petrograd and Moscow they were able to exhaust the enemy as an attacking force and then drive them back on the major fronts until they scattered or surrendered.

Red and White brutality

As in most civil wars, the opposing sides accused each other of committing atrocities. Both Reds and Whites did undoubtedly use terror to crush opposition in the areas they seized. The actual fighting was not unduly bloody; it was in the aftermath, when the civilian population had been cowed, that the savagery usually occurred. The Reds gained recruits by offering defeated enemy troops and neutral civilians the stark choice of enlistment or execution. Although the Reds imposed a reign of terror, the Whites' own record in ill-treating local populations was equally notorious. A White general wrote revealingly (see Source D) of the way atrocities committed by his side provided a propaganda gift to the Reds.

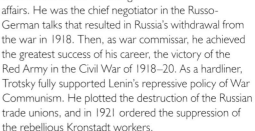

Leon Trotsky 1879–1940

1879	Born Leon Bronstein, into a Ukrainian Jewish family
1905	Became chairman of St Petersburg soviet
1907–17	Lived in various European countries and in the USA
1917	Principal organiser of the October coup
1918	Negotiated the Treaty of Brest-Litovsk
1918–20	Created the Red Army
1924–27	Outmanoeuvred in the power struggle with Stalin
1940	Assassinated in Mexico on Stalin's orders

As a young revolutionary, Trotsky was drawn to Menshevism and it was as a Menshevik that he became chairman of the St Petersburg soviet during the 1905 Revolution. His activities led to his arrest and exile. Between 1906 and 1917 he developed his theory of 'permanent revolution', the notion that revolution was not one event but a continuous process of international class warfare.

Following the February Revolution, Trotsky returned to Petrograd and immediately joined the Bolshevik Party. He became chairman of the Petrograd soviet, a position that he used to organise the Bolshevik uprising, which overthrew the Provisional Government in October 1917.

In the Bolshevik government that then took over, Trotsky became commissar for foreign affairs. He was the chief negotiator in the Russo-German talks that resulted in Russia's withdrawal from the war in 1918. Then, as war commissar, he achieved the greatest success of his career, the victory of the Red Army in the Civil War of 1918–20. As a hardliner, Trotsky fully supported Lenin's repressive policy of War Communism. He plotted the destruction of the Russian trade unions, and in 1921 ordered the suppression of the rebellious Kronstadt workers.

Never fully accepted by his fellow Bolsheviks, despite his brilliance, Trotsky lost to Stalin in the power struggle that followed Lenin's death. Trotsky's concept of permanent revolution was suppressed in favour of 'socialism in one country', Stalin's term for the consolidation of Communist rule in the USSR.

In 1929 Trotsky was exiled from the USSR. In 1939 he founded the vocal but ineffectual anti-Stalin Fourth International. Trotsky's end came in 1940 in Mexico City, when a Soviet agent acting on Stalin's direct orders killed him by driving an ice-pick into his head.

SOURCE D

From the diary of General Budberg, 3 May 1919, quoted in Edward Acton, editor, *The Soviet Union: A Documentary History*, volume 1, University of Exeter Press, 2005, p. 80.

The lads think that, if they have killed and tortured a few hundred or thousand Bolsheviks and beaten up a certain number of commissars, then they have done a great job, inflicted a decisive blow on Bolshevism and brought the restoration of the old order nearer … The lads do not seem to realise that if they rape, flog, rob, torture and kill indiscriminately and without restraint, they are thereby instilling such hatred for the government they represent that the swine in Moscow must be delighted at having such diligent, valuable and beneficial collaborators.

What impression of White terror methods is offered in Source D?

?

To the ordinary Russian there was little to choose between the warring sides in the matter of brutality. By the end of the Civil War any initial sympathy gained by the Reds from the peasants was lost by the severity of their grain-requisitioning methods. However, the Whites were unable to present themselves as a better alternative. All they could offer was a return to the pre-revolutionary situation. This was particularly damaging to them in relation to the land question. The Reds continually pointed out that all the lands that the peasants had seized in the revolutions of 1917 would be forfeit if ever the Whites were to win the war. It was this fear more than any other that stopped the peasants from giving their support to the Whites.

The importance of morale

Waging war is not just a matter of resources and firepower. Morale and dedication play a vital role. Throughout the struggle, the Reds were sustained by a driving sense of purpose. Trotsky as the Bolshevik war commissar may have been extreme in his methods, but he created an army that proved capable of fighting with an unshakeable belief in its own eventual victory (see page 160). Set against this, the Whites were never more than an uncoordinated group of forces, whose morale was seldom high. They were a collection of dispossessed socialists, liberals and moderates, whose political differences often led them into bitter disputes among themselves. Save for their hatred of Bolshevism, the Whites lacked a common purpose. Throughout the Civil War, the White cause was deeply divided by the conflicting interests of those who were fighting for national or regional independence and those who wanted a return to strong central government. Furthermore, no White leader emerged of the stature of Trotsky or Lenin around whom an effective anti-Bolshevik army could unite.

The effects of the Civil War on the Bolsheviks

Toughness

On the domestic front, the Civil War proved to be one of the great formative influences on the Bolsheviks (renamed the Communist Party in 1919). Their attempts at government took place during a period of conflict in which their very survival was at stake. The development of the party and the government has to be set against this background. The revolution had been born in war, and the government had been formed in war. Of all the members of the Communist Party in 1927, a third had joined in the years 1917–20 and had fought in the Red Army. This had created a tradition of military obedience and loyalty. The Bolsheviks of this generation were hard men, forged in the fires of war.

Authoritarianism

A number of modern analysts have emphasised the central place that the Civil War had in shaping the character of Communist rule in Soviet Russia. Robert Tucker stresses that it was the military aspect of early Bolshevik government that left it with a 'readiness to resort to coercion, rule by **administrative fiat**, centralised administration and summary justice'. No regime placed in the Bolshevik predicament between 1917 and 1921 could have survived without resort to authoritarian measures.

Centralisation

The move towards centralism in government increased as the Civil War dragged on. The emergencies of war required immediate day-to-day decisions to be made. This led to effective power moving away from the Central Committee of the Communist (Bolshevik) Party, which was too cumbersome, into the hands of the two key subcommittees, the **Politburo** and the **Orgburo**, set up in 1919, that could act with the necessary speed. In practice, the authority of *Sovnarkom*, the official government of Soviet Russia, became indistinguishable from the rule of these party committees, which were served by the **Secretariat**.

KEY TERMS

Politburo The Political Bureau, responsible for major policy decisions.

Orgburo Organisation Bureau, which turned policies into practice.

Secretariat A form of civil service that administered the policies.

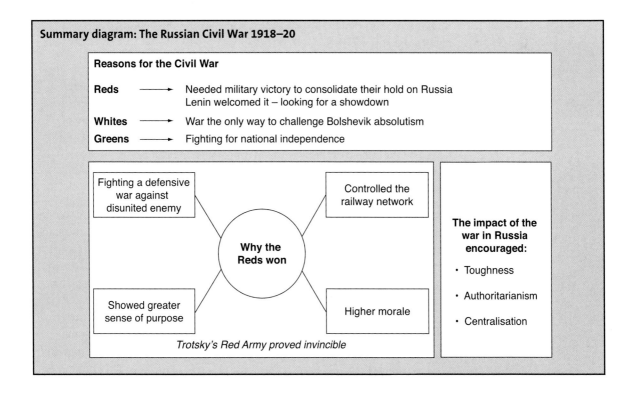

Summary diagram: The Russian Civil War 1918–20

Reasons for the Civil War

Reds → Needed military victory to consolidate their hold on Russia. Lenin welcomed it – looking for a showdown

Whites → War the only way to challenge Bolshevik absolutism

Greens → Fighting for national independence

Fighting a defensive war against disunited enemy / Controlled the railway network / **Why the Reds won** / Showed greater sense of purpose / Higher morale

Trotsky's Red Army proved invincible

The impact of the war in Russia encouraged:
- Toughness
- Authoritarianism
- Centralisation

The foreign interventions 1918–20

▶ *What led foreign powers to intervene in Russia?*

Russia and the Western Allies

When tsardom collapsed in 1917, the immediate worry for the Western Allies was whether the new regime would keep Russia in the war. If revolutionary Russia made a separate peace, Germany would be free to divert huge military resources from the eastern to the western front. To prevent this, the Allies offered large amounts of capital and military supplies to Russia to keep it in the war. The new government eagerly accepted the offer; throughout its eight months in office from February to October 1917 the Provisional Government remained committed to the war against Germany in return for Allied war-credits and supplies.

This produced an extraordinary balance. On one side stood Lenin and his anti-war Bolsheviks financed by Germany; on the other the pro-war Provisional Government funded by the Allies. However, the October Revolution destroyed the balance. The collapse of the Provisional Government and the seizure of power by the Bolsheviks had precisely the effect hoped for by Germany and feared by the Allies. Within weeks, an armistice had been agreed between Germany and the new government, and fighting on the eastern front ended in December 1917.

The initial response of France and Britain was cautious. In the faint hope that the Bolsheviks might be persuaded to continue the fight against Germany, the same support was offered to them as to their predecessors. David Lloyd George, the British prime minister, declared that he was neither for nor against Bolshevism, but simply anti-German. He was willing to side with any group in Russia that would continue the war against Germany.

Allied and Bolshevik attitudes harden

However, the Treaty of Brest-Litovsk in March 1918 ended all hope of Lenin's Russia renewing the war against Germany. From now on, any help given by Britain to anti-German Russians went necessarily to anti-Bolshevik forces. It appeared to the Bolsheviks that Britain and its allies were intent on destroying them. This was matched by the Allies' view that in making a separate peace with Germany the Bolsheviks had betrayed the Allied cause. The result was a fierce determination among the Allies to prevent their vital war supplies, previously loaned to Russia and still stockpiled there, from falling into German hands.

Soon after the signing of the Treaty of Brest-Litovsk, British, French and US troops occupied the ports of Murmansk in the Arctic and Archangel in the

White Sea (see the map on page 152). This was the beginning of a two-year period during which armed forces from a large number of countries occupied key areas of European, central and far-eastern Russia.

Once the First World War had ended in Europe in November 1918, the attention of the major powers turned to the possibility of a full offensive against the Bolsheviks. Among those most eager for an attack were Winston Churchill, the British cabinet minister, and Marshal Foch, the French military leader. They were alarmed by the creation of the **Comintern** and by the spread of revolution in Germany and central Europe:

- In January 1918, the **Spartacists**, a Communist movement in Germany, tried unsuccessfully to mount a coup in Berlin.
- In 1919, a short-lived Communist republic was established in Bavaria.
- In March 1919 in Hungary, a Marxist government was set up under Bela Kun, only to fall five months later.

The interventions spread

There was also a strong financial aspect to anti-Bolshevism in Western Europe. One of the first acts of the Bolshevik regime had been to declare that the new government had no intention of honouring the foreign debts of its predecessors. In addition, it nationalised a large number of foreign companies and froze all foreign assets in Russia. The bitter reaction to what was regarded as international theft was particularly strong in France, where many financiers had invested in tsarist Russia. It was the French who now took the lead in proposing an international campaign against the Reds:

- In 1918, British land forces entered Transcaucasia in southern Russia and also occupied part of central Asia.
- British warships entered Russian Baltic waters and the Black Sea, where French naval vessels joined them.
- The French also established a major land base around the Black Sea port of Odessa.
- In April 1918, Japanese troops occupied Russia's far-eastern port of Vladivostok.
- Four months later, units from France, Britain, the USA and Italy joined them.
- Czech, Finnish, Lithuanian, Polish and Romanian forces crossed into Russia.
- In 1919, Japanese and US troops occupied parts of Siberia.

An important point to stress is that these were not co-ordinated attacks. There was little co-operation between the occupiers. The declared motive of Britain, France, Germany, Italy, Japan and the USA was the legitimate protection of their individual interests. The objective of Czechoslovakia, Finland, Lithuania, Poland and Romania, all of whom directly bordered western Russia, was to achieve their separatist aim, going back to tsarist times, of gaining independence from Russia.

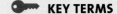

KEY TERMS

Comintern The Communist International, a body set up in Moscow in March 1919 to organise worldwide revolution.

Spartacists Named after Spartacus, the leader of a slave rebellion in ancient Rome.

Figure 6.3 The foreign interventions, 1918–20.

Principal armies attempting to destroy Bolshevism in bold italic font

— Under Bolshevik rule November 1918

– – Maximum advance of the anti-Bolshevik forces 1918–19

■ Remnant of anti-Bolshevik forces, defeated 1920–1

- - - Established Russian western frontiers, March 1921–October 1939

The failure of the interventions

Despite the preaching of an anti-Bolshevik crusade by influential voices in Western Europe, no concerted attempt was ever made to unseat the Bolshevik regime. This was shown by the relative ease with which the interventions were resisted. The truth was that after four long years of struggle against Germany the interventionists had no stomach for a prolonged campaign. There were serious threats of mutiny in some British and French regiments ordered to embark for Russia. Trade unionists who were sympathetic towards the new 'workers' state' refused to transport military supplies bound for Russia.

After the separate national forces had arrived in Russia, there was seldom effective contact between them. Furthermore, such efforts as the foreign forces made to liaise with the White armies were half-hearted and had little effect. The one major exception to this was in the Baltic states, where the national forces, backed by British warships and troops, crushed a Bolshevik invasion and obliged Lenin's government to recognise the independence of Estonia, Latvia and Lithuania, a freedom which they maintained until taken over by Stalin in 1940.

Such interventionist success was not repeated elsewhere. After a token display of aggression, the foreign troops began to withdraw. By the end of 1919, all French and US troops had been recalled, and by the end of 1920, all other Western forces had left. It was only the Japanese who remained in Russia for the duration of the Civil War, not finally leaving until 1922.

Propaganda success for the Bolsheviks

In no real sense were the foreign withdrawals a military victory for the Bolsheviks, but that was exactly how they were portrayed in Soviet propaganda. Lenin's government presented itself as the saviour of the nation from foreign conquest; all the interventions had been imperialist invasions of Russia intent on overthrowing the revolution. This apparent success over Russia's enemies helped the Bolshevik regime to recover the esteem it had lost over its 1918 capitulation to Germany. It helped to put resolve into the doubters in the party and it lent credibility to the Bolshevik depiction of the Whites as agents of foreign powers, intent on restoring reactionary tsardom.

War against Poland

The failure of the foreign interventions encouraged the Bolsheviks to undertake what proved to be a disastrous attempt to expand their authority outside Russia. In 1920, the Red Army marched into neighbouring Poland expecting the Polish workers to rise in rebellion against their own government. However, the Poles saw the invasion as traditional Russian aggression and drove the Red Army back across the border. Soviet morale was seriously damaged, which forced Lenin and the Bolsheviks to rethink the whole question of international revolution.

Lenin's approach to foreign affairs

Lenin adopted an essentially realistic approach. He judged that the Polish reverse, the foreign interventions in Russia, and the failure of the Communist risings in Germany and Hungary all showed that the time was not ripe for world revolution. The capitalist nations were still too strong. The Bolsheviks would, therefore, without abandoning their long-term revolutionary aims, adjust their foreign policy to meet the new situation. The Comintern would continue to call for world revolution, but Soviet Russia would soften its international attitude.

Lenin's concerns were very much in the tradition of Russian foreign policy. Western encroachment into Russia had been a constant fear of the tsars. That long-standing Russian worry had been increased by the hostility of European governments towards the October Revolution and by their support of the Whites during the Civil War. Lenin's reading of the international situation led him to conclude that discretion was the better part of valour. Under him, Soviet foreign policy was activated not by thoughts of expansion but by the desire to avoid conflict.

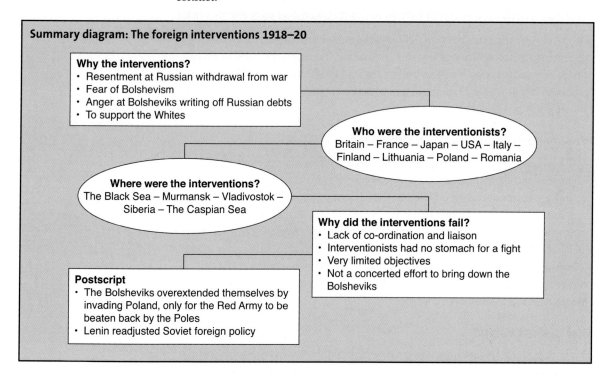

Summary diagram: The foreign interventions 1918–20

Why the interventions?
- Resentment at Russian withdrawal from war
- Fear of Bolshevism
- Anger at Bolsheviks writing off Russian debts
- To support the Whites

Who were the interventionists?
Britain – France – Japan – USA – Italy – Finland – Lithuania – Poland – Romania

Where were the interventions?
The Black Sea – Murmansk – Vladivostok – Siberia – The Caspian Sea

Why did the interventions fail?
- Lack of co-ordination and liaison
- Interventionists had no stomach for a fight
- Very limited objectives
- Not a concerted effort to bring down the Bolsheviks

Postscript
- The Bolsheviks overextended themselves by invading Poland, only for the Red Army to be beaten back by the Poles
- Lenin readjusted Soviet foreign policy

6 Lenin's methods for imposing control 1917–21

▶ *Were Lenin's terror tactics a temporary response to a desperate situation or an expression of Russian communism's true character?*

The repression that accompanied the spread of Bolshevik control over Russia between 1918 and 1921 became known as the Terror; whether it was justified remains a controversial question. One argument is that the extreme measures that Lenin's government adopted were the only response possible to the problems confronting the Bolsheviks after the October Revolution, in particular the need to win a desperate civil war.

An opposing view is that repression was not a reaction to circumstances but was a defining characteristic of **Marxism–Leninism**, a creed that regarded itself as uniquely superior to all other ideologies. An extension of this argument is that there was something essentially totalitarian about Lenin himself. He did not know how to act in any other way. He had always accepted the necessity of terror as an instrument of political control. Before 1917 he had often made it clear that a Marxist revolution could not survive if it were not prepared to smash its enemies: 'Coercion is necessary for the transition from capitalism to socialism. There is absolutely no contradiction between Soviet democracy and the exercise of dictatorial powers.' The chief instruments by which the Bolsheviks exercised their policy of terror were the *Cheka* and the Red Army, both of which played a critical role during the civil war.

The *Cheka*

This state police force, often likened historically to the *Gestapo* in Nazi Germany, had been created in December 1917 under the direction of **Felix Dzerzhinsky**, a Polish intellectual and aristocrat who pathologically despised his own class and wanted them to suffer. Lenin found him the ideal choice to lead the fight against the enemies of the revolution. Dzerzhinsky never allowed finer feelings or compassion to deter him from the task of destroying the enemies of Bolshevism. His remorseless attitude was shown in his first address as head of the *Cheka*, as given in Source E.

SOURCE E

From Dzerzhinsky's address, 20 December, 1917, in N. Zubov, *Dzerzhinsky*, Moscow, 1933, p. 9.

This is no time for speech-making. Our Revolution is in serious danger. We are ready to do all to defend the attainments of our Revolution. Do not think that I am on the look-out for forms of revolutionary justice. We have no need for justice now. Now we have need of a battle to the death! I propose, I demand the use of the revolutionary sword, which will put an end to all counter-revolutionaries. We must act not tomorrow, but today, at once.

The *Cheka*, which was to change its title several times over the years, but never its essential character, remains the outstanding expression of Bolshevik ruthlessness. Operating as a law unto itself, and answerable only to Lenin, it was granted unlimited powers of arrest, detention and torture, which it used in the most arbitrary and brutal way. It was the main instrument by which Lenin and his successors terrorised the Russian people into subservience and conformity.

What does Dzerzhinsky mean in Source E by saying, 'We have no need for justice'?

The murder of the Romanovs, July 1918

In July 1918, a group of SRs assassinated the German ambassador as a protest against the Treaty of Brest-Litovsk. A month later an attempt was made on Lenin's life (see page 104), followed by the murder of the Petrograd chairman of the *Cheka*. These incidents were made the pretext for a Bolshevik reign of terror across the greater part of Russia. It was in this atmosphere that a local *Cheka* detachment, on Lenin's personal order, executed the ex-tsar and his family in Ekaterinburg in July 1918.

The *Cheka* wages class war

The summary shooting of the Romanovs without the benefit of trial was typical of the manner in which the *Cheka* went about its business throughout Russia. In accordance with Dzerzhinsky's instructions, all pretence of legality was abandoned; the basic rules relating to evidence and proof of guilt no longer applied. Persecution was directed not simply against individuals, but against whole classes. This was class war of the most direct kind. 'Do not demand evidence to prove that the prisoner has opposed the Soviet government; your first duty is to ask him to which class he belongs, what are his origins. These questions should decide the fate of the prisoner.'

Labour camps

One of the most sinister developments was Dzerzhinsky's setting up of forced labour camps in which 'enemies of the revolution', a blanket term for all those the Bolsheviks considered to be actual or potential enemies, were incarcerated. By the time of Lenin's death there were 315 such camps. Developed as part of the Red Terror, they held White prisoners of war, uncooperative peasants and political prisoners, such as SRs, who were considered a threat to Soviet authority. The regime in the camps was deliberately harsh; severe hunger and beatings were the everyday lot of the prisoners.

Show trials

The *Cheka* was also involved in the arrest of those subsequently prosecuted in a series of show trials. On Lenin's instruction, between April and August 1922, leading members of the Soviet Union's outlawed parties and of the Moscow clergy were put on humiliating public trial, before being sentenced to imprisonment. Lenin's authority was also behind an accompanying campaign to politicise the law. Under the new regime, the law was operated not as a means of protecting society and the individual but as an extension of political control. Lenin declared that the task of the courts was to apply revolutionary justice. 'The court is not to eliminate terror but to legitimise it.'

Some Bolsheviks were uneasy about the relentless savagery of the *Cheka* but there were no attempts to restrict its powers. The majority of party members accepted that the hazardous situation they were in justified the severity of the

SOURCE F

What does Source F suggest about the public relationship between Lenin and Trotsky?

Lenin addressing a crowd in Moscow in May 1920. Trotsky and Kamenev are on the steps of the podium. This photo later became notorious when in Stalin's time it was airbrushed to remove Trotsky from it. Despite such later attempts to deny Trotsky's role in the revolution he had undoubtedly been Lenin's right-hand man.

repression. The foreign interventions and the Civil War, fought out against the background of famine and social disorder, threatened the existence of the Communist Party and the government. This had the effect of stifling criticism of the *Cheka*'s methods. Dzerzhinsky declared that the proletarian revolution could not be saved except by 'exterminating the enemies of the working class'.

Trade unions crushed

The activities of Trotsky as war commissar, a post he took after the signing of the Treaty of Brest-Litovsk, complemented Dzerzhinsky's work. Trotsky used his powers to end the independence of the trade unions, which had first been legalised in 1905. Trotsky dismissed the unions as 'unnecessary chatterboxes' and told them: 'The working classes cannot be nomads. They must be commanded just like soldiers. Without this there can be no serious talk of industrialising on new foundations.' Early in 1920, the workers were brought under military discipline on the same terms as soldiers. Among the restrictions put into effect were:

- A total ban was placed on the questioning of orders and instructions.
- Rates of pay or conditions were no longer negotiable.
- Severe penalties were imposed for poor workmanship or not meeting production targets.

555

SOURCE G

What does Source G illustrate about the scope of Trotsky's activities as war commissar?

A montage, showing the enormous efforts Trotsky put into his work as commissar of war. One of the most remarkable features of Trotsky's activities was the use of his special train in which he travelled over 100,000 km (63,000 miles) during the Civil War. It was not just a train. It was a town on wheels, serving as mobile command post, military headquarters, troop transporter, radio station, court martial, propaganda unit, publishing centre, arsenal and administrative office. In Trotsky's own words: 'The train linked the front with the base, solved urgent problems on the spot, educated, appealed, supplied, rewarded and punished.'

Organisation of the Red Army

Trotsky's outstanding achievement as commissar for war was his creation of the Red Army, which more than any other factor explains the survival of the Bolshevik government. This has obvious reference to the Reds' triumph in the Civil War, but the Red Army also became the means by which the Bolsheviks imposed their authority on the population at large.

Lenin showed his complete trust in Trotsky by giving him a totally free hand in military matters. From his heavily armed special train, which served as his military headquarters and travelled vast distances, Trotsky supervised the development of a new fighting force in Russia. He had inherited 'The Workers' and Peasants' Red Army', formed early in 1918. Within two years he had turned an unpromising collection of tired Red Guard veterans and raw recruits into a formidable army of 3 million men. Ignoring the objections of many fellow Bolsheviks, he enlisted large numbers of ex-tsarist officers to train the rank and file into efficient soldiers. As a precaution, Trotsky attached **political commissars** to the army. These became an integral part of the Red Army structure. No military order carried final authority unless a commissar countersigned it.

Trotsky tolerated no opposition within the Red Army from officers or men. The death sentence was imposed for desertion or disloyalty. In the heady revolutionary days before Trotsky took over, the traditional forms of army discipline had been greatly relaxed. Graded ranks, special uniforms, saluting and deferential titles were dropped as belonging to the reactionary past. Trotsky, however, had no truck with such fanciful experiments. He insisted that the demands of war meant that discipline had to be tighter, not looser.

Although 'commander' replaced the term 'officer', in all other key respects the Red Army returned to the customary forms of rank and address, with the word 'Comrade' usually prefixing the standard terms, as in 'Comrade Captain'. The practice of electing officers, which had come into favour in the democratic atmosphere of the February Revolution, was abandoned, as were soldiers' committees.

Conscription

Trotsky responded to the Civil War's increasing demand for manpower by enforcing conscription in those areas under Bolshevik control. (The Whites did the same in their areas.) Under the slogan 'Everything for the Front', Trotsky justified the severity of the Red Army's methods by referring to the dangers that Russia faced on all sides. Those individuals whose social or political background made them suspect as fighting men were nevertheless conscripted, being formed into labour battalions for back-breaking service behind the lines, such as digging trenches, loading ammunition and pulling heavy guns.

Most of the peasants who were drafted into the Red Army proved reluctant warriors, and were not regarded as reliable in a crisis. Desertions were commonplace, in spite of the heavy penalties. The Bolsheviks judged that the only dependable units were those drawn predominantly from among the workers. Such units became in practice the élite corps of the Red Army. Heroic stories of the workers as defenders of the Revolution quickly became legend.

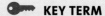

KEY TERM

Political commissars Party officials who accompanied the officers and reported on their political correctness.

Red Army idealism

Not everything was achieved by coercion; there were idealists among the troops who believed sincerely in the Communist mission to create a new proletarian world. Theirs was a vital contribution to the relatively high morale of the Reds. Although, by the standards of the European armies of the time, the Red Army was short of equipment and expertise, within Russia it soon came to outstrip its White opponents in its efficiency and sense of purpose.

Despite Trotsky's military triumphs, his authority did not go unchallenged. He met opposition from local Red commanders and commissars over tactics. His most notable dispute was with Joseph Stalin, who acted as political commissar in the Caucasus. Their legendary personal hostility dates from the Civil War days. Nonetheless, whatever the disputes, there was no doubting that Trotsky's organisation and leadership of the Red Army was the major factor in the survival of Bolshevik Russia.

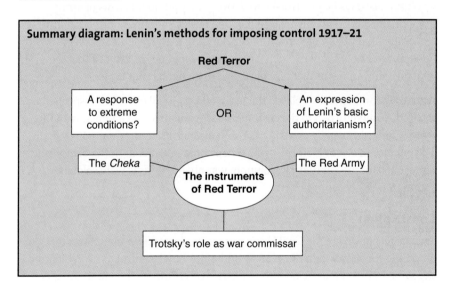

Summary diagram: Lenin's methods for imposing control 1917–21

 7 # War Communism 1918–21

▶ *What was the impact of War Communism on the economy?*

In the summer of 1918, Lenin began to introduce a series of harshly restrictive economic measures, which were collectively known as War Communism. The chief reason for the move away from the system of state capitalism, which had operated up to then, was the desperate situation created by the Civil War. Lenin judged that the White menace could be met only by an intensification of authority in those regions that the Reds controlled (approximately 30 of the 50 provinces of European Russia). The change in economic strategy has to be seen, therefore, as part of the Terror that the Bolsheviks operated in these years. Every aspect of life, social, political and economic, had to be subordinated to the task of winning the Civil War.

Impact on industry

The first step towards War Communism as a formal policy was taken in June 1918. The existence of the *Cheka* and the Red Army enabled Lenin to embark on a policy of centralisation knowing that he had the means of enforcing it. By that time also, there had been a considerable increase in Bolshevik influence in the factories. This was a result of the infiltration of the workers' committees by political commissars. This development helped to prepare the way for the issuing of the **Decree on Nationalisation** in June 1918, which within two years brought practically all the major industrial enterprises in Russia under central government control.

Nationalisation by itself did nothing to increase production. It was imposed at a time of severe industrial disruption, which had been caused initially by the strains of the war of 1914–17 but which worsened during the Civil War. Military needs were given priority, thus denying resources to those industries not considered essential. The situation was made more serious by the factories being deprived of workers. This was a consequence both of conscription into the Red Army and of the flight from the urban areas of large numbers of inhabitants, who left either in search of food or to escape the Civil War. The populations of Petrograd and Moscow dropped by a half between 1918 and 1921.

The problems for industry were deepened by hyperinflation. The scarcity of goods and the government's policy of continuing to print currency notes effectively destroyed the value of money. By the end of 1920, the rouble had fallen to one per cent of its worth in 1917. All this meant that while War Communism tightened the Bolshevik grip on industry it did not lead to economic growth. Table 6.2 shows the failure of War Communism in economic terms.

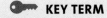

KEY TERM

Decree on Nationalisation Laid down a programme for the takeover by the state of the larger industrial concerns.

Table 6.2 A comparison of industrial output in 1913 and in 1921

Output	1913	1921
Index of gross industrial output	100	31
Index of large-scale industrial output	100	21
Electricity (million kWh)	2039	520
Coal (millions of tonnes)	29	8.9
Oil (millions of tonnes)	9.2	3.8
Steel (millions of tonnes)	4.3	0.18
Imports (at 1913 rouble value, millions)	1374	208
Exports (at 1913 rouble value, millions)	1520	20

Impact on agriculture

For Lenin, the major purpose of War Communism was to tighten government control over agriculture and force the peasants to provide more food. But the peasants proved difficult to bring into line. As a naturally conservative class, they were resistant to central government, whether tsarist or Bolshevik. The government blamed the resistance on the **kulaks** who, it was claimed, were hoarding their grain stocks in order to keep prices artificially high. This was untrue; there was no hoarding. The plain truth was that the peasants saw no point in producing more food until the government, which had become the main grain purchaser, was willing to pay a fair price for it. Moreover, the existence of a *kulak* class was a myth. Rather than being a class of exploiters, the *kulaks* were simply the more efficient farmers who were marginally more prosperous.

KEY TERM

Kulaks The Bolshevik term for the class of allegedly rich, exploiting peasants.

Grain requisitioning

Exasperated by the peasants' refusal to conform, the government condemned them as counter-revolutionaries and resorted to coercion. *Cheka* requisition units were sent into the countryside to take the grain by force. In August 1918, the people's commissar for food issued the orders shown in Source H.

? What explains the severity of the measures laid down in Source H?

SOURCE H

From 'Instructions for Requisitioning Grain', 20 *August* 1918, quoted in M. McCauley, editor, *The Russian Revolution and the Soviet State*, Macmillan, 1975, p. 184.

A commander is to head each detachment. The tasks of the requisition detachments are to: harvest winter grain in former landlord-owned estates; harvest grain on the land of notorious kulaks; *every food requisition detachment is to consist of not less than 75 men and two or three machine guns. The political commissar's duties are to ensure that the detachment carries out its duties and is full of revolutionary enthusiasm and discipline. The food requisition detachments shall be deployed in such a manner as to allow two or three detachments to link up quickly. Continuous cavalry communication shall be maintained between the various food requisition detachments.*

Between 1918 and 1921, the requisition squads systematically terrorised the countryside. The *kulaks* were targeted for particularly brutal treatment. Lenin ordered that they were to be 'mercilessly suppressed'. In a letter of 1920, he gave instructions that 100 *kulaks* were to be hanged in public in order to terrify the population 'for hundreds of miles around'.

Yet, the result was largely the reverse of the one intended. Even less food became available. Knowing that any surplus would simply be confiscated, the peasant produced only the barest minimum to feed himself and his family. Nevertheless, throughout the period of War Communism, the Bolsheviks persisted in their belief that grain hoarding was the basic problem. Official reports continued to speak of 'concealment everywhere, in the hopes of selling grain to town speculators at fabulous prices'.

Famine

By 1921, the combination of requisitioning, drought and the general disruption of war had created a national famine. The grain harvests in 1920 and 1921 produced less than half that gathered in 1913. Even *Pravda*, the government's propaganda newspaper, admitted in 1921 that one in five of the population was starving. Matters became so desperate that the Bolsheviks, while careful to blame the *kulaks* and the Whites, were prepared to admit there was a famine and to accept foreign assistance. A number of countries supplied Russia with aid. The outstanding contribution came from the USA, which through the **ARA**, provided food for some 10 million Russians.

Despite such efforts, foreign help came too late to prevent mass starvation. Of the 10 million fatalities of the Civil War period, over half starved to death. Lenin resented having to accept aid from the ARA and ordered it to withdraw from Russia in 1923 after two years, during which time it had spent over $60 million in relief work.

> **KEY TERM**
>
> **ARA** The American Relief Association, formed to provide food and medical supplies for post-war Europe.

SOURCE I

> How does the photo in Source I help to explain why Lenin abandoned War Communism in 1921?

A pile of unburied bodies in a cemetery in Buzuluk, grim testimony to the famine that struck the region in 1921. Similar tragedies were common across Russia, reducing some areas to cannibalism.

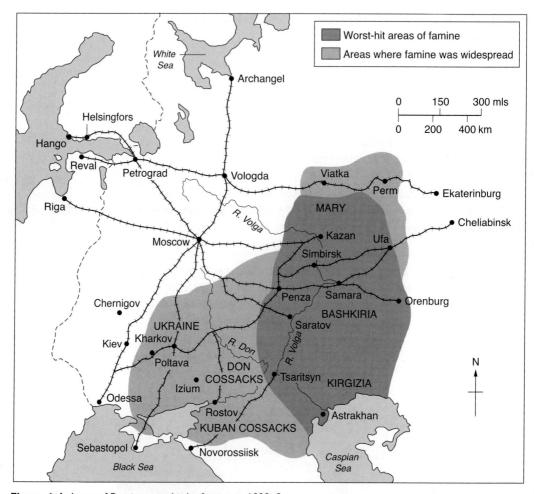

Figure 6.4 Areas of Russia worst hit by famine in 1932–3.

Enforcing War Communism

What is now known is that Lenin positively welcomed the famine as providing an opportunity to pursue his destruction of the Orthodox Church. In a letter of 1922, he ordered the Politburo to exploit the famine by shooting priests, 'the more, the better'. He went on: 'It is precisely now when in the starving regions people are eating human flesh and thousands of corpses are littering the roads that we can (and therefore must) carry out the confiscation of the church valuables with the most savage and merciless energy.'

By 1921, the grim economic situation had undermined the original justification for War Communism. During its operation, industrial and agricultural production had fallen alarmingly. Yet, this did not mean that the policy necessarily became unpopular among the Bolsheviks themselves. Indeed, there were many in the party who, far from regarding it as a temporary measure to meet an extreme situation, believed that it represented true revolutionary communism. The party's leading economists, **Nikolai Bukharin** and **Yevgeny Preobrazhensky**, urged that War Communism should be retained as the permanent economic strategy of the Bolshevik government. They saw it as true socialism in action since it involved:

- the centralising of industry
- the ending of private ownership
- the squeezing of the peasants.

The policy of War Communism was maintained even after the victory of the Red Army in the Civil War. The systematic use of terror by the *Cheka*, the spying on factory workers by political commissars and the enforced requisitioning of peasant grain stocks all continued. As a short-term measure the policy had produced the results Lenin wanted, but its severity had increased Bolshevik unpopularity. As long as the Whites were seen as the greater threat, the peasants had been prepared to put up with the strict control imposed by the Reds. However, with the Whites defeated, the peasants expected grain requisitioning to end. But the opposite happened. Even greater amounts of grain and fodder were seized by Red requisition squads. The abused peasants reacted violently.

The Tambov Rising

Throughout 1920 there were outbreaks of fierce resistance, the scale of the disturbances being evident in a *Cheka* admission that they had been involved in supressing 120 different uprisings. Ukraine witnessed many of these but the most serious trouble occurred in the central Russian province of Tambov. There, what were, in effect, peasant armies, were formed. The principal leader of these was **Alexander Antonov**, a Social Revolutionary. Attacking and seizing arms, including machine guns, from the requisition squads, the peasants took over whole areas and regions in the countryside. In retaliation for the past ill-treatment they had received from the requisition detachments, the peasants hunted down Red sympathisers, venting their anger with particular savagery on any officials they captured. Execution by shooting, bayonetting or beheading was often preceded by torture which including the victims' being branding with irons. Even after death, the vengeance continued, with bodies being mutilated and left in obscene postures.

By the end of 1920, Antonov commanded a guerrilla army of some 20,000. It was only with the greatest difficulty that sufficient Red Army detachments were gathered and sent into Tambov to re-establish government control. The Reds then resorted to the same vicious tactics that the peasants had used. Mass arrests, deportations and summary executions continued the cycle of violence. Whole families were taken hostage and their houses burnt to the ground. Such measures eventually worked and by the summer of 1921 peasant resistance had been broken. Antonov himself eluded capture for another year but in June 1922, after his hiding place had been revealed by a former supporter, he was cornered by a *Cheka* unit and killed in an exchange of gunfire.

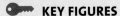

KEY FIGURES

Nikolai Bukharin (1888–1938)

Ally of Lenin since 1906, later executed under Stalin.

Yevgeny Preobrazhensky (1886–1937)

A Bolshevik since 1903, later executed under Stalin.

Alexander Antonov (1888–1922)

A former SR member, he had been imprisoned by the tsarist authorities for robbery and political crimes. He initially supported the Reds during the civil war but turned against them because of their repression of the peasants.

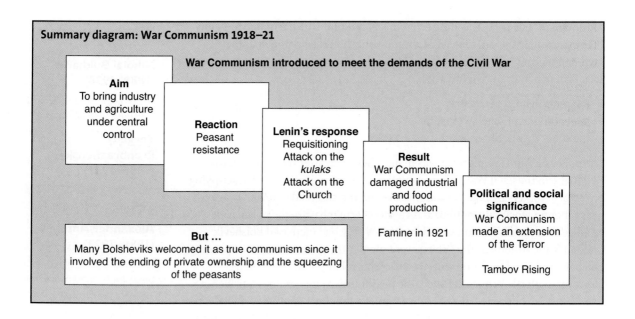

Summary diagram: War Communism 1918–21

War Communism introduced to meet the demands of the Civil War

Aim
To bring industry and agriculture under central control

Reaction
Peasant resistance

Lenin's response
Requisitioning
Attack on the *kulaks*
Attack on the Church

Result
War Communism damaged industrial and food production

Famine in 1921

Political and social significance
War Communism made an extension of the Terror

Tambov Rising

But ...
Many Bolsheviks welcomed it as true communism since it involved the ending of private ownership and the squeezing of the peasants

⑧ The Kronstadt Rising 1921

▶ *What developments led to the Kronstadt Rising?*

Lenin himself clung to War Communism as long as he could. However, the failure of the economy to recover and the scale of the famine led him to consider possible alternative policies. He was finally convinced of the need for change by widespread anti-Bolshevik uprisings in 1920–1. These were a direct reaction against the brutality of requisitioning. One in particular was so disturbing that Lenin described it as a lightning flash that illuminated the true reality of things. He was referring to the Kronstadt Rising of 1921, the most serious challenge to Bolshevik control since the October Revolution.

The 'Workers' Opposition'

As long as unrest was confined to the peasants and to the Bolsheviks' political enemies it was a containable problem. What became deeply worrying to Lenin in 1921 was the development of opposition to War Communism within the party itself. Two prominent Bolsheviks, Alexander Shlyapnikov, the labour commissar, and **Alexandra Kollontai**, the outstanding woman in the party, led a 'Workers' Opposition' movement against the excesses of War Communism. Kollontai produced a pamphlet in which she accused the party leaders of losing touch with the proletariat. Speaking for the workers, she asked rhetorically, 'Are we really the prop of the class dictatorship, or just an obedient flock that serves as a support for those, who, having severed all ties with the masses, carry out their own policy without any regard to our opinions?'

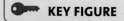 **KEY FIGURE**

Alexandra Kollontai (1872–1952)

Pioneering Russian feminist and adviser to Lenin on family and social policy.

Picking up the cue given by the 'Workers' Opposition', groups of workers in Petrograd went on strike early in 1921, justifying their actions in an angrily worded proclamation, reproduced in Source J.

SOURCE J

From the Petrograd Workers' Proclamation, 27 February 1921, quoted in David Shub, *Lenin*, Penguin, 1976, p. 407.

A complete change is necessary in the policies of the government. First of all, the workers and peasants need freedom. They don't want to live by the decrees of the Bolsheviks; they want to control their own destinies. Comrades, preserve revolutionary order! Determinedly and in an organised manner demand: liberation of all the arrested Socialists and non-partisan working-men [workers not belonging the Communist party]; abolition of martial law; freedom of speech, press and assembly for all who labour.

According to Source J, what are the main complaints of the Petrograd workers?

By February 1921, thousands of Petrograd workers had crossed to the naval base on Kronstadt. There they linked up with the sailors and dockyard workers to demonstrate for greater freedom. They demanded that in a workers' state, which the Bolshevik government claimed Soviet Russia to be, the workers should be better, not worse, off than in tsarist times. In an attempt to pacify the strikers, Lenin sent a team of political commissars to Kronstadt. They were greeted with derision. Petrechenko, a spokesman for the demonstrators, rounded bitterly on the commissars at a public meeting, as described in Source K.

SOURCE K

From Petrechenko's speech in February 1921, quoted in David Shub, *Lenin*, Penguin, 1976, p. 408.

You are comfortable; you are warm; you commissars live in the palaces … Comrades, look around you and you will see that we have fallen into a terrible mire. We were pulled into this mire by a group of Communist bureaucrats, who, under the mask of Communism, have feathered their nests in our republic. I myself was a Communist, and I call on you, Comrades, drive out these false Communists who set worker against peasant and peasant against worker. Enough shooting of our brothers!

In Source K, whom does Petrechenko identify as 'false Communists'?

The Kronstadt manifesto

Early in March, the sailors and workers of Kronstadt elected Petrechenko as chairman of a fifteen-man revolutionary committee, responsible for representing their grievances to the government. This committee produced a manifesto that included the following demands:

- New elections to the soviets, to be held by secret ballot.
- Freedom of speech and of the press.
- Freedom of assembly.
- Rights for trade unions and release of imprisoned trade unionists.

- Ending of the right of Communists to be the only permitted socialist political party.
- Ending of special food rations for Communist Party members.
- Freedom for individuals to bring food from the country into the towns without confiscation.
- Withdrawal of political commissars from the factories.
- Ending of the Communist Party's monopoly of the press.

It was not the demands themselves that frightened the Bolsheviks; it was the people who had drafted them: the workers and sailors of Kronstadt. They had been the great supporters of the Bolsheviks in 1917. Trotsky had referred to them as 'the heroes of the revolution'. It was these same heroes who were now insisting that the Bolshevik government return to the promises that had inspired the revolution. For all the efforts of the Bolshevik press to brand the Kronstadt protesters as White agents, the truth was that they were genuine socialists who had previously been wholly loyal to Lenin's government, but who had become appalled by the regime's betrayal of the workers' cause.

The uprising crushed

Angered by the growing number of strikers and their increasing demands, Trotsky ordered the Red Army under General Tukhachevsky to cross the late-winter ice linking Kronstadt to Petrograd and crush 'the tools of former tsarist generals and agents of the interventionists'. An ultimatum was issued to the demonstrators. When this was rejected, Tukhachevsky gave the signal for his force, made up of Red Army units and *Cheka* detachments, to attack. After an artillery bombardment, 60,000 Red troops stormed the Kronstadt base. The sailors and workers resisted fiercely. Savage fighting occurred before they were finally overcome. Source L describes Tukhachevsky's report to Trotsky.

SOURCE L

According to Source L, how fierce was resistance of the workers to their suppression by Tukhachevsky's forces?

From Tukhachevsky's report, quoted in Roman Gool, *Tukhachevsky*, Berlin, 1922, p. 159.

The sailors fought like wild beasts. I cannot understand where they found the might for such rage. Each house where they were located had to be taken by storm. An entire company fought for an hour to capture one house and when the house was captured it was found to contain two or three soldiers at a machine-gun. They seemed half-dead, but they snatched their revolvers and gasped, 'Too little did we shoot at you scoundrels.'

Aftermath of the uprising

Immediately after the uprising had been suppressed, the ringleaders who had survived were condemned as White reactionaries and shot. In the succeeding months the *Cheka* hunted down and executed those rebels who had escaped from Kronstadt. Lenin justified the severity on the grounds that the uprising had been the work of the bourgeois enemies of the October Revolution: 'Both the Mensheviks and the Socialist Revolutionaries declared the Kronstadt movement to be their own.' However, as well as being a propagandist, Lenin was a realist. He took the lesson of Kronstadt to heart. To avoid the scandal and embarrassment of another open challenge to his party and government, he decided it was time to soften the severity of War Communism. At the tenth conference of the Communist Party, which opened in March 1921, Lenin declared that the Kronstadt rising had 'lit up reality like a lightning flash'. This was the prelude to his introduction of the New Economic Policy, a move intended to tackle the famine and in doing so to lessen the opposition to Bolshevism. However, this was to be a purely economic adjustment. Lenin was not prepared to make political concessions: Communist control was to be made even tighter.

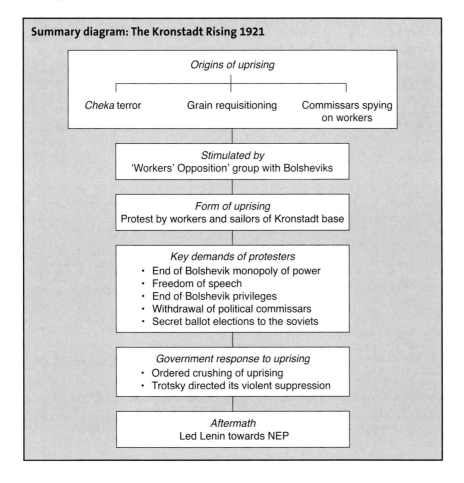

Summary diagram: The Kronstadt Rising 1921

Origins of uprising

Cheka terror   Grain requisitioning   Commissars spying on workers

Stimulated by
'Workers' Opposition' group with Bolsheviks

Form of uprising
Protest by workers and sailors of Kronstadt base

Key demands of protesters
- End of Bolshevik monopoly of power
- Freedom of speech
- End of Bolshevik privileges
- Withdrawal of political commissars
- Secret ballot elections to the soviets

Government response to uprising
- Ordered crushing of uprising
- Trotsky directed its violent suppression

Aftermath
Led Lenin towards NEP

9 The New Economic Policy

▶ *Why did NEP prove such a divisive issue for the Bolsheviks?*

As with the policy it replaced, the New Economic Policy (NEP) was intended by Lenin primarily to meet Russia's urgent need for food. Whatever the purity of the revolutionary theory behind War Communism, it had clearly failed to deliver the goods. State terror had not forced the peasants into producing larger grain stocks. Pragmatic as ever, Lenin judged, that, if the peasants could not be forced, they must be persuaded. The stick had not worked, so now was the time to offer the carrot. Source M recalls what Lenin told the delegates at the 1921 party congress.

SOURCE M

From *Lenin's Collected Works*, quoted in David Shub, *Lenin*, Penguin, 1976, p. 411.

We must try to satisfy the demands of the peasants who are dissatisfied, discontented, and cannot be otherwise. In essence the small farmer can be satisfied with two things. First of all, there must be a certain amount of freedom for the small private proprietor; and, secondly, commodities and products must be provided.

According to Lenin in Source M, how does he intend to relieve the pressure on the peasants?

Despite the deep disagreements that were soon to emerge within the Bolshevik Party over NEP, the famine and the grim economic situation in Russia led the delegates to give unanimous support to Lenin's proposals when they were first introduced. The decree making NEP official government policy was published in the spring of 1921. Its essential features were:

- central economic control to be relaxed
- the requisitioning of grain to be abandoned and replaced by a **tax in kind**
- the peasants to be allowed to keep their food surpluses and sell them for a profit
- public markets to be restored
- money to be reintroduced as a means of trading.

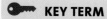 **KEY TERM**

Tax in kind The peasants surrendered a certain amount of their produce, equivalent to a fixed sum of money.

Lenin was aware that the new policy marked a retreat from the principle of state control of the economy. It restored a mixed economy in which certain features of capitalism existed alongside socialism. Knowing how uneasy this made many Bolsheviks, Lenin stressed that NEP was only a temporary concession to capitalism. He emphasised that the party still retained control of 'the commanding heights of the economy', by which he meant large-scale industry, banking and foreign trade. He added: 'we are prepared to let the peasants have their little bit of capitalism as long as we keep the power'.

The adoption of NEP showed that the Bolshevik government since 1917 had been unable to create a successful economy along purely ideological lines. Lenin admitted as much. He told party members that it made no sense for Bolsheviks to pretend that they could pursue an economic policy that took no account of the circumstances.

Bolshevik objections to NEP

Lenin's realism demanded that political theory take second place to economic necessity. It was this that troubled the members of the party, such as Trotsky and Preobrazhensky, who had regarded the repressive measures of War Communism as the proper revolutionary strategy for the Bolsheviks to follow. To their mind, bashing the peasants was exactly what the Bolsheviks should be doing since it advanced the revolution. It disturbed them, therefore, that the peasants were being given in to and that capitalist ways were being tolerated. Trotsky described NEP as 'the first sign of the degeneration of Bolshevism'.

A main complaint of the objectors was that the reintroduction of money and private trading was creating a new class of profiteers whom they derisively dubbed **Nepmen**. It was the profiteering that Victor Serge, a representative of the Left Bolsheviks, had in mind when he described the immediate social effects of NEP: 'the cities we ruled over assumed a foreign aspect; we felt ourselves sinking into the mire. Money lubricated and befouled the entire machine just as under capitalism.'

Lenin's ban on factionalism

NEP became such a contentious issue among the Bolsheviks that Lenin took firm steps to prevent the party being torn apart over it. At the tenth party congress in 1921, at which the NEP had been formally announced, he introduced a resolution 'On Party Unity'. The key passage read: 'Congress orders the immediate dissolution of all groups that have been formed on the basis of some platform or other, and instructs all organisations to be very strict in ensuring that no **factionalism** of any sort be tolerated.' Members were warned that non-compliance with the resolution would lead to immediate expulsion.

The object of Lenin's ban on factionalism was to prevent criticism of government or Central Committee decisions. An accompanying resolution condemned the 'Workers' Opposition', the group that had opposed the brutalities of War Communism and had been involved in the Kronstadt Rising. The two resolutions on party loyalty provided a highly effective means of stifling criticism of NEP. At the same time as Lenin condemned factionalism, he also declared that all socialist parties other than the Bolsheviks were now outlawed in Soviet Russia. 'Marxism teaches that only the Communist Party is capable of training and organising a vanguard of the proletariat and the whole mass of the working people.' This was the logical climax of the policy, begun in 1918, of suppressing all opposition to Bolshevik rule. Lenin's announcements at this critical juncture made it extremely difficult for doubting members to come out and openly challenge NEP, since this would appear tantamount to challenging the party itself.

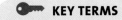 **KEY TERMS**

Nepmen Those who stood to gain from the free trading permitted under NEP: rich peasants, retailers, traders and small-scale manufacturers.

Factionalism The forming within the party of groups with a particular complaint or grievance.

Bukharin's role

A further boost to Bolshevik unity was the decision by Bukharin, the outstanding party economist, to abandon his opposition to NEP and become its most enthusiastic supporter. His new approach was expressed in his appeal to the peasants: 'Enrich yourselves under NEP.' Bukharin believed that the greater amount of money the peasants would now have, after selling their surplus grain, would stimulate industry since their extra income would be spent on buying manufactured goods. It is significant that during the final two years of Lenin's life, when he became increasingly exhausted by a series of crippling strokes, it was Bukharin who was his closest colleague. The last two articles published under Lenin's name, *On Co-operation* and *Better Fewer, But Better*, were justifications of NEP. Both were the work of Bukharin.

Economic results of NEP

In the end, the most powerful reason for the party to accept NEP proved to be a statistical one. The production figures suggested that the policy worked. By the time of Lenin's death in 1924, the Soviet economy had begun to make a marked recovery. Table 6.3 indicates the scale of this.

Table 6.3 Growth under NEP

Output	1921	1922	1923	1924
Grain harvest (millions of tonnes)	37.6	50.3	56.6	51.4
Value of factory output (millions of roubles)	2004	2619	4005	4660
Electricity (millions of kWh)	520	775	1146	1562
Average monthly wage of urban worker (roubles)	10.2	12.2	15.9	20.8

Lenin's claim that under NEP the Bolsheviks would still control 'the commanding heights of the economy' was shown to be substantially correct by the census of 1923. Figure 6.5 and Table 6.4 indicate that, in broad terms, NEP had produced an economic balance: while agriculture and trade were largely in private hands, the state dominated Russian industry.

Table 6.4 Balance between main types of enterprise

Enterprise	Proportion of industrial workforce	Average number of workers in each factory
Private	12%	2
State	85%	155
Co-operative	3%	15

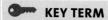 **KEY TERM**

Co-operatives Groups of workers or farmers working together on their own enterprise.

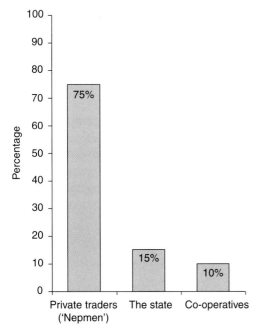

Figure 6.5 Share of trade under NEP, 1923.

NEP was not a total success. Its opponents criticised it on the grounds that the balance it appeared to have achieved was notional rather than real. The fact was that industry failed to expand as rapidly as agriculture. The Nepmen may have done well, but there was high unemployment in the urban areas. NEP would continue to be a matter of dispute and division among the Bolsheviks long after Lenin's death.

Lenin's legacy

At his death in 1924 Lenin left Russia the following legacy:

- The one-party state: all parties other than the Bolsheviks had been outlawed by 1922.
- The bureaucratic state: despite the Bolsheviks' original belief in the withering away of the state, central power increased under Lenin and the number of government institutions and officials grew.
- The police state: the *Cheka* was the first of a series of secret police organisations in Soviet Russia whose task was imposing government control over the people.
- Democratic centralism: the requirement that party members obey and act on orders handed down by the party leaders.
- The ban on factionalism: prevented criticism of leadership within the party, in effect a prohibition of free speech.

- The destruction of the trade unions: with Lenin's encouragement, Trotsky had destroyed the independence of the trade unions, with the result that the Russian workers were entirely at the mercy of the state.
- The politicising of the law: under Lenin, the law was operated not as a means of protecting society and the individual, but as an extension of political control.
- The system of purges and show trials which were to become a notorious feature of Stalinism were created under Lenin.
- Labour camps: at the time of Lenin's death there were 315 such camps.
- Prohibition of public worship.
- The Soviet Union's attitude towards the outside world based on the notion of delayed revolution.

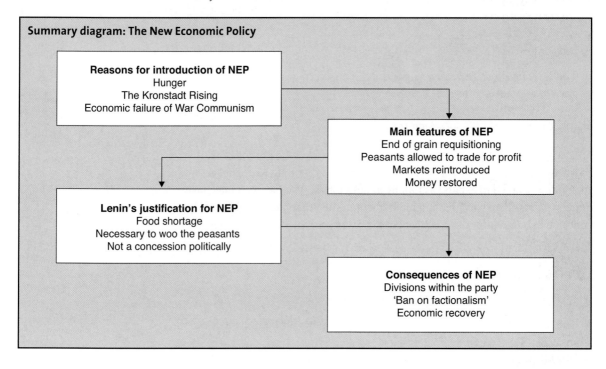

Summary diagram: The New Economic Policy

Reasons for introduction of NEP
Hunger
The Kronstadt Rising
Economic failure of War Communism

Main features of NEP
End of grain requisitioning
Peasants allowed to trade for profit
Markets reintroduced
Money restored

Lenin's justification for NEP
Food shortage
Necessary to woo the peasants
Not a concession politically

Consequences of NEP
Divisions within the party
'Ban on factionalism'
Economic recovery

Chapter summary

Faced with major domestic and foreign problems, it was questionable whether Lenin's Bolsheviks could retain power. But a combination of their ruthlessness, which included the forcible dissolution of the Constituent Assembly, and their opponents' weaknesses enabled their new regime to survive. Lenin's acceptance of the punitive peace treaty imposed by Germany left his government free to concentrate on internal consolidation. A savage civil war (1918–20) ended with Bolshevik victory and the repulsing of a series of foreign interventions.

The oppressive political methods by which Lenin governed were extended into the economic field in the form of War Communism, a programme of centralised economic control whose main purpose was to provide the resources for war. However, such was the disruption, that famine set in. Deprivation and state oppression stimulated a resistance movement from within the Bolsheviks' own ranks. The most threatening challenge came at Kronstadt, where workers previously loyal to the party rose in protest. Trotsky crushed the movement bloodily, but it had taught Lenin that the rigidities of War Communism had to be eased. He did this by introducing NEP, a policy of concessions, which aroused opposition from some party members, a development which Lenin immediately suppressed by his ban on factionalism.

 Refresher questions

Use these questions to remind yourself of the key material covered in this chapter.

1 Who were the opposing sides in the Civil War?
2 Was the Bolshevik victory a result of Red strength or White weakness?
3 What strategy did Trotsky follow as war commissar?
4 How big a factor was morale in the Reds' victory?
5 How much did the victory of the Reds in the Civil War owe to Trotsky?
6 What influence did the Civil War have on the character of Bolshevism?
7 Why did the foreign interventions fail?
8 What was Lenin's attitude towards foreign affairs?
9 What role did Trotsky play in the Red Terror?
10 What was the impact of War Communism on industry?
11 What was the impact of War Communism on agriculture?
12 In what ways was War Communism an extension of the Red Terror?
13 What led to the Kronstadt Rising of 1921?
14 Why was the Kronstadt Rising so disturbing for Lenin and the Bolsheviks?
15 How did Lenin preserve party unity over NEP?

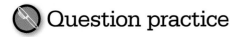 Question practice

ESSAY QUESTIONS

1 'The victory of the Reds in the Civil War of 1918–20 was a result of their opponents' weaknesses rather than their own strengths.' How far do you agree with this statement?

2 To what extent did their repelling of the foreign interventions help to consolidate the Bolsheviks' hold on power?

3 How accurate is it to say that the Kronstadt Rising in 1921 was a clear sign that War Communism had failed?

4 How far were the problems faced by Lenin's government solved by the introduction of NEP in 1921?

SOURCE QUESTIONS

1 How far could the historian make use of Sources 1 and 2 together to investigate the Kronstadt Rising in 1921 and its suppression by the Soviet government? Explain your answer, using both sources, the information given about them and your own knowledge of the historical context.

2 Why is Source 1 valuable to the historian for an enquiry into the grievances of the Kronstadt workers in 1921? Explain your answer using the source, the information given about it and your own knowledge of the historical context.

3 How much weight do you give the evidence of Source 2 for an enquiry into the reasons for the suppression of the Kronstadt Rising in 1917? Explain your answer using the source, the information given about it and your own knowledge of the historical context.

4 How far were the problems faced by Lenin's government in 1921 solved by the introduction of NEP?

SOURCE 1

From a proclamation of 28 February 1921 by the Kronstadt Workers' Committee, stating their grievances against the Soviet government and listing their demands. In M. Matthews, editor, *Soviet Government: A Selection of Official Documents on Internal Policies*, Jonathan Cape, 1974, p. 148.

1 *In view of the fact that the present soviets do not represent the will of the workers, to re-elect the soviets immediately by secret voting.*

2 *Freedom of speech and press for workers, peasants, Anarchists and Left Socialist Parties.*

3 *Freedom of meetings, trade unions and peasant associations.*

4 *To convene not later than 1 March 1921, a non-party conference of workers, soldiers and sailors of Petrograd City, Kronstadt and Petrograd Province.*

5 *To liberate all political prisoners of Socialist Parties and also all peasants, soldiers and sailors who have been imprisoned in connection with working class and peasant movements.*

6 *To elect a commission to review the cases of those who are imprisoned in jails and concentration camps.*

7 *To abolish all Political Propaganda departments because no single party may enjoy privileges in the propagation of its ideas.*

8 *To equalize rations for all workers.*

9 *To abolish all Communist fighting detachments in all military units, and also the various Communist guards at factories.*

10 *To appoint a travelling bureau for supervising and checking on the work of officials … .*

President of the Meeting

PETRICHENKO

SOURCE 2

From a decree of 6 March 1921, issued by Trotsky and distributed by General Tukhachevsky, who at the head of 60,000 troops was about to cross the ice linking the mainland to the island of Kronstadt. Quoted in David Shub, *Lenin*, Penguin, 1976, pp. 408–9.

To the garrison and population of Kronstadt and the rebel forts. The Workers' and Peasants' Government has decided that Kronstadt and the naval ships should all at once be turned over to the Soviet Republic and therefore I order all those who raise their hands against the Socialist Fatherland to lay down their arms immediately. Those who refuse must be immediately disarmed and surrendered to the Soviet officials. The arrested commissars must be released at once. Only those who surrender unconditionally can hope for the mercy of the Soviet Republic. Simultaneously I also give an order to prepare for the suppression of the rebellion and the destruction of the rebels by armed forces. The responsibility for all the misfortune that will fall on the peaceable elements will be on the heads of the White Guard rebels. This warning is the last one.

Signed

Chairman of the Revolutionary Military Council of the Republic

TROTSKY

Edexcel A level History

Essay guidance

Edexcel's Paper 2, Option 2C.2: Russia in revolution, 1894–1924 is assessed by an exam comprising two sections:

- Section A tests the depth of your historical knowledge through source analysis (see page 182 for guidance on this).
- Section B requires you to write one essay from a choice of two from your own knowledge.

The following advice relates to Paper 2, Section B. It is relevant to A level and AS level questions. Generally, the AS exam is similar to the A level exam. Both examine the same content and require similar skills; nonetheless, there are differences, which are discussed below.

Essay skills

In order to get a high grade in Section B of Paper 2 your essay must contain four essential qualities:

- focused analysis
- relevant detail
- supported judgement
- organisation, coherence and clarity.

This section focuses on the following aspects of exam technique:

- understanding the nature of the question
- planning an answer to the question set
- writing a focused introduction
- deploying relevant detail
- writing analytically
- reaching a supported judgement.

The nature of the question

Section B questions are designed to test the depth of your historical knowledge. Therefore, they can focus on relatively short periods, or single events, or indeed on the whole period from 1894 to 1924.

Moreover, they can focus on different historical processes or 'concepts'. These include:

- cause
- consequence
- change/continuity
- similarity/difference
- significance.

These different question focuses require slightly different approaches:

Cause	1	'The inadequacy of Nicholas II's rule was primarily responsible for the February Revolution of 1917.' How far do you agree with this statement?
Consequence	2	To what extent did the policies of Peter Stolypin, 1906–11, reform tsarist government?
Continuity and change	3	'The Russian economy changed radically between 1906 and 1924.' How far do you agree with this statement?
Similarities and differences	4	'As an economic programme, NEP differed radically from War Communism.' How far do you agree with this statement?
Significance	5	How significant was the Civil War (1918–20) in the consolidation of Bolshevik power in the period 1917 to 1924?

Some questions include a 'stated factor'. The most common type of stated factor question would ask how far one factor caused something. For example, for the first question in the table: 'The inadequacy of Nicholas II's rule was primarily responsible for the February Revolution of 1917.' In this type of question you would be expected to evaluate the importance of 'Nicholas II' – the 'stated factor' – compared to other factors.

AS and A level questions

AS level questions are generally similar to A level questions but the wording will be slightly less complex.

A level question	AS level question	
To what extent did the policies of Count Witte lead to the modernisation of the Russian economy?	To what extent did Count Witte's policies improve the Russian economy?	The A level question focuses on the complex notion of 'modernisation' whereas the AS question focuses on the relatively simple issue of 'change'
'As an economic programme, NEP differed radically from War Communism.' How far do you agree with this statement?	How far did economic policy change between the launch of War Communism and the introduction of NEP?	The AS question asks how far economic policies changed. The A level question asks you to make the more complex judgement: how far the policies 'differed radically'

To achieve the highest level at A level, you will have to deal with the full complexity of the question. For example, if you were dealing with question 4, about changing economic policy, you would have to deal with the question of how far NEP policies 'differed radically', not merely how far they changed things.

Planning your answer

It is crucial that you understand the focus of the question. Therefore, read the question carefully before you start planning. Check the following:

- The chronological focus: which years should your essay deal with?
- The topic focus: what aspect of your course does the question deal with?

- The conceptual focus: is this a causes, consequences, change/continuity, similarity/ difference or significance question?

For example, for question 3 you could point these out as follows:

'The Russian economy[1] changed radically[2] between 1906 and 1924[3].' How far do you agree with this statement?

1 Topic focus: the character of the economy.
2 Conceptual focus: continuity/change.
3 Chronological focus: 1906–24.

Your plan should reflect the task that you have been set. Section B asks you to write an analytical, coherent and well-structured essay from your own knowledge, which reaches a supported conclusion in around 40 minutes.

- To ensure that your essay is coherent and well structured, your essay should comprise a series of paragraphs, each focusing on a different point.
- Your paragraphs should come in a logical order. For example, you could write your paragraphs in order of importance, so you begin with the most important issues and end with the least important.
- In essays where there is a 'stated factor', it is a good idea to start with the stated factor before moving on to the other points.
- To make sure you keep to time, you should aim to write three or four paragraphs plus an introduction and a conclusion.

The opening paragraph

The opening paragraph should do four main things:

- answer the question directly
- set out your essential argument
- outline the factors or issues that you will discuss
- define key terms used in the question – where necessary.

Different questions require you to define different terms, for example:

A level question	Key terms
To what extent did the policies of Count Witte lead to the modernisation of the Russian economy?	Here it is worth defining 'modernisation'
'As an economic programme, NEP differed radically from War Communism.' How far do you agree with this statement?	In this example, it is worth defining 'differed radically'

The judgement is supported in part by evaluating the evidence, and in part by linking it to valid criteria. In the case of the first question above, the criterion is the definition of modernisation set out in the introduction. Significantly, this criterion is specific to this essay, and different essays will require you to think of different criteria to help you make your judgement.

Here's an example introduction in answer to question 2 in the table on page 178: 'To what extent did the policies of Peter Stolypin, 1906–11, reform tsarist government in Russia?'

Stolypin's policies after 1906 strengthened the tsarist government in the short term but they did not reform it.[1] It is true his twin policies of political repression and economic improvement reasserted control over the groups likely to give trouble in Russia: the liberals, the workers, and the peasants. However, these policies did not reform government itself since those who ran government remained highly resistant to change.[2] This became clear in the three years after Stolypin's death when the government refused to consider reforming itself and blundered on in the face of rising opposition[3].

1 The essay starts with a clear answer to the question.
2 This sentence simultaneously defines Stolypin's principal aim and the obstacles in his path.
3 Finally, the essential argument is stated.

The opening paragraph: advice

- Don't write more than a couple of sentences on general background knowledge. This is unlikely to focus explicitly on the question.
- After defining key terms, refer back to these definitions when justifying your conclusion.
- The introduction should reflect the rest of the essay. Don't make one argument in your introduction, then make a different argument in the essay.

Deploying relevant detail

Paper 2 tests the depth of your historical knowledge. Therefore, you will need to deploy historical detail. In the main body of your essay your paragraphs should begin with a clear point, be full of relevant detail and end with explanation or evaluation. A detailed answer might include statistics, proper names, dates and technical terms. For example, if you are writing a paragraph about how Stolypin dealt with the peasant problem, you might include statistics showing the number of farms 'consolidated' between 1906 and 1913.

Writing analytically

The quality of your analysis is one of the key factors that determines the mark you achieve. Writing analytically means clearly showing the relationships between the ideas in your essay. Analysis includes two key skills: explanation and evaluation.

Explanation

Explanation means giving reasons. An explanatory sentence has three parts:

- a claim: a statement that something is true or false
- a reason: a statement that justifies the claim
- a relationship: a word or phrase that shows the relationship between the claim and the reason.

Imagine you are answering question 1 in the table on page 178: 'The inadequacy of Nicholas II's rule was primarily responsible for the February Revolution of 1917.' Your paragraph on Nicholas II's responsibility should start with a clear point, which would be supported by a series of examples. Finally, you would round off the paragraph with some explanation:

Therefore, Nicholas II's own inadequacy as ruler was certainly a major factor in the onset of the revolution[1] since[2] they undermined his authority and encouraged the growth of resistance to him[3].

1 Claim.
2 Relationship.
3 Reason.

Make sure of the following:

- The reason you give genuinely justifies the claim you have made.
- Your explanation is focused on the question.

Reaching a supported judgement

Finally, your essay should reach a supported judgement. The obvious place to do this is in the conclusion of your essay. Even so, the judgement should reflect the findings of your essay. The conclusion should present the following:

- a clear judgement that answers the question
- an evaluation of the evidence that supports the judgement
- finally, the evaluation should reflect a valid criteria.

Evaluation and criteria

Evaluation means weighing up to reach a judgement. Therefore, evaluation requires you to:

- summarise both sides of the issue
- reach a conclusion that reflects the proper weight of both sides.

So for question 2 in the table on page 178: 'To what extent did the policies of Peter Stolypin, 1906–11, reform tsarist government in Russia?', the conclusion might look like this:

In conclusion, it can be said that while Stolypin had temporally strengthened the government he had not reformed it significantly[1]. By the time of his death in 1911, he had certainly reasserted government control. But this did not mean the government had been reformed[2]. The tsar and his government remained reactionary, unwilling to consider genuine reform. Once Stolypin's strong hand was removed in 1911, industrial troubles and general dissatisfaction grew. The unreformed government's only response was repression. The blindness of the tsar's government to the true needs of Russia meant Stolypin had never received Nicholas II's full backing[3]. The very limited extent to which Stolypin had achieved basic reform was evident in the troubled years 1911–14[4].

1 The conclusion starts with a clear judgement that answers the question.
2 This sentence considers the extent of the strength that Stolypin's policies restored to the government.
3 The conclusion also considers evidence of the limits of government strength.
4 The essay ends with a final judgement that is supported by the evidence of the essay.

Sources guidance

Edexcel's Paper 2, Option 2C.2: Russia in revolution, 1894–1924 is assessed by an exam comprising two sections:

- Section A tests the depth of your historical knowledge through source analysis.
- Section B requires you to write one essay from a choice of two from your own knowledge (see page 178 for guidance on this).

The following advice relates to Paper 2, Section A. It is relevant to A level and AS level questions. Generally, the AS exam is similar to the A level exam. Both examine the same content and require similar skills; nonetheless, there are differences, which are discussed below.

The questions in Paper 2, Section A, are structured differently in the A level and AS exams.

AS exam	Full A level exam
Section A: contains one compulsory question divided into two parts. Part a) is worth 8 marks. It focuses on the value of a single source for a specific enquiry. Part b) is worth 12 marks. It asks you to weigh the value of a single source for a specific enquiry. Together the two sources will comprise about 350 words.	Section A: contains a single compulsory question worth 20 marks. The question asks you to evaluate the usefulness of two sources for a specific historical enquiry. Together the two sources will comprise about 400 words.
Questions will start with the following stems: a) Why is Source 1 valuable to the historian for an enquiry about … b) How much weight do you give the evidence of Source 2 for an enquiry into …	Questions will start with the following stem: How far could the historian make use of Sources 1 and 2 together to investigate …

Practice questions

AS style question

a) Study Sources 1 and 2 before you answer this question.

Why is Source 1 valuable to the historian for an enquiry about the causes of the February Revolution?

Explain your answer using the source, the information given about it and your own knowledge of the historical context.

b) How much weight do you give the evidence of Source 2 for an enquiry into attitudes to the tsar's government in late 1916?

Explain your answer using the source, the information given about it and your own knowledge of the historical context.

A level style question

Study Sources 1 and 2 before you answer this question.

How far could the historian make use of Sources 1 and 2 together to investigate the causes of the February Revolution?

Explain your answer using both sources, the information given about them and your own knowledge of the historical context.

Sources 1 and 2

SOURCE I

From a Petrograd *Okhrana* police report, October 1916. The report describes the threatening atmosphere and increasing tensions created by rising prices and food shortages in the capital.

Despite the great increase in wages, the economic condition of the masses is worse than terrible. Even if we estimate the rise in earnings at 100 per cent, the prices of products have risen on the average, 300 per cent. The impossibility of even buying many food products and necessities, the time wasted standing idle in queues to receive goods, the increasing incidence of disease due to malnutrition and unsanitary living conditions (cold and dampness because of lack of coal and wood), and so forth, have made the workers as a whole, prepared for the wildest excesses of a 'hunger riot'.

If, in the future, grain continues to be hidden, the very fact of its disappearance will be sufficient to provoke in the capitals and in the other most populated centres of the empire the greatest disorders, attended by pogroms and endless street rioting. The mood of anxiety, growing daily more intense, is spreading to ever wider sections of the populace. Never have we observed such nervousness as there is now. The slightest incident is enough to provoke the biggest brawl. This is especially noticeable in the vicinity of shops, stores, banks, and similar institutions, where 'misunderstandings' occur almost daily.

SOURCE 2

From a speech made by Paul Milyukov, the leader of the liberal Kadet Party, to the Fourth *Duma* on 1 November 1916. Here, Milyukov criticises the tsar's government.

This present government has sunk beneath the level on which it stood during normal times in Russian life. And now the guilt between us and that government has grown wider and become impassable. Today we are aware that with this government we cannot legislate, and we cannot, with this government, lead Russia to victory. We are telling this government, as the declaration of the [Progressive Bloc] stated: We shall fight you, we shall fight you with all legitimate means until you go.

When the Duma declares again and again that the home front must be organized for a successful war and the government continues to insist that to

organize the country means to organize a revolution, and consciously chooses chaos and disorganization – is this stupidity or treason? We have many reasons for being discontented with the government. But all these reasons boil down to one general one: the incompetence and evil intentions of the present government. We shall fight until we get a responsible government. Cabinet members must agree unanimously as to the most urgent tasks. They must agree and be prepared to implement the programme of the Duma majority. They must rely on this majority, not just in the implementation of this programme, but in all their actions.

Understanding the questions

- To answer the question successfully you must understand how the question works.
- The question is written precisely in order to make sure that you understand the task. Each part of the question has a specific meaning.
- You must use the source, the information given about the source, and your own knowledge of the historical context when answering the question.

Understanding the AS question

a) Why is Source 1 valuable to the historian[1] for an enquiry about the causes of the February Revolution[2]?

1 You must focus on the reasons why the source could be helpful to a historian. Indeed, you can get maximum marks without considering the source's limitations.
2 The final part of the question focuses on a specific topic that a historian might investigate. In this case: the causes of the February Revolution.

b) How much weight do you give the evidence of Source 2[1] for an enquiry[2] into attitudes towards the tsar's government in late 1916?[3]

1 This question focuses on evaluating the extent to which the source contains evidence. Therefore, you must consider the ways in which the source is valuable and the limitations of the source.
2 This is the essence of the task: you must focus on what a historian could legitimately conclude from studying this source.
3 This is the specific topic that you are considering the source for: 'attitudes towards the tsar's government in late 1916'.

Understanding the A level question

How far[1] could the historian make use of Sources 1 and 2[2] together[3] to investigate the causes of the February Revolution[4]? Explain your answer using both sources, the information given about them and your own knowledge of the historical context[5].

1 You must evaluate the extent of something, rather than giving a simple 'yes' or 'no' answer.
2 This is the essence of the task: you must focus on what a historian could legitimately conclude from studying these sources.
3 You must examine the sources as a pair and make a judgement about both sources, rather than simply making separate judgements about each source.
4 The final part of the question focuses on a specific topic that a historian might investigate. In this case: 'attitudes towards the tsar's government in late 1916?'
5 This instruction lists the resources you should use: the sources, the information given about the sources and your own knowledge of the historical context that you have learnt during the course.

Source skills

Generally, Section A of Paper 2 tests your ability to evaluate source material. More specifically, the sources presented in Section A will be taken from the period that you have studied: 1894–1924, or be written by people who witnessed these events. Your job is to analyse the sources by reading them in the context of the values and assumptions of the society and the period that produced them.

Examiners will mark your work by focusing on the extent to which you are able to:

- Interpret and analyse source material:
  - At a basic level, this means you can understand the sources and select, copy, paraphrase and summarise the source or sources to help answer the question.
  - At a higher level, your interpretation of the sources includes the ability to explain, analyse and make inferences based on the sources.
  - At the highest levels, you will be expected to analyse the source in a sophisticated way. This includes the ability to distinguish between information, opinions and arguments contained in the sources.
- Deploy knowledge of the historical context in relation to the sources:
  - At a basic level, this means the ability to link the sources to your knowledge of the context in which the source was written, using this knowledge to expand or support the information contained in the sources.
  - At a higher level, you will be able to use your contextual knowledge to make inferences, and to expand, support or challenge the details mentioned in the sources.

- At the highest levels, you will be able to examine the value and limits of the material contained in the sources by interpreting the sources in the context of the values and assumptions of the society that produced them.
- Evaluate the usefulness and weight of the source material:
  - At a basic level, evaluation of the source will be based on simplistic criteria about reliability and bias.
  - At a higher level, evaluation of the source will be based on the nature and purpose of the source.
  - At the highest levels, evaluation of the source will based on a valid criterion that is justified in the course of the essay. You will also be able to distinguish between the value of different aspects of the sources.

Make sure your source evaluation is sophisticated. Avoid crude statements about bias, and avoid simplistic assumptions such as that a source written immediately after an event is reliable, whereas a source written years later is unreliable.

Try to see things through the eyes of the writer:

- How does the writer understand the world?
- What assumptions does the writer have?
- Who is the writer trying to influence?
- What views is the writer trying to challenge?

Basic skill: comprehension

The most basic source skill is comprehension: understanding what the sources mean. There are a variety of techniques that you can use to aid comprehension. For example, you could read the sources included in this book and in past papers:

- Read the sources out loud.
- Look up any words that you don't understand and make a glossary.
- Make flash cards containing brief biographies of the writers of the sources.

You can demonstrate comprehension by copying, paraphrasing and summarising the sources. However, keep this to the minimum as comprehension is a low-level skill and you need to leave room for higher-level skills.

Advanced skill: contextualising the sources

First, to analyse the sources correctly you need to understand them in the context in which they were written. People in Russia in 1916 (see Sources 1 and 2 on page 183) saw the world differently to people in early twenty-first-century Britain. The sources reflect this. Your job is to understand the values and assumptions behind the source:

- One way of contextualising the sources is to consider the nature, origins and purpose of the sources. However, this can lead to formulaic responses.
- An alternative is to consider two levels of context. First, you should establish the general context. In this case, Sources 1 and 2 refer to a period in which tsarist Russia was moving towards revolution.

Second, you can look for specific references to contemporary events or debates in the sources. For example:

Sources 1 and 2 both refer to the situation in Petrograd in late 1916. However, Source 1 is mainly concerned with the impact the grim economic circumstances have had on people living in Petrograd, while Source 2 deals with the political breakdown that has occurred at government level. Thus, in their different ways, they both paint a picture of a mounting crisis caused by anger, bitterness and confusion caused by poor leadership. The police report speaks of the strong possibility of the people's desperation leading to a hunger riot. Milyukov's fierce denunciation also points to a looming crisis now that effective government no longer operates. Both sources concur in seeing the war as the critical factor leading to crisis.

Use context to make judgements

- Start by establishing the general context of the source:
  - Ask yourself, what was going on at the time that the source was written, or the time of the events described in the source?
  - What are the key debates that the source might be contributing to?
- Next look for key words and phrases that establish the specific context. Does the source refer to specific people, events or books that might be important?
- Make sure your contextualisation focuses on the question.
- Use the context when evaluating the usefulness and limitations of the source.

For example:

Source 1 is valuable to a historian investigating the causes of the February Revolution because it shows the desperate economic conditions to which the people of Petrograd have been reduced by the privations of war. The report is particularly informative because the police are in a perfect position to observe the attitudes and feelings of the people. Source 2 is valuable because it complements the description in the police report by illustrating that the anger of the political opponents of the government is of the same intensity as the suffering people. Thus, taken together, the sources provide vital information regarding the combination of economic and political frustration, a development that would ultimately lead to the February Revolution a few months later.

Glossary of terms

Accommodationism   The idea that the Bolsheviks should co-operate with the Provisional Government and work with the other revolutionary and reforming parties.

Administrative fiat   An unchallengeable command from above.

Agents provocateurs   Government agents who infiltrate opposition movements with the aim of stirring up trouble so that the ringleaders can be exposed.

Agrarian economy   Food and goods produced by arable and dairy farming, and then traded.

All-Russian Congress of Soviets   A gathering of representatives from all the soviets formed in Russia since February 1917.

Amazons   A special corps of female soldiers recruited by Kerensky to show the patriotism of Russia's women in the anti-German struggle.

Anarchy   Absence of government or authority, leading to disorder.

ARA   The American Relief Association, formed to provide food and medical supplies for post-war Europe.

Autocrat   A ruler with absolute authority.

Autonomy   National self-government.

Balkans   The area of south-eastern Europe (fringed by Austria-Hungary to the north, the Black Sea to the east, Turkey to the south and the Aegean Sea to the west), which had largely been under Turkish control.

Bi-cameral   A parliament made up of two chambers: an upper and a lower.

Bolsheviks   From *bolshinstvo*, Russian for majority.

Borsch   A thin soup made from rotting beetroot.

Bosphorus   The narrow waterway linking the Black Sea with the Dardanelles.

Bourgeoisie   The owners of capital, the boss class, who exploited the workers but who supposedly would be overthrown by them in revolution.

Buffer state   An area that lies between two states, providing protection for each against the other.

Capital   The essential supply of money that provides investment for economic expansion.

Capitalists   Financiers and factory owners.

Catechism   A primer of religious instruction, explaining essential dogmas.

Central Powers   Germany, Austria-Hungary and Turkey.

Cheka   All-Russian Extraordinary Commission for Fighting Counter-Revolution, Sabotage and Speculation.

Class struggle   A continuing conflict at every stage of history between those who possessed economic and political power and those who did not – in simple terms, 'the haves' vs 'the have-nots'.

Comintern   The Communist International, a body set up in Moscow in March 1919 to organise worldwide revolution.

Commissar for foreign affairs   Equivalent to the secretary of state in the USA or the foreign secretary in the UK.

Commissars   Russian for ministers; Lenin chose the word because he said 'it reeked of blood'.

Commissions   Official appointments of individuals to the various officer ranks.

Committee system   A process in which the *duma* deputies formed various subgroups to discuss and advise on particular issues.

Confidant   A person in whom another places a special trust and to whom one confides intimate secrets.

Conscription   Compulsory enlistment of people (in Russia's case, largely peasants) into the armed services.

Constitutional monarchy   A system of government in which the king or emperor rules but only through elected representatives whose decisions he cannot countermand.

Co-operatives   Groups of workers or farmers working together on their own enterprise.

Cossacks   The remnants of the élite cavalry regiment of the tsars.

Counter-revolution   A term used by the Bolsheviks to cover any action of which they disapproved by branding it as reactionary.

Dark masses   The dismissive term used in the royal court and government circles to describe the peasants.

De facto   'By the very fact' – a term used to denote the real situation, as compared to what it should or might be in theory or in law.

De jure   By legitimate legal right.

Decree on Nationalisation   Laid down a programme for the takeover by the state of the larger industrial concerns.

'Democratic centralism'   Lenin's notion that democracy in the Bolshevik Party lay in obedience to the authority and instructions of the leaders. In practice, Bolsheviks did what Lenin told them to do.

Dialectic   The violent struggle between opposites which takes place in nature and in human society.

Diktat   A settlement imposed on a weaker nation by a stronger one.

Double-agent   A government spy who pretends to be working for the opposition against the authorities but who reports plans and secrets back to the authorities.

Dual Authority   Lenin first coined this term to describe the balance of power between the Provisional Government and the Petrograd soviet.

Duma   The Russian parliament, which existed from 1906 to 1917.

Economism   Putting the improvement of the workers' conditions before the need for revolution.

Emancipation Decree of 1861   Granting of freedom to the serfs (peasant land workers), who had formerly been bound to the landowners.

Émigré   One who fled from Russia after the Revolution, from fear or a desire to plan a counter-strike against the Bolsheviks.

Entente   An agreement to remain on friendly terms.

Entrepreneurialism   The dynamic attitude associated with individual commercial and industrial enterprise.

Factionalism   The forming within the party of groups with a particular complaint or grievance.

Fait accompli   An established situation that cannot be changed.

Finance capital   The resource used by stronger countries to exploit weaker ones. By investing heavily in another country, a stronger power made that country dependent on it.

Fundamental Laws of the Empire   These defined the powers of the tsar. Article 1 declared: 'The Emperor of all the Russias is an autocratic and unlimited monarch. God himself ordains that all must bow to his supreme power, not only out of fear but also out of conscience.'

'German woman'   The disparaging term used by anti-tsarists to describe Empress Alexandra.

Ghettos   Discrete districts where Jews were concentrated and to which they were restricted.

God's anointed   The anointing of the tsar with holy oil at his coronation symbolised that he governed by divine right.

Gold standard   The system in which the rouble had a fixed gold content, thus giving it strength when exchanged with other currencies.

Great spurt   The spread of industry and the increase in production that occurred in Russia in the 1890s.

Greens   Groups from the national minorities, struggling for independence from central Russian control.

Haemophilia   A genetic condition in which the blood does not clot, leaving the sufferer with painful bruising and internal bleeding, which can be life threatening.

Indemnities   Payment of war costs demanded by the victors from the defeated.

Intelligentsia   Educated and more enlightened members of Russian society who had been influenced by Western ideas and wanted to see Russia adopt progressive changes.

International revolutionaries   Marxists who were willing to sacrifice mere national interests in the cause of the worldwide rising of the workers.

Kulaks   The Bolshevik term for the class of allegedly rich, exploiting peasants.

Labourists   The Social Revolutionaries as a party officially boycotted the elections to the first *duma*, but stood as Labourists.

Left SRs   Social revolutionaries who sided with the Bolsheviks in their recognition of the legitimacy of the peasant land-seizures and in their demand that Russia withdraw from the war.

Legislative *duma*   A parliament with law-making powers.

Liberal   A conviction that the powers of rulers and governments should be restricted and the freedom of the people enlarged.

Little Father   A traditional term denoting the tsar's paternal care of his people.

Martial law   The placing of the population under direct military authority.

Marxism–Leninism   The notion that Marx's theory of class war, as interpreted by Lenin, was an unchallengeable scientific truth.

Mensheviks   From *menshinstvo*, Russian for minority.

Militia   Local citizens called together and given arms to control social disorder.

Mir   The traditional village community.

Monarchists   Reactionaries who wanted a restoration of tsardom.

Moscow   In 1918, for security reasons, Moscow replaced Petrograd as the capital of Soviet Russia.

National insurance   A system of providing workers with state benefits, such as unemployment pay and medical treatment, in return for the workers' contributing regularly to a central fund.

Nationalism   The conviction that the nation state is the highest form of social organisation; in Russian tradition, the belief that Russia was a 'holy' nation that did not need to embrace modernity.

Nepmen   Those who stood to gain from the free trading permitted under NEP: rich peasants, retailers, traders and small-scale manufacturers.

Nepotism   The corrupt practice in which officials distributed positions and offices to their family or friends.

Non-determinist approach   Rejection of the idea that history follows a fixed, inevitable course.

Obschina   Peasant communes set up within the localities.

Okhrana   Tsarist secret police, responsible for hunting down opponents of the regime.

Orgburo   Organisation Bureau, which turned policies into practice.

Orthodoxy   Conformity to an unchanging set of political ideas or religious beliefs.

Papacy   The governmental system of the Roman Catholic branch of western Christianity headed by the Pope.

Parliamentary-bourgeois republic   Lenin's contemptuous term for the Provisional Government, which he dismissed as an unrepresentative mockery that had simply replaced the rule of the tsar with the rule of the reactionary *duma*.

Passive disobedience   Opposing government not by violent challenge but by refusing to obey particular laws.

People   That part of the population that the Social Revolutionaries believed truly represented the character and will of the Russian nation.

People's militia   A new set of volunteer law-enforcement officers drawn from ordinary people.

Per capita   'Per head', calculated by dividing the amount produced by the number of people in the population.

Petrograd   For patriotic reasons, soon after the war began, the German name for the capital, St Petersburg, was changed to the Russian form of 'Petrograd'.

Pogroms   Fierce state-organised persecutions that often involved the wounding or killing of Jews and the destruction of their property.

Politburo   The Political Bureau, responsible for major policy decisions.

Political activists   People who believe that change can be achieved only by direct action.

Political commissars   Party officials who accompanied the officers and reported on their political correctness.

Political subversives   Kornilov's term for the SDs and SRs in Russia.

Popular mandate   The authority to govern granted by a majority of the people through elections.

Populists   *Narodniks*, from the Russian word for 'the people'.

Pragmatic   An approach in which policies are changed according to circumstance rather than in accordance with a fixed theory.

Private enterprise   Economic activity organised by individuals or companies, not the government.

Progressists   A party of businessmen who favoured moderate reform.

Progressives   Those who believed in parliamentary government for Russia.

Prohibition   The state's banning of the production and sale of alcohol.

Proletariat   The exploited industrial workers who would supposedly triumph in the last great class struggle.

Quantitative easing   Printing extra currency to meet the demand for ready money; a risky process since the money is not tied to an actual increase in genuine wealth.

Radicalisation   A movement towards more sweeping or revolutionary ideas.

Radicalism   The desire to change society fundamentally – literally at its roots.

Rasputin   By an interesting coincidence, the word 'rasputin' in Russian also means lecher.

Reactionary   Resistant to any form of progressive change.

Red Guards   Despite the Bolshevik legend that these were the crack forces of the revolution, the Red Guards, some 10,000 in number, were largely made up of elderly men recruited from the workers in the factories.

Reds   The Bolsheviks and their supporters.

Reformers   Strong critics of the tsarist system who believed it could be changed for the better by pressure from without and reform from within.

Reparations   Payment of war costs by the loser to the victor.

Representative government   A system in which the people of a nation elect a government into office, and subsequently vote it out if they so choose.

Requisitioning   State-authorised takeover of property or resources.

Revolutionaries   Those who believed that Russia could not progress unless the tsarist system was destroyed.

Revolutionary socialism   The belief that change could be achieved only through the violent overthrow of the tsarist system.

Rightists   Not a single party; they represented a range of conservative views from right of centre to extreme reaction.

Romanov dynasty   The Russian monarchy was hereditary. Between 1613 and 1917, Russia was ruled by members of the house of Romanov.

Rouble   Russia's basic unit of currency.

Rural crisis   Land shortage and overpopulation in the countryside resulting from the huge number of people living in Russia by the late nineteenth century.

Russian constituent assembly   A full gathering of the elected representatives of the Russian people.

Russification   Russian was declared to be the official first language; all legal proceedings and all administration had to be conducted in Russian. Public office was closed to those not fluent in the language.

Samogon   Illicitly distilled vodka, the equivalent of 'moonshine' or 'hooch', Western forms of unlicensed alcohol.

Secretariat   A form of civil service that administered policies.

Serbian nationalists   Activists struggling for Serbia's independence from Austria-Hungary.

Smolny   The Bolshevik headquarters in Petrograd, housed in what had been a young ladies' finishing school.

Social Democrats   The All-Russian Social Democratic Workers' Party.

Soviet   Russian word for a council made up of elected representatives.

Sovnarkom   Russian for government or cabinet.

Spartacists   Named after Spartacus, the leader of a slave rebellion in ancient Rome.

Starets   Russian for holy man, the name given to Rasputin by the impressionable peasants who believed he had superhuman powers.

State capitalism   The direction and control of the economy by the government, using its central authority.

Stavka   The high command of the Russian army.

System of dating   Until February 1918, Russia used the Julian calendar, which was 13 days behind the Gregorian calendar, the one used in most Western countries by this time. That is why different books may give different dates for the same event. This book uses the older dating for the events of 1917.

Tariffs   Duties imposed on foreign goods to keep their prices high and thereby discourage importers from bringing them into the country.

Tax in kind   The peasants surrendered a certain amount of their produce, equivalent to a fixed sum of money.

Total war   A struggle in which the whole nation, people, resources and institutions, are involved.

Trade recession   A fall in the demand for goods, which leads to production being cut back and workers laid off.

Triple Entente   Not a formal alliance, but a declared willingness by three powers to co-operate.

Troika   A three-person team.

Union of Municipal Councils   A set of patriotic urban local councils.

Union of *Zemstvos*   A set of patriotic rural local councils.

Universal suffrage   An electoral system in which all adults have the right to vote.

Vesenkha   Supreme Council of the National Economy.

War-credits   Money loaned on easy repayment terms to Russia to finance its war effort.

Whites   The Bolsheviks' opponents, including monarchists looking for a tsarist restoration, and those parties who had been outlawed or suppressed by the new regime.

Zemgor   The joint body that devoted itself to helping Russia's war wounded.

Zemstvos   Local elected councils, dominated by the landowners since the voting regulations largely excluded peasants.

Further reading

Books of overall relevance

E.H. Carr, *A History of Soviet Russia*, 14 volumes (Macmillan, 1950–78)

Often regarded now as dated and too pro-Soviet, this monumental study is still worth dipping into

David Christian, *Imperial and Soviet Russia* (Macmillan, 1997)

A very helpful combination of documents, commentary and analysis across the whole period

Michael Court, *The Soviet Colossus History and Aftermath* (M.E. Sharpe, 1996)

A clear, informed narrative that begins with the reign of Nicholas II

Sheila Fitzpatrick, *The Russian Revolution 1917–1932* (Oxford University Press, 1994)

A short, stimulating survey by a celebrated expert in the field

Geoffrey Hosking, *Russia and the Russians* (Allen Lane, 2001)

A very readable coverage of the whole period by a leading authority

Lionel Kochan, *The Making of Modern Russia* (Penguin, 1977)

First published over 50 years ago but still one of the best short introductions to the period

Martin Malia, *The Soviet Tragedy: A History of Socialism in Russia, 1917–1991* (Free Press, 1994)

The earlier chapters of this survey offer an informed analysis of the period up to 1924

Martin McCauley, *Who's Who in Russian History since 1900* (Routledge, 1997)

An exceptionally helpful reference book of mini-biographies of key figures

Richard Pipes, *The Russian Revolution 1899–1919* (Collins Harvill, 1990)

Strongly critical of Lenin and the Bolsheviks, but a very detailed and readable account by a Polish–American historian

Robert Service, *Lenin: A Biography* (2000); *Trotsky: A Biography* (2004); *Stalin: A Biography* (2009) (originally published by Macmillan, now all in Pan paperbacks, 2010)

The writer's classic trilogy of the three great revolutionaries figures of the period

Robert Service, *The Penguin History of Modern Russia: From Tsarism to the Twenty-first Century* (Penguin, 2009)

Informed coverage of the whole period by an outstanding Western historian

S.A. Smith, *The Russian Revolution: A Very Short Introduction* (Oxford University Press, 2002)

Despite its disarming subtitle, this is a brilliantly concise coverage of the critical developments of the 1917–24 period

Leon Trotsky, *The History of the Russian Revolution* (Pluto Press, 1985)

Notwithstanding its obvious bias, this survey, written in the 1930s by one of the major participants in the revolution, remains a highly readable account

Dmitri Volkogonov, *The Rise and Fall of the Soviet Empire: Political Leaders from Lenin to Gorbachev* (HarperCollins, 1998)

Intrinsically valuable as an analysis and made more so by the fact that the Russian author lived and worked under Stalin

J. N. Westwood, *Endurance and Endeavour: Russian History 1812–2001* (Oxford University Press, 2003)

Long established as a very reliable guide to the period

Website

http://www.marxists.org/history/ussr/events/revolution/index.htm

Soviet History Archive: a rich set of sources, starting with 1917 and covering politics, economics, culture and foreign affairs

Chapter 1

Dominic Lieven, editor, *The Cambridge History of Russia: volume 2, Imperial Russia, 1689–1917* (Cambridge University Press, 2006)

Heavy going occasionally but its later chapters provide an invaluably comprehensive coverage of the last years of tsardom

Richard Pipes, *Russia Under the Old Regime* (Weidenfeld & Nicolson, 1974)

Established as the most authoritative description of the social structure of late Imperial Russia

Ian D. Thatcher, editor, *Late Imperial Russia: Problems and Perspectives* (Manchester University Press, 2005)

A collection of stimulating essays by a group of leading scholars

Chapter 2

George Katkov and Harold Shukman, *Lenin's Path to Power* (Macdonald, 1971)

Short, readable account of Lenin's rise during the last years of Imperial Russia

Lionel Kochan, *Russia in Revolution* (Palladin, 1974)

A clear, informative analysis enlivened with a well-chosen set of documents

Dominic Lieven, *Nicholas II: Twilight of the Empire* (St Martin's Press, 1994)

Regarded by the author's fellow historians as an unmatchable analysis of Nicholas II as a person and of the problems he faced as the Romanov dynasty approached its end

Robert K. Massie, *Nicholas and Alexandra* (Head of Zeus, 2013)

Over-romantic perhaps, but an absorbing account of the fateful end of the Romanovs

Chapter 3

Anna Geifman, editor, *Russia Under the Last Tsar: Opposition and Subversion 1894–1917* (Blackwell, 1999)

A set of essays by leading scholars on the ideas and activities of the opponents of tsardom

Martin McCauley, *The Rise and Fall of the Soviet Union: 1917–1991* (Routledge, 2013)

Especially strong on political and cultural developments

Hans Rogger, *Russia in the Age of Modernisation and Revolution 1881–1917* (Longman, 1983)

An informed treatment of the political, social and economic pressures that built up in Imperial Russia by 1917

Robert Service, editor, *Society and Politics in the Russian Revolution* (St Martin's Press, 1992)

A set of authoritative essays on the key revolutionary developments

Chapter 4

Edward Action, editor, *Critical Companion to the Russian Revolution 1914–21* (Bloomsbury Academic, 2001)

A voluminous set of essays covering all the major aspects of the 1917 Revolution in its origins and outcome

John L.H. Keep, *The Russian Revolution: A Study in Mass Mobilization* (Littlehampton Books, 1976)

A pioneering study of ordinary Russians and their role in revolution

Norman Stone, *The Eastern Front* (Penguin, 1998)

A very readable account of Russia at war between 1914 and 1917 by a lively, provocative historian

Dmitri Volkogonov, *Lenin: Life and Legacy* (HarperCollins, 1994)

Fascinating insights from a Russian perspective into Lenin's revolutionary activities pre-1917

Chapter 5

Edward Acton, *Rethinking the Russian Revolution* (Edward Arnold, 1990)

An interesting survey of many of the major interpretations of 1917

E.H. Carr, *The Russian Revolution from Lenin to Stalin 1917–1929* (Palgrave, 2004)

A much shortened version of a monumental study by a pioneer historian in Russian studies

Richard Pipes, *Three Whys of the Russian Revolution* (Pimlico, 1998)

A short, powerful, committed explanation of why the 1917 revolution occurred

Richard Sakwa, *The Rise and Fall of the Soviet Union 1917–1991* (Routledge, 1999)

A highly useful selection of key documents, linked with a very well-informed commentary

Robert Service, *Trotsky: A Biography* (Macmillan, 2004)

A detailed study of Trotsky's revolutionary activities in 1917

Rex Wade, *The Russian Revolution, 1917* (Cambridge University Press, 2005)

An important study of the political and social antecedents and major interpretations of the 1917 revolution

Chapter 6

R.W. Davies, *From Tsarism to the New Economic Policy* (Cornell University Press, 1990)

Essays surveying economic developments In Russia between 1914 and 1921 by the foremost economic historian in this field

Stephen Kotkin, *Stalin: Paradoxes of Power 1878–1928* (Allen Lane, 2014)

The first volume of a major reappraisal of Stalin

E. Mawdsley, *The Russian Civil War* (Allen & Unwin, 1987)

Widely acknowledged as the clearest analysis of a pivotal event in Soviet history

Richard Pipes, *Russia Under the Bolshevik Regime, 1919–24* (Collins Harvill, 1994)

A detailed study of the Bolshevik consolidation of power

J.D. White, *The Russian Revolution, 1917–21* (Edward Arnold, 1994)

Written in the period following the collapse of the USSR, this study reflects absorbingly on the 1917 revolution and its aftermath

Index